INTERACTIONS II
A Communicative Grammar

SECOND EDITION

INTERACTIONS II
A Communicative Grammar

Patricia K. Werner
University of Wisconsin, Madison

Mary Mitchell Church
Madison Metropolitan School District

Lida R. Baker
University of California at Los Angeles

McGraw-Hill Publishing Company

New York   St. Louis   San Francisco   Auckland   Bogotá   Caracas
Hamburg   Lisbon   London   Madrid   Mexico   Milan
Montreal   New Delhi   Oklahoma City   Paris   San Juan
São Paulo   Singapore   Sydney   Tokyo   Toronto

This is an ⌐BⁱI book

Interactions II: A Communicative Grammar
Second Edition

1 2 3 4 5 6 7 8 9 0   RMT RMT   9 5 4 3 2 1 0

ISBN 0-07-557536-1

Cover illustration: Frantisĕk Kupka: *Lines, Planes, Depth,* c. 1920–22. Oil on canvas, 31½″ x 28½″. Albright-Knox Art Gallery, Buffalo, New York. Charles Clifton and George B. and Jenny R. Mathews Funds, 1977.

Sponsoring editor: Eirik Børve
Developmental editor: Mary McVey Gill
Project editor: Cathy de Heer
Production supervisor: Renée Reeves
Copyeditor: Pat Campbell
Proofreader: Karen Kevorkian
Illustrations: Sally Richardson
Photo research: Judy Mason
Interior and cover design: Cheryl Carrington
Composition: Graphic Typesetting Service
Color separation: Color Tech
Printing and binding: Rand McNally

Grateful acknowledgment is made for the graph on page 329, © *U.S. News and World Report,* 21 November 1983.

CONTENTS

√ Chapter 8   9   TASTES AND PREFERENCES   222

Adjectives and Adverbs; Clauses and Phrases of
    Comparison

Chapter 9   THE SKY ABOVE US   252

The Passive Voice

Chapter 10   MEDICINE, MYTHS, AND MAGIC   278

Adjective Clauses

PREFACE
to the Second Edition

INTERACTIONS: THE PROGRAM

Interactions consists of ten texts plus two instructor's manuals for in-college or college-bound nonnative English students. *Interactions I* is for high-beginning to low-intermediate students, while *Interactions II* is for low-intermediate to intermediate students. Within each level, I and II, the books are carefully coordinated by theme, vocabulary, grammar structure, and, where possible, language functions. A chapter in one book corresponds to and reinforces material taught in the same chapter of the other three books at that level for a truly integrated, four-skills approach.

Each level, I and II, consists of five books plus an instructor's manual. In addition to *A Communicative Grammar,* they include:

A Reading Skills Book I, II: The selections in these books are written by the authors and carefully graded in level of difficulty and amount of vocabulary. They include many vocabulary-building exercises and emphasize reading strategies: for example, skimming, scanning, guessing meaning from context, understanding the structure and organization of a selection, increasing reading speed, and interpreting the author's point of view.

A Writing Process Book I, II: These books use a process approach to writing, including many exercises on prewriting and revision. Exercises build skills in exploring and organizing ideas, developing vocabulary, using correct form and mechanics, using coherent structure, editing, revising, and using feedback to create a final draft.

A Listening/Speaking Skills Book I, II: These books use lively, natural language from a variety of contexts—dialogues, interviews, lectures, and announcements. Listening strategies emphasized include summarizing main ideas, making inferences, and listening for stressed words, reductions, and intonation. A cassette tape program with instructor's key accompanies each text.

A Speaking Activities Book I, II: These books are designed to give students the opportunity to practice their speaking and listening skills in English by promoting realistic use of the language through individual, pair, and small-group work. Task-oriented and problem-solving activities simulate real-life situations and help develop fluency.

Instructor's Manual I, II: These manuals provide instructions and guidelines for use of the books separately or in any combination to form a program. For each of the core books except *Speaking Activities,* there is a separate section with teaching tips, additional activities, and other suggestions. The Instructor's Manual also includes sample tests for the grammars and readers.

INTERACTIONS II: A COMMUNICATIVE GRAMMAR

This text introduces, practices, and applies grammatical structures through contexts relevant to the needs of the students. It progresses with the intermediate-level student by gradually shifting from basic structures and conversational topics to complex structures and academic topics.

Chapter Organization and Teaching Suggestions

The text is organized by structure and by theme. The first several chapters review basic use of verbs, articles, prepositions, and modal auxiliaries in conversational contexts such as student life, money and banking, and city living. Later chapters treat more complex structures through more sophisticated topics such as traditional and modern medicine, the known universe, and the history and traditions of North America.

All chapters are divided into four parts, each of which opens with artwork and a short passage or conversation that introduce the theme and target structures. The part openers can be used to introduce key vocabulary and to make sure the students have a basic understanding of the part's content. The introductory passage can be covered with the class as a whole, or it can be used as a homework assignment, timed reading, or listening comprehension exercise.

All structures are presented in boxes and introduced with general rules. Examples are accompanied by further explanation that may include notes on particular usages and variations, spelling or punctuation guidelines, or exceptions to general rules.

Every section, or part, includes a wide variety of exercises and activities that progress from more to less controlled while continuing to target specific structures. The exercises are both traditional and innovative, including transformations, sentence completions, sentence combining, and personal questions. Most may be used as either oral or written work and done as a class, in pairs, or in small groups.

In addition, over two hundred speaking and writing activities—such as minidramas, language games, presentations, and compositions—appear in the text. These activities are optional, but we encourage their use. They are designed to encourage the use of target structures and vocabulary in natural, personalized communication.

Finally, several chapters end with summaries of grammar points, spelling rules, and punctuation guidelines. These summaries provide easy reference for key points and include information on exceptions to or variations on the general rules covered in the chapter.

Flexibility

Because ESL/EFL courses vary greatly in length and focus, this text includes more material than may be necessary for many of them. When instructors do not want or have time to cover all the material in the text, they are encouraged to be selective: Cover structures that students have the most difficulty with, and omit structures that they already have a command of. In addition, instructors may want to omit diagnostic or review material, reading passages, and activities; of course, the extra material may be used as the basis for quizzes or tests, if desired.

Changes to the Second Edition

1. More practice is given for many of the key structures. New exercises have been added, most of which are tightly controlled.
2. Several grammar explanations now include more detail.
3. All material has been updated as necessary, and some reading passages have been changed. In certain readings and exercises, vocabulary has been simplified.
4. The present perfect tense with *ever, never,* etc. and the present perfect continuous have been moved from Chapter 1 to Chapter 4, and work on questions, short responses, and prepositions has been expanded. The future present tense has been omitted from the book, as well as material on indefinite pronouns and adjectives. In Chapter 5, the number of phrasal verbs has been reduced.
5. The new edition has a clearer design and layout. New photos and artwork have been included as needed to accompany exercises and readings. Verb charts were modified for improved clarity.
6. The second edition includes an index.

ACKNOWLEDGMENTS

Numerous people contributed their ideas, energy, time, and faith to the development of this text. The authors are very grateful to all colleagues, friends, and family who helped. We would like to thank the following reviewers, whose comments, both favorable and critical, were of great value in the development of the text: Tiby Applestein, Newbury Junior College; Lois Locci, De Anza College; and Margaret Segal. A special thanks to Elaine Kirn for her assistance throughout the project.

Also, thanks to the following reviewers of the first edition for their help in shaping the second edition: Barbara Flaharan Aghai, Tacoma Community College; James Burke, El Paso Community College; Sylvia Carlson, Mountain View College, Dallas; David Fein, UCLA Extension; Ardis Flenniken, California State University, Northridge; Marie Greco, Springfield Technical Community College; Matthew Handelsman, St. Michael's College; Vivian P. Hefley, Iowa State University; George Krikorian, Boston University; Michael Kuhlmann, University of California Extension, Berkeley; Martina Kusi-Mensah, Mountain View College, Dallas; Karen O'Neill, San Jose State University; Laurie Roberts, City College of San Francisco; Simin Rooholamini, County College of Morris; Helen Schley, Portland State University; Webster J. Van De Mark, Valencia Community College; Bill VanderWerft, City College of San Francisco, and Ellen Wall, City College of San Francisco.

Appreciation goes to Cathy de Heer for her work on the production of the text. And above all, heartfelt thanks to Mary McVey Gill and Eirik Børve, whose constant encouragement and support made the completion of this project possible.

P. K. W.
M. M. C.
L. R. B.

INTERACTIONS II
A Communicative Grammar

EDUCATION AND STUDENT LIFE

Review of Basic Verb Tenses

THE SIMPLE PRESENT AND PRESENT CONTINUOUS TENSES; FREQUENCY AND TIME EXPRESSIONS

How do you usually feel during your first few days at a new school? Share your ideas and experiences while answering the following questions about the picture.

1. Who are these people and where are they?
2. Describe the two young men in the center of the picture. What problem does one of the students have? How will he solve it?

The First Day

STEVE: Do you need some help? You seem lost.

MIGUEL: Thanks, I *am* lost! I'm looking for the foreign student office. Can you help me?

STEVE: Sure, I'm going near there. Do you want to come with me? By the way, my name's Steve. What's yours?

MIGUEL: I'm Miguel.

STEVE: Where do you come from, Miguel?

MIGUEL: I come from Colombia. I'm here to study architecture. Are you from here?

STEVE: No, I'm not from Madison. I'm from Canada, from Toronto. I started college in Canada, but I'm finishing my degree here.

MIGUEL: What are you studying?

STEVE: I'm majoring in engineering. I'm taking a lot of computer courses now. They're very crowded this semester.

MIGUEL: Do you live in a dorm?

STEVE: No, I don't. I'm here with my wife and baby daughter. We have an apartment on the other side of town. Where do you live?

MIGUEL: I was in a hotel, but I'm moving into Meyer Dormitory this afternoon.

STEVE: There's the foreign student office. Good luck!

Discussing the Passage

1. What is Miguel looking for? Where is he from?
2. What is Steve majoring in? Where does he live?
3. What are dormitories? Are you living in one now?

The Simple Present Tense

The simple present tense can describe habits, routines, or events that happen regularly. It can also express opinions or make general statements of fact. Time expressions such as the following often appear with this tense: *always, often, never, rarely, sometimes, usually, every day, in general.*

Statements of fact:	I **go** to City College.
	He **goes** to City College.
Opinions:	I **like** my classes.
	He **doesn't like** his classes.
Regular events, habits, or routines:	I **have** classes every day from 9:00 to 2:45.
	He **has** classes three days a week.

The Verb *Be*

	Affirmative Statements	**Negative Statements**
Long Forms	I **am** a student. He She **is** at the college. It We You **are** in the library. They	I **am not** a student. He She **is not** at the college. It We You **are not** in the library. They
Contracted Forms	**I'm** here. **He's** **She's** here. **It's** **We're** **You're** here. **They're**	**I'm** not there. He She **isn't** there. It We You **aren't** there. They

	Questions	Affirmative Answers	Negative Answers

Yes/No Questions and Short Answers	**Am** I a student?
	
	   he
	Is she at the college?
	   it
	
	   we
	Are you in the library?
	   they
		Yes, **I am.**
		
		   he
		Yes, she **is.**
		   it
		
		   we
		Yes, you **are.**
		   they
			No, **I'm not.**
			
			   he
			No, she **isn't.**
			   it
			
			   we
			No, you **aren't.**
			   they

Have and Other Verbs

	Affirmative Statements	Negative Statements
Long Forms	I We You **have** classes today. They He She **has** many books. It I We You **study** a lot. They He She **works** every day. It	I We You **do not have** classes today. They He She **does not have** many books. It I We You **do not study** a lot. They He She **does not work** every day. It
Contracted Forms		I We You **don't** know. They He She **doesn't** work. It

	Questions	Affirmative Answers	Negative Answers
Yes/No Questions and Short Answers	**Do** I we you they **have** classes today?	Yes, I we you they **do.**	No, I we you they **don't.**
	Does he she it **have** classes today?	Yes, he she it **does.**	No, he she it **doesn't.**
	Do I we you they **study** a lot?		
	Does he she it **work** every day?		

Note: See pages 50–51 for spelling rules for the *-s* ending of present tense verbs. See Part Four of this chapter for more information on questions and responses.

A. Exercise: Underline all uses of the simple present tense in the conversation "The First Day," at the beginning of the chapter.

B. Exercise: We often use the simple present tense to give information about ourselves. Complete the sentences with appropriate forms of the following verbs. Use each verb at least once.

be   have
be interested in   live
come

1. His name *is* Miguel.

2. Miguel _____ Colombian.

3. He _____ from Bogotá.

4. He _____ in Meyer Dormitory.

5. He _____ an American roommate.

6. He _____ architecture.

7. Their names _____ Steve, Nancy, and Barbara.

8. They _____ Canadian.

9. They _____ from Toronto.

10. They _____ in an apartment.

C. Activity: **Telling about Yourself.** Introduce yourself to your class. Use ideas from the opening conversation and Exercise B and add any other information you would like to share with the class.

D. Exercise: Complete the following conversation with the simple present form of the verbs in parentheses. Use contractions when possible.

MARIA: Hi, Daniel! How _are_ (be) you?

It _'s_ (be) good to see you!

DANIEL: Hi, Maria! I _____ (be) fine.
                                        1
And you?

MARIA: Great! Daniel, I _____ (want)
                                          2
to introduce you to Isabelle. She

_____ (come) from France.
        3

She _____ (have) a
              4

scholarship to study here. Her

brother _____ (live) here, too.
                    5

DANIEL: It _____ (be) nice to meet you,
                      6

Isabelle. How _____ you

_____ (like) the United States?
        7

ISABELLE: I _____ (like) Madison a lot. It
                    8

_____ (be) very pretty. I
        9

_____ (not know) about other places,
        10

though. I _____ (hope) to visit many places with my brother.
                11

DANIEL: My brother _____ (be) here, too. We _____ (share) an apartment
                          12   13

with another student.

MARIA: _____ you _____ (have) classes now? Let's all go to the Student
                            14

Union for lunch. They _____ (make) great hamburgers, and the food
                                15

there _____ (not cost) very much.
              16

Daniel, this is my friend Isabelle. She's from Paris.

E. **Exercise**: In pairs, make statements, questions, and responses in the simple present tense using the following cues. Use the examples as models.

Examples: I / have a professor for history class
            a teaching assistant →
            S1: **I have a professor for history class. Do you have a professor, too?**
            S2: **No, I don't. I have a teaching assistant.**

            my brother / study here
            a technical school →
            S1: **My brother studies here. Does your brother study here, too?**
            S2: **No, he doesn't. He studies at a technical school.**

1. I / live in a dorm
    an apartment
2. I / have classes every day
    three days a week
3. my roommate / come from the United States
    Canada
4. my roommate / always study at the library
    in our apartment
5. my neighbors / play the stereo all night
    go to bed early
6. my professors / assign work every night
    about twice a week
7. I / always do my homework at the last minute
    ahead of time
8. my math teacher / have office hours three times a week
    once a week

Adverbs of Frequency and Other Time Expressions

A common use of the simple present tense is to describe habits or routines. The following adverbs and time expressions are often used with this tense to indicate frequency.

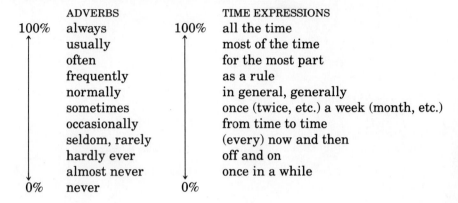

	ADVERBS		TIME EXPRESSIONS
100%	always	100%	all the time
	usually		most of the time
	often		for the most part
	frequently		as a rule
	normally		in general, generally
	sometimes		once (twice, etc.) a week (month, etc.)
	occasionally		from time to time
	seldom, rarely		(every) now and then
	hardly ever		off and on
	almost never		once in a while
0%	never	0%	

Here are some guidelines for placement of these expressions.

	Examples	**Notes**
With the Verb *Be*	I am **usually** on time. She is **rarely** late.	One- or two-word adverbs of frequency come after *be*.
With All Other Verbs and Verb Tenses	I **seldom** go to class late. She **rarely** goes to class. He has **never** been late.	One- or two-word adverbs of frequency normally come before the main verb or between the auxiliary and main verbs in a statement.
Longer Time Expressions with All Verbs	They are late **once in a while.** **Once in a while** they come late.	Longer time expressions usually come at the beginning or end of a sentence.
***Ever* with Questions**	Is he **ever** late? Do you **ever** come late?	*Ever* means "any time." *Ever* and other adverbs of frequency come after the subject in a question.

F. Exercise: Use a variety of appropriate adverbs of frequency to complete the following.

1.

I'm a terrible student. I'm _____ late for class. I'm ___*never*___ on time. I _____ do my assignments, and I fail at least one class. . . .

2. I'm a good student, but I like to have fun, too. I'm _____ late for class, and I ___*seldom*___ forget assignments. I _____ go out on week-ends, and I _____ go out on weeknights. . . .

3.

I'm an excellent student. I _____ get straight A's. I ___*hardly ever*___ go out. I am _____ in the library studying.

G. Activity: Telling About Yourself. What kind of student are you? Tell about yourself by completing the following. Add other information if you like.

I'm a _____ student. I'm _____ late for class.

I'm _____ on time. I _____ do my assign-

ments. I _____ get good grades. . . . On weekends,

I. . . . On weeknights, I. . . .

H. Exercise: Use the cues in each picture to make complete statements about these people.

Example: **Paul almost always does his assignments. Every now and then Christine forgets assignments.**

Do my assignments? Almost always...

Forget assignments? Every now and then.

(Am I on time?) As a rule, yes...

(Late?) Well, occasionally.

1.

Study at the library? Hardly ever.

The library? Off and on.

2.

(Go to the language lab?) Once in a while.

(Language lab?) Almost never.

3.

Do I write my family and friends? Never! Call? Always.

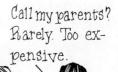

Call my parents? Rarely. Too expensive.

4.

I. Activity: Getting and Giving Information. Most colleges and universities have a variety of facilities, such as libraries, sports centers, theaters, and museums. In pairs, ask one another the following questions.

1. How often do you study at the library? Do you ever check out books?
2. How frequently do you use the language lab?
3. Do you ever go to movies or plays on campus?
4. Do you usually buy your lunch at the campus cafeteria?
5. How often do you use the gym? The pool? The tennis courts?
6. Do you ever go to a museum on campus? Which one?

J. Exercise: Underline all uses of the present continuous tense in the conversation at the beginning of this chapter. Tell whether the activities are happening at the moment of speaking, are currently in progress, or are plans for the future.

K. Exercise: Look at the picture at the beginning of the chapter and describe what is happening in it. Use the following cues to help you.

Example: look at a map → **Miguel is looking at a map.**

1.   look for the foreign student office
2.   try to help Miguel
3.   ride bicycles
4.   carry books
5.   read a college catalog
6.   talk in front of the student union

The Present Continuous Tense

The present continuous tense can describe activities that are happening at the moment of speaking, activities that are currently in progress, or plans for the future. Time expressions such as these often appear with this tense: *now, right now, at the moment, today, this week (month), these days, nowadays.*

Activities at the moment of speaking:	**I'm doing** my homework right now. She**'s studying** at the library now.
Activities currently in progress:	**I'm taking** math this semester. He**'s majoring** in chemistry.
Plans for the future:	**I'm not moving** tomorrow. **I'm moving** on Saturday. My roommate **is arriving** on Sunday.

	Affirmative Statements	**Negative Statements**
Long Forms	I **am studying** now. He She **is working.** It We You **are taking** math. They	I **am not studying** now. He She **is not working.** It We You **are not taking** math. They
Contracted Forms	**I'm** working. **He's** **She's** working. **It's** **We're** **You're** working. **They're**	**I'm** not working. He She **isn't** working. It We You **aren't** working. They

	Questions	**Affirmative Answers**	**Negative Answers**
Yes/No Questions and Short Answers	**Am I studying** now? he **Is** she **working?** it we **Are** you **taking** math? they	Yes, I **am.** he Yes, she **is.** it we Yes, you **are.** they	No, I'm **not.** he No, she **isn't.** it we No, you **aren't.** they

Note: See pages 50–51 for spelling rules for the *-ing* ending of present participles. See Part Four of this chapter for more information on questions and responses.

L. Exercise: Complete the following conversation with present continuous forms of the verbs in parentheses. Use contractions when possible. Pay close attention to the spelling of the *-ing* forms.

DANIEL: How ___*are*___ your classes ___*going*___ (go), Maria? _____

you _____ (take) a lot of different subjects?

1

MARIA: Well, this semester I _____ (finish) all the basic psychology

2

courses, so I _____ (take) six classes. I _____ (try)

3   4

to find a part-time job, too. This afternoon, I _____ (inter-

5

view) for a job at a psychology lab.

DANIEL: You _____ (work) too hard! I _____ (not

6   7

study) as much this semester, and I _____ (enjoy) life much

8

more. My brother and I _____ (play) on a soccer team, and

9

we _____ (learn) about photography. We _____

10   11

(plan) some trips, too. Next weekend, we _____ (visit) some

12

friends in Chicago.

MARIA: That's great! Maybe next semester I'll take it easy.

M. Exercise: In pairs, take turns asking and answering questions in the present continuous tense using the following cues. Use the example as a model.

Example: you / live in the dorm this semester

         in an apartment →

        MARIA: **Are you living in the dorm this semester?**

        DANIEL: **No, I'm not. I'm living in an apartment now.**

1. you / take Russian history this semester

European history
2. your roommate / still major in economics

political science
3. your friends / still learn word processing

data processing
4. your boyfriend (girlfriend) / study African history this semester

African languages

Nonaction Verbs and the Continuous Tenses

Verbs that express feelings or thoughts are not normally used in continuous tenses. Verbs that express possession or perceptions are used in continuous tenses only in very specific cases.

	Examples	**Verbs/Notes**
Feelings, Opinions, or Thoughts	I **don't understand** your question. What **do** you **mean?** I **want** to know. **Do** you **mind** explaining?	appear mean appreciate need be prefer believe recognize dislike remember hate seem know sound like understand love want
Possession	She **owns** a house. She also **has** a car. *Compare:* She **is having** problems with her car. We're **having** dinner at 6:00. I'm **having** a party on Friday.	belong to own have possess The *-ing* form is used with *have* in some idiomatic expressions.
Perceptions (Senses)	This pizza **tastes** good. It **smells** delicious. *Compare:* I **am tasting** the pizza now.	wear look see smell taste The *-ing* form is used to express an action.

Note: The verbs *hear, mean, need,* and *want* sometimes appear in the present perfect continuous.

 Examples: I've been meaning to call you.

      I've been hearing stories about you.

N. Exercise: Contrast of the Simple Present and Present Continuous Tenses.
Complete the following conversation with appropriate forms of the verbs in
parentheses.

Dorm Food

DANIEL: This food __*smells*__ (smell) awful!

MARIA: If you _____ (think) that it _____ (smell) bad, wait until
                1   2

you _____ (taste) it!
         3

DANIEL: Why _____ this cafeteria _____ (have) such terrible
                                          4

food? I _____ (remember) the food at the cafeteria at my univer-
         5

sity. It was much better than this. I _____ (not understand)!
                                           6

Why _____ the cook at this dorm _____ (use /
                                                7

always) so much grease? And, why _____ he _____
                                                     8

(cook) everything too long?

MARIA: Well, if you _____ (not like) greasy, tasteless food, this
                                     9

_____ (not be) the place to eat. Today they _____ (serve)
        10   11

"mystery meat" again. _____ you _____ (see) my room-
                                            12

mate over there? She _____ (try) to cut the meat with a plastic
                                  13

fork. Good luck!

DANIEL: I _____ (not want) to eat here tonight, that _____ (be)
               14   15

for sure! I _____ (get) a stomach ache just looking at this food.
                        16

MARIA: I _____ (have) an idea. How about getting a hamburger
              17

somewhere?

DANIEL: That _____ (sound) like a great idea. Let's go.
              18

O. Activity: Expressing Opinions. What are your opinions about American food, or food at your school cafeteria or nearby lunch spot? Make at least five original statements using the following verbs: *like, dislike, appear, look, seem, smell, taste.*

P. Activity: Getting to Know Your Classmates. Take this opportunity to get to know more about your new classmates. Make a chart like the one below and use it to find classmates with similar backgrounds and interests. After you've finished, give a brief summary of all the interests you share with other students.

Example: **Toshio and I have the same birthday! Also, both of us play tennis and golf....**

NAME	BIRTHDAY	FAMILY	EDUCATION	INTERESTS	OTHER
José Rico	May 2	single 2 brothers	B.A. in French lit.	playing guitar	works in an ice cream store

PART TWO

THE PAST CONTINUOUS AND SIMPLE PAST TENSES

Is homesickness a problem for you? Share your ideas and experiences while answering the following questions about the picture.

1. Describe the picture. Who is in it? Where is it?
2. How is the student probably feeling? What is he probably thinking about? How do you know?
3. What can he do about this?

Studying Abroad

Over 300,000 foreign students are studying in the United States, and homesickness is often a problem. Having a friend to talk to is sometimes the best remedy for it.

TOM: Hi, Miguel! How is it going?

MIGUEL: Well, . . . okay, . . . no, terrible. I was thinking about home, and I was getting a little homesick.

TOM: I know what you mean. I'm homesick, too.

MIGUEL: You know, a year ago now, I was studying at the university. I was really busy. While I was taking classes, I was also working for my father on weekends.

TOM: Why did you leave your country, then? Didn't you get a degree there?

MIGUEL: When I won a scholarship to study here, I decided to leave. It was a great opportunity. And, of course, I wanted to have the experience of studying abroad. I made the right decision, but sometimes it's hard.

Discussing the Passage

1. What was Miguel doing a year ago? Why did he leave his country?
2. Are you studying away from home? Do you get homesick? What do you miss the most about your home town or country?

The Past Continuous Tense

The past continuous tense describes activities that were happening or in progress in the past: in the recent past, at a specific time in the past, or during a period of time in the past. It often describes or "sets" a scene. Time expressions such as *just a moment, (week, month, year) ago, at that time, at this time last week (month, year),* or *in (during, by) the summer (June, etc.)* often appear with this tense. Chapter 7 includes information on the use of the past continuous with *when* and *while.*

Recent past:	I **was watching** the news a moment ago. The announcer **was just telling** about the fire at the library.
Specific time in the past:	My roommate **was studying** at the library at the time of the fire. Lots of students **were studying** at that time.
Period of time in the past:	My classmates **were working** on the project during the summer. I **was doing** homework all morning.

	Affirmative Statements	**Negative Statements**
Long Forms	I He She **was working** then. It We You **were studying then.** They	I He She **was not working** then. It We You **were not studying** then. They
Contracted Forms	I He She **wasn't** working. It We You **weren't** working. They	

	Questions	**Affirmative Answers**	**Negative Answers**
Yes/No Questions and Short Answers	I **Was** he **working** then? she it we **Were** you **studying** then? they	I Yes, he **was.** she it we Yes, you **were.** they	I No, he **wasn't.** she it we No, you **weren't.** they

Note: See pages 50–51 for spelling rules for the *-ing* ending of present participles. See page 15 for information on verbs that do not normally appear in the continuous tenses. See Part Four for more information on questions and responses.

A. Exercise: Use the following cues to form sentences with the past continuous and various time expressions.

Example: a year ago / Miguel / study at the university in his country →
          A year ago Miguel was studying at the university in his country.

1. in 1988 / Miguel / still live in Colombia
2. at that time / he / study at the university
3. he / not work
4. during the summer of 1988 / Tom / travel in Europe
5. by the end of the summer / he / start to get homesick

B. **Exercise**: Homesickness brings back memories of special moments. Use the following cues to describe the scene of a special evening Miguel had a year ago. Use the past continuous in your sentence.

Example: My girlfriend and I / celebrate her birthday →
   My girlfriend and I were celebrating her birthday.

1. she / wear a beautiful black dress
2. I / wear my best suit
3. we / hold hands and drink champagne
4. the waiters / smile at us
5. the band / play romantic music

C. **Exercise**: Imagine that you are sitting in your American history class. The lecture is boring, and you are having trouble concentrating. Answer the following questions in complete sentences using the past continuous.

1. Were you paying attention to the professor a moment ago?
2. What (Who) were you looking at a moment ago?
3. What (Who) were you thinking about a few minutes ago?
4. Were you sitting in class yesterday at this time?
5. What were you doing last Sunday at this time?

D. **Activity: Describing Scenes or Special Events.** What special events do you think of when you look back at the past? A party, a vacation, or a special dinner? Briefly describe the scene, telling who was there, what everyone was wearing and doing, and how you were feeling.

E. **Exercise: Contrast of the Past Continuous and Present Continuous Tenses.** Tom is complaining that nothing in his life ever changes. Use the following cues to compare past and present activities in Tom's life.

Example: study chemistry →
   A year ago I was studying chemistry, and I'm still studying chemistry.

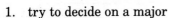

My life is really boring compared to yours. What was I doing a year ago? A year ago....

It was so romantic....

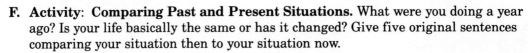

1. try to decide on a major
2. live in the dorm
3. save money for a car
4. look for a part-time job
5. plan to learn French

F. **Activity: Comparing Past and Present Situations.** What were you doing a year ago? Is your life basically the same or has it changed? Give five original sentences comparing your situation then to your situation now.

Examples: **A year ago I was studying English, and today I'm still studying English.**

   A year ago I was living in Tokyo, but now I'm living in Canada.

The Simple Past Tense

The simple past tense describes actions or situations that began and ended in the past. Time expressions such as these often appear with this tense: *yesterday, last Monday (week, year),* or *two days (a week) ago.*

Past actions: I **studied** at a South American university for three years.
      I **won** a scholarship a year ago.

Past situations: He **enjoyed** most of his classes.
       He **didn't like** math or chemistry.

	Affirmative Statements	Negative Statements
Long Forms	I He She It **worked** last night. We You They	I He She It **did not work** last night. We You They
Contracted Forms		I He She It **didn't** work. We You They

	Questions	Affirmative Answers	Negative Answers

Yes/No Questions and Short Answers	I
	  he
	  she
	Did it **work** last night?
	  we
	  you
	  they
		I
		   he
		   she
		Yes, it **did.**
		   we
		   you
		   they
			I
			   he
			   she
			No, it **didn't.**
			   we
			   you
			   they

Note: See pages 50–51 for spelling rules for the *-ed* ending of regular past verbs. See pages 48–50 for a list of irregular past verbs. See Part Four for more information on questions and responses.

G. Exercise: The Simple Past Tense with Regular Verbs. Miguel's roommate, Tom, is from the U.S. Midwest. Tell a little about Tom's life by forming complete sentences with the following cues. Pay careful attention to the spelling and pronunciation of the verb endings.

Example: Tom / enjoy his childhood a lot →
         Tom enjoyed his childhood a lot.

1. Tom / live with his parents until college
2. Tom / attend a public high school
3. He / play many sports in high school
4. He / work in a restaurant during high school
5. He / save money from his job
6. Tom / travel a lot during high school
7. He / apply to three universities
8. Tom / want to study business
10. He / decide to go to a large, public university

H. Exercise: The Simple Past Tense with Irregular Verbs. Miguel is a Colombian studying at a large U.S. university. Tell about Miguel's life by forming complete sentences with the following cues.

Example: Miguel / grow up in Colombia →
         Miguel grew up in Colombia.

1. his parents / meet each other in Bogotá
2. they / get married in 1960
3. they / have six children
4. Miguel / go to a bilingual school
5. he / become fluent in English
6. he / begin university studies in Bogotá
7. he / take a test for a scholarship
8. Miguel / win the scholarship
9. he / choose to study architecture in the United States
10. he / leave Colombia to complete his education

I. Exercise: Complete the following conversation with the simple past form of the verbs in parentheses or a form of *do* + simple verb.

TOM: Miguel, guess what? Your sister ___*called*___ (call) an hour ago.

MIGUEL: Really? From Colombia?

TOM: Yes, and she _____ (speak) to me in English. Her English is very
     1
good.

MIGUEL: It should be good. She _____ (study) here, too. At first, she
₂

_____ (plan) to stay for only one summer, and she just
₃

_____ (take) English courses. She _____ (become)
₄   ₅

fluent very fast. Then she _____ (apply) to the University of
₆

Texas. They _____ (accept) her and she _____ (begin)
₇   ₈

studying there that fall.

TOM: She must be very smart. What _____ she _____ (major)
₉

in?

MIGUEL: When we _____ (be) small, she _____ (tell/always)
₁₀   ₁₁

everyone that she was going to be a scientist. Well, she _____
₁₂

(start) in engineering, but she _____ (change) majors. In the end,
₁₃

she _____ (get) her degree in computer science—with honors!
₁₄

We all _____ (feel) very proud of her.
₁₅

J. Exercise: In pairs, use the following cues to make short conversations. Use the
example as a model. Change nouns to pronouns when necessary.

Example: take Biology 110 →
    S1: **Did you take Biology 110?**
    S2: **No, I didn't, but my best friend (roommate, etc.) took it.**

1. study calculus in high school
2. pass the math exam
3. meet the new biology professor
4. get the last computer assignment
5. fail the accounting test yesterday
6. buy the lab manual for chemistry

K. Exercise: Contrast of the Simple Past and Past Continuous Tenses. Fill in the blanks with the correct forms of the verbs in parentheses.

ANA: What _____ you _____ (do) two hours ago?
                                    1

HON MAY: I _____ (sleep), of course. It was only six-thirty A.M.!
                    2

ANA: _____ you _____ (not feel) the earthquake?
                                    3

HON MAY: Earthquake? I _____ (not know) there was an earthquake.
                                4

ANA: Well, there was. It _____ (start) at exactly six-thirty-eight A.M.
                                5

I _____ (do) my exercises at the time. Suddenly the floor
            6

_____ (start) to move. It _____ (last) for about fifteen
        7   8

seconds.

HON MAY: _____ (Be) you afraid?
                9

ANA: To tell you the truth, I _____ (enjoy) it!
                                        10

L. Exercise: Contrast of Tenses. Complete the following letter with the simple present, simple past, present continuous, or past continuous forms of the verbs in parentheses.

Madison
September 10

Dear Mom and Dad,

I ___*miss*___ (miss) all of you, and I _____ (hope) everything
                                                            1

_____ (be) fine at home.
        2

Let me tell you about my first few days. I _____ (arrive) in
                                                        3

Madison three weeks ago. At that time it _____ (rain) a lot. My first
                                                4

few days _____ (not be) very good because I _____ (feel)
            5   6

depressed and homesick. I immediately _____ (notice) a lot of things
                                            7

that _____ (be) new to me. The students, especially, _____
        8   9

(seem) so different from students at home. Students here _____
                                                                10

(wear/usually) very casual clothing, and there _____ (be) some
                                                        11

students who _____ (not take) school very seriously. To give you
                12

an idea, I'll describe one situation. Last Monday I _____ (study) in
                                                            13

the library. I _____ (try) hard to concentrate, but several students
                14

around me _____ (talk) and some _____ (laugh). I
                15   16

_____ (get) upset. But then I _____ (ask) them to be
        17   18

quiet, and they _____ (be) very nice about it.
                        19

Now I _____ (understand) that at first I _____ (be)
    20   21
just too nervous about going to school in a new country. And, I
_____ (begin) to enjoy my life here. It _____ (be) autumn,
    22   23
and the leaves on the trees _____ (change) color. Right now some
                                24
students _____ (play) football—American football—outside. Yes-
            25
terday, my roommate Tom _____ (ask) me to play with them, and
                            26
I _____ (score) two touchdowns! But we _____ (lose)
    27   28
anyway.

This _____ (be) all for now. I _____ (have) to study.
        29   30
My teachers _____ (give/always) us a lot of homework.
                31

Love,

Miguel

M. Activity: Describing Schools and Comparing Educational Experiences.
Where were you studying a year ago (two years ago, etc.)? Were you in high school
or college? Were you studying in another country? Think about the differences
between this school and the schools that you attended before now. In small groups,
tell each other a little about your education. If you are from a foreign country, tell a
little about your system of education, too.

PART THREE

BE GOING TO, THE SIMPLE FUTURE TENSE, AND THE FUTURE CONTINUOUS TENSE

Have you ever taken a lecture class? Are classes in your native country primarily lectures or small group discussions? Share your ideas and experiences while answering the following questions about the picture.

1. Who is the man walking into the room?
2. What kind of a class is this and what are these students going to learn?

Computer Science 104

"Good morning. This is Computer Science 104. My name is John Andrews, and I will be your instructor for this course. Tomorrow I am going to choose two teaching assistants who will teach the discussion sections and help grade the assignments. I will introduce the new T.A.s to you at our next meeting.

"During the course, you'll be learning about three important computer languages: BASIC, PASCAL, and FORTRAN. For the next three weeks, we will be spending a lot of time on BASIC. You are going to write programs in BASIC first. Then we'll begin PASCAL. There will be a midterm and a final exam. If you do well on the programming assignments, you will have no trouble with the tests.

"Are there any questions before I begin today's lecture?"

Discussing the Passage

1. What languages will these students learn? What exams will they take?
2. What is a lecture? What is a discussion section? Are there other types of classes at the college level?
3. What is a teaching assistant? Do you have T.A.s in any of your courses? What will they be teaching?

Be Going to

Be going to + verb often expresses specific future plans or intentions. It is common in conversation and often sounds like "gonna" or "gunna."

Future plans: **I'm going to** study tonight.
My roommate **is going to** help me with my work.

Future intentions: **I'm going to** get good grades this semester.
I'm not going to go to so many parties.

	Affirmative Statements	**Negative Statements**
Long Forms	I **am going to** study tonight. He She **is going to** work. It We You **are going to** finish now. They	I **am not going to** study tonight. He She **is not going to** work. It We You **are not going to** finish now. They
Contracted Forms	**I'm** going to work. **He's** **She's** going to work. **It's** **We're** **You're** going to work. **They're**	**I'm** not going to work. He She **isn't** going to work. It We You **aren't** going to work. They

	Questions	**Affirmative Answers**	**Negative Answers**
Yes/No Questions and Short Answers	**Am I going to** study tonight? he **Is** she **going to** work? it we **Are** you **going to** finish now? they	Yes, I **am.** he Yes, she **is.** it we Yes, you **are.** they	No, I'm **not.** he No, she **isn't.** it we No, you **aren't.** they

Note: See Part Four of this chapter for more information on questions and responses.

A. Exercise: Use *be going to* with the following cues to ask your teacher questions about your English course. Then ask your teacher at least five additional questions about plans for this quarter or semester.

Example: you / assign homework every night →
Are you going to assign homework every night?

1. we / finish this book
2. we / have many tests
3. you / give homework on the weekends
4. the class / take any field trips
5. we / have any class parties

B. Exercise: When students begin a new quarter or semester, they usually have good intentions to study a lot, to get good grades, and so forth. List four things that you are going to do this semester and then list four things that you are *not* going to do. You may use the following cues or form your own sentences.

Examples: **I'm going to study every night.**

I'm not going to go to parties during the week.

- go to the language lab every week
- study my notes after every lecture
- wait until the last minute to begin studying for exams
- visit my professors during office hours
- do my homework with the T.V. on
- turn assignments in late
- fall asleep in class

The Simple Future Tense

Like *be going to,* the simple future tense expresses future intentions. In some cases, *will* and *be going to* are interchangeable. However, *will* (not *going to*) is normally used to express predictions, requests, offers, and promises. In spoken English, the short forms of *will* (*'ll*) and *will not* (*won't*) are common.

Intentions:	I'll **work** much harder this semester, Mom.
Predictions:	By studying more, I'll **get** better grades.
Requests:	**Will** you **help** me with my work?
Offers:	I'll **find** some books for you.
Promises:	I'll **help** you on Saturday.

	Affirmative Statements	Negative Statements
Long Forms	I He She It **will finish** at 10:00. We You They	I He She It **will not finish** at 10:00. We You They
Contracted Forms	**I'll** **He'll** **She'll** **It'll** work. **We'll** **You'll** **They'll**	I He She It **won't** work. We You They

	Questions	Affirmative Answers	Negative Answers
Yes/No Questions and Short Answers	I he she **Will** it **work?** we you they	I he she Yes, it **will.** we you they	I he she No, it **won't.** we you they

Note: See Part Four of this chapter for more information on questions and responses. Chapter 6 includes information on the use of this tense with *if, unless, when,* and other conjunctions.

C. Exercise: Mothers always worry when their children go away to school. In pairs, take turns asking and answering this worried mother's questions. You may give short or long answers.

Example: study hard →
    S1: **Will you study hard?**
    S2: **Yes, Mom, I'll study very hard.**

1. get plenty of sleep
2. eat well
3. go to bed early
4. do all of your assignments
5. be polite in class
6. ask a lot of questions

D. Activity: **Making Promises.** Imagine the things your mother or father might say to you or ask you to do while you're in school. In pairs, take turns making requests and promises, using Exercise C as a model.

The Future Continuous Tense

The future continuous tense normally describes actions that will be in progress in the future. This means that they will begin before, and perhaps continue after, a specific time in the future. Specific time expressions such as *at 3:00 (noon), at that time, at this time tomorrow (next week), the day after tomorrow, a week (month) from today* often appear with this tense.

Actions in progress in the future:	At this time tomorrow, I'**ll be taking** a test.
	Will you **be taking** the test, too?
	A week from today, we'**ll be flying** home.

	Affirmative Statements	**Negative Statements**
Long Forms	I He She It **will be working** at noon. We You They	I He She It **will not be working** at noon. We You They
Contracted Forms	**I'll** **He'll** **She'll** **It'll** be working. **We'll** **You'll** **They'll**	I He She It **won't** be working then. We You They

	Questions	**Affirmative Answers**	**Negative Answers**
Yes/No Questions and Short Answers	I he she **Will** it **be working** at noon? we you they	I he she Yes, it **will.** we you they	I he she No, it **won't.** we you they

Note: See pages 50–51 for spelling rules for the *-ing* ending of present participles. See Part Four of this chapter for more information on questions and responses. See page 15 for a list of verbs that do not normally appear in the continuous tenses.

E. Exercise: Underline all uses of the future continuous tense in the passage "Computer Science 104" at the beginning of Part Three.

F. Exercise: In pairs, take turns asking and answering the following questions using the future continuous tense.

1. What will you be doing at 3:00 P.M. today?
2. I want to come to your apartment at seven o'clock this evening. Will you still be eating dinner then?
3. What will you be doing at this time tomorrow?
4. Where will you be living at this time next year?
5. Will you still be studying two years from now, or will you be working?
6. What will you be doing five years from now?

G. Exercise: Use the following syllabus to describe the coursework expected in Computer Science 104. Use *going to,* the simple future, and the future continuous to form at least ten sentences.

```
Week 1 -  read Chapters 1, 2, 3 of text
          form study groups for research
          projects

Week 2 -  read Chapters 4, 5 of text
          hand in outline for the research project
          start the first program in BASIC

Week 3 -  critique outlines
          finish the first program in BASIC

Week 4 -  work on the research project
          read Chapters 6, 7 of text
          write a program in PASCAL

Week 5 -  review for the exam
          complete first draft of the research
          project

Week 6 -  take midterm exam
          read Chapter 8 of text
```

Examples: **In the first week, we are going to read Chapters 1, 2, and 3 of the text.**

During the first week, we will be forming study groups.

There will be a midterm exam the sixth week.

A class in English as a second language

H. **Exercise: Review of Tenses.** Review all the tenses in this chapter by using appropriate forms of the verbs in parentheses. In some cases, more than one form may be appropriate. Be prepared to explain your choices.

Foreign Students in the United States

The first foreign students _____ (come) to the United States to study over two hundred years ago. For two centuries, until World War II, the percentage of foreign students in the United States _____ (stay) about the same. Then, after the war, foreign student enrollment _____ (start) to change. In the 1950s, the number of foreign students _____ (begin) to increase tremendously. This trend _____ (continue) through the 1960s and 1970s. During 1980 and 1981, for example, more than 300,000 foreigners _____ (study) in U.S. schools. At that time, 47,000 _____ (be) from Iran and almost 20,000 _____ (be) from Taiwan. As a region, South and East Asia _____ (send) the greatest number of students in 1980.

Today, Asian countries _____ (sponsor) even more students, but other nations, like the OPEC countries, _____ (send) fewer students than in the past. In the future, countries _____ (continue/certainly) to send students to the United States, but the numbers and the nationalities of the students _____ (change/probably).

I. Activity: **Discussing Plans for the Future.** What are your academic plans for the future? In small groups, share your plans with your classmates. Include in your discussion:

1. What courses will you need for your major? How interesting and/or difficult will those courses be?
2. Did you do well enough in all your coursework up to now to enter that major? Do many other students also want to major in that field?

A student in an English language lab

PART FOUR

QUESTIONS AND SHORT RESPONSES; PREPOSITIONS

At Miguel's university, every foreign student has an advisor.
Do you have an advisor or counselor at your school? Share
your information about advisors while answering the following questions about the picture.

1. Where is Miguel?
2. What kinds of questions do you think the advisor
   is asking Miguel?

The Foreign Student Advisor

ADVISOR: It's nice to meet you, Miguel. Now, tell me a little about yourself. First of all,
you're from Colombia, aren't you? Did your family come with you?

MIGUEL: Yes, I'm from Colombia. And, no, my family didn't come with me. They're in
Bogota now. My sister studied in the United States several years ago, though.
She won a scholarship to study here, and so did I.

ADVISOR: That's great, Miguel. Well, this is your first visit to the U.S., isn't it? When
did you arrive? How do you like it so far?

MIGUEL: I arrived on Saturday, August 28th. It was a long trip, and I finally got here
at 11:00 P.M. This is my first visit to the States, so I'm a little nervous, of
course! But I know that I'm going to like it here a lot.

ADVISOR: How many hours does it take to fly here from Bogotá?

MIGUEL: Well, it normally takes about twelve hours.

ADVISOR: That's a long trip! Now, tell me about your university work. You began your
studies in Colombia, didn't you? Where did you study? How many semesters
did you complete? I have a copy of your transcripts, don't I? . . .

Discussing the Passage

1. Is this Miguel's first visit to the United States? When did he arrive? How long
   did the trip take him?
2. What are three questions Miguel's advisor asks him?

A. Exercise: Review of Auxiliaries in Questions and Short Answers. In pairs, make complete questions from these shortened forms. Add the appropriate auxiliary (and pronoun, when necessary). Then answer the questions using short answers.

Example: Studying accounting? →
         S1: **Are you studying accounting?**
         S2: **Yes, I am.**

1. Want to see a movie?
2. Going to study tonight?
3. Have a lot of work to do?
4. Get a bad grade on the accounting test?
5. Yesterday's test difficult?
6. Know where Jack is?
7. Jack say where he went?
8. Sally still at the library?
9. Be here when I get back?
10. Studying tomorrow night, too?

Auxiliary Verbs in Short Responses with *Too, Either, So,* and *Neither*

If two sentences have different subjects but the same verb, you can change the second sentence to a short response with auxiliary verbs (or the verb *be*). *Too* or *so* appears in the affirmative, and *either* or *neither* appears in the negative.

	Two Statements	**Statements and Responses**	**Notes**
Affirmative	I like to study. John likes to study.	I like to study. John **does, too.** I like to study. **So** does John.	*Too* follows the auxiliary verb or *be* in the short response. The auxiliary verb or *be* follows *so* in the short response.
Negative	You don't like to study. Mary doesn't like to study.	You don't like to study. Mary **doesn't either.** You don't like to study. **Neither does** Mary.	*Either* follows the auxiliary verb or *be* in the short response. The auxiliary verb or *be* follows *neither* in the short response.

B. Exercise: Complete the following with the appropriate auxiliary verb and *too* or *either*.

Example: My sister hates to study, and I ___*do*___ ___*too*___ .

   She doesn't get good grades, and I ___*don't*___ ___*either*___ .

1.   My sister always gets C's, and I _____ _____ .

2.   I'm not a good student, and she _____ _____ .

3.   I got bad grades last semester, and she _____ _____ .

4.   She's planning to work harder, and I _____ _____ .

5.   I'll go to the library every night, and she _____ _____ .

6.   I won't go to parties every night, and she _____ _____ .

C. Exercise: Work in pairs and take turns making statements and responding. Use the words in parentheses to give short responses with *so* or *neither*. Pay attention to the order of the subject and auxiliary verb in each.

Examples: The textbook for chemistry is expensive. (the lab manual) →
   S1: **The textbook for chemistry is expensive.**
   S2: **So is the lab manual.**

   The books for math are not expensive. (the books for English) →
   S1: **The books for math are not expensive.**
   S2: **Neither are the books for English.**

1.   My dormitory is always noisy. (my apartment building)
2.   The dorm food isn't very good. (the cafeteria food)
3.   Gino's has good pizza. (the student union)
4.   The student union wasn't crowded last night. (Smith Library)
5.   A lot of foreign students study at Smith Library. (many graduate students)
6.   Smith Library closed early last night. (the language lab)

D. Exercise: In pairs, practice making short responses with *so* and *neither*. Student 1 shculd make a true statement. Student 2 should respond truthfully. Use *so* or *neither* in responses that show agreement.

Example: I (don't) like the food at the student union. →
   S1: **I don't like the food at the student union.**
   S2: **Oh, really? I do.** *or*
   Neither do I.

1. I (don't) like the food at the dormitory.
2. I'm (not) going to eat at the dorm tonight.
3. I'm (not) going to study after dinner.
4. I'll (I won't) finish everything tonight.
5. I (don't) have a car.
6. I (don't) think chemistry (biology, English grammar, etc.) is interesting.
7. I got (didn't get) a good grade on the last test.
8. I had (didn't have) a great time during my last vacation.

Tag Questions

Tag questions are short questions at the ends of sentences. They use the same auxiliary verbs as yes/no questions. If the statement is affirmative, the tag question is negative. If the statement is negative, the tag question is affirmative. In general, people use tag questions when they expect a certain response. An affirmative statement and a negative tag question normally receive an affirmative response. A negative statement and an affirmative tag question normally receive a negative response. Note that this is not always the case, however.

	Affirmative Statement + Negative Tag; Expected Response	**Negative Statement + Affirmative Tag; Expected Response**
Simple Present and Past Tenses	"You study a lot, **don't you?**" "Yes, I do." "You studied a lot, **didn't you?**" "Yes, I did."	"You don't study a lot, **do you?**" "No, I don't." "You didn't study a lot, **did you?**" "No, I didn't."
The Verb *Be*; Present and Past Continuous Tenses; *Be Going To*	"You're a student, **aren't you?**" "Yes, I am." "She's studying, **isn't she?**" "Yes, she is." "They were studying, **weren't they?**" "Yes, they were." "He's going to study, **isn't he?**" "Yes, he is."	"You aren't a student, **are you?**" "No, I'm not." "She isn't studying, **is she?**" "No, she isn't." "They weren't studying, **were they?**" "No, they weren't." "He isn't going to study, **is he?**" "No, he isn't."
Simple Future and Future Continuous Tenses	"You will study a lot, **won't you?**" "Yes, I will." "He'll be studying at 3:00, **won't he?**" "Yes, he will."	"You won't study this weekend, **will you?**" "No, I won't." "He won't be studying at 3:00, **will he?**" "No, he won't."

E. Exercise: In pairs, take turns making statements with tag questions and giving responses. Complete the tag question for each statement using the correct form of the verb *be* and the correct pronoun. Then give short responses.

Examples: S1: You aren't studying now, *are* *you* ?
S2: *No,* *I'm* *not* .
S1: Your roommate is studying now, *isn't* *she* ?
S2: *Yes,* *she* *is* .

1.   Your roommate is at the library, _____ _____ ?

2.   He/She was studying at the library last night, _____ _____ ?

3.   You're not going to play soccer tonight, _____ _____ ?

4.   We're playing soccer tonight, _____ _____ ?

5.   Your friends aren't coming tonight, _____ _____ ?

6.   They were here last night, _____ _____ ?

F. Exercise: In pairs, take turns making statements with tag questions and giving responses. Use the simple present, simple past, or simple future tenses.

Example: always ask a lot of questions →
S1: **You always ask a lot of questions, don't you?**
S2: **Yes, I do. I don't always understand everything.**
or **No, I don't.**

not ask a lot of questions yesterday →
S1: **You didn't ask a lot of questions yesterday, did you?**
S2: **No, I didn't, because I understood everything.**

1.   almost always do your homework
2.   not finish your work last night
3.   do your homework tomorrow
4.   not study next Friday night
5.   have fun on the weekend

Information Questions

Information questions ask *who, what, when, where, why, how often, how far,* and so on. As in yes/no questions, in most information questions the auxiliary verb comes *before* the subject. However, in questions about the subject (with *who, which,* and *what*) there is *no* auxiliary verb.

Information Questions with *When, What Time, Where, Why,* etc.

	Question Word	Auxiliary Verb	Subject	Main Verb
With *Be* and *Will*	**When**	**is**	Kim	**coming?**
	What time	**is**	she	**going to arrive?**
	Where	**was**	she	**going?**
	What	**will**	she	**do** here?
	How long	**will**	she	**be staying** in Dallas?
With Other Verbs	**When**	**does**	the bus	**arrive?**
	How long	**does**	the trip	**take?**
	How	**did**	the accident	**happen?**
	Where	**did**	it	**happen?**
	Which hospital	**did**	Kim	**go to?**

Information Questions About the Subject with *Who, Which,* and *What*

	Question Word	Verb
With All Verbs	**Who**	**was hurt** in the accident?
	Who	**is** in the hospital?
	Who	**saw** the accident?
	Which person	**was driving?**
	What	**happened?**

Common Question Words

Question Words	Notes
how	asks about manner
how . . . like	asks for an opinion
how + adjective or adverb	
how cold (hot, far, late, fast, slow, etc.**)**	asks about a characteristic (such as temperature, distance, or speed)
how long	asks about length of time
how many	asks about quantity (count nouns)
how much	asks about quantity (noncount nouns)
how often	asks about frequency
what	asks about things
what . . . be like	asks for a description*
what + noun	
what kind of	asks about category
what color (country, size, etc.**)**	asks for specific details
what time	asks for a specific time
when	asks about time (specific or general)
where	asks about place or direction
which (+ noun)	
which book (city, one, etc.**)**	asks about a specific person, place, or thing
who(m)	asks about people
whose	asks about ownership or possession
why	asks for reasons

* *What does she (he, it) look like?*   asks for a physical description
What is he (she, it) like?   asks about qualities or characteristics (*interesting, nice, fun,* etc.)

Prepositions

Common Prepositions of Time

QUESTION: When (What time) did Kim arrive?
RESPONSE: She arrived **in the morning.**

Example	Notes
in (**during**) the morning (July, the summer, 1984)	Use *in* or *during* with periods of time.
during the week (the month, the year)	
on Tuesday (August 13)	Use *on* with days or dates.
at 3:00 (noon, midnight, the beginning, the end)	Use *at* with specific times. *Exception: at* night
from 9:00 **to** (**until, till**) 5:00	Use *from . . . to* (*until, till*) with beginning and ending times.
for eight hours (three days)	Use *for* with durations of time.

Common Prepositions of Place and Direction

QUESTION: Where did you see Kim?
RESPONSE: I saw her **in class.**

Example	Notes
in class (Ellison Hall, Santa Barbara, California, the West, Canada)	Use *in* with buildings, cities, states, regions, and countries.
on Milpas Street (the Ohio River, Lake Michigan, the East Coast, the Pacific Ocean)	Use *on* with streets and bodies of water.
at 423 Orilla Drive (the corner, home, work, school, church, the office)	Use *at* with specific addresses and certain idiomatic expressions.

QUESTION: Where is the book?
RESPONSE: It's **next to** the typewriter.

QUESTION: Where is the market?
RESPONSE: It's **across** (**up, down**) the street from the theater.

above	**down**	**over**
across	**in front (back) of**	**under**
beside	**near**	**up**
by	**on top of**	

G. **Exercise**: Miguel is talking to his advisor. Complete their conversation with question words.

Example: ADVISOR: Tell me, Miguel . . . ___*What*___'s new?
        MIGUEL: I have a lot to tell you about!

1. ADVISOR: _____ are your classes like?

   MIGUEL: They're all interesting, but my English class is difficult.

2. ADVISOR: _____ English class are you taking?

   MIGUEL: English 117.

3. ADVISOR: _____ is your instructor?

   MIGUEL: Professor Burnson.

4. ADVISOR: _____ does it seem difficult?

   MIGUEL: Because we have to do a lot of writing.

5. ADVISOR: _____ of assignments does he give?

   MIGUEL: The assignments are long essays, but I'm learning a lot from them.

6. ADVISOR: I suggest that you talk to Professor Burnson. _____ is his office?

   MIGUEL: It's in Smith Library.

7. ADVISOR: _____ does he have office hours?

   MIGUEL: From 10:00 A.M. to noon on Tuesdays.

8. ADVISOR: Now, please tell me about your other classes. _____ history class are you taking?

   MIGUEL: Dr. Fendler's.

H. Exercise: Complete the following questions with *how* or with *how + adjective* or *adverb*.

Example: MIGUEL: Tom, ___*how far*___ is the Science Center from here?
          TOM: About five blocks.

1. MIGUEL: _____ computers do they have at the Science Center?

    TOM: About fifty, I think.

2. MIGUEL: _____ does it cost to use a computer?

    TOM: Three dollars an hour, I think.

3. MIGUEL: _____ can you use a computer there?

    TOM: As often as you want, but you should make a reservation first.

4. MIGUEL: _____ can you work at one time?

    TOM: Two hours is the maximum time, I think.

5. MIGUEL: _____ do I get to the Science Center from here?

    TOM: Walk straight down Broadway Avenue.

6. MIGUEL: _____ do you like using a computer?

    TOM: I really like it. I can work much faster.

I. Exercise: Use the catalog pages below to fill in appropriate prepositions of time in the following sentences.

Biology	100	T TH	1:20
	lab[1]	M	7–10 P.M.
		T	7–10
		W	2–5
		TH	7–10
Business	100	M–F	9:20
	110	T TH	8:20
	210[2]	T TH	10:30
Chemistry	101	T TH	11:20
	210	T TH	9:20–11:20
		M W	7–9
		T TH	7–9
English[3]	101	M–F	9:20
	102	MTWTH	10:30
	225	T TH	12:00–1:30

[1] Open hours, biology lab: January 15–March 15
                    April 15–June 1
                    June 15–July 15
                    September 10–December 10

[2] Not offered in summer or winter.

[3] Open hours, language lab: M–F   6–10
                       Sat   8–12

Example: Chemistry 210 has one section *in (during)* the morning and two sections ___*at*___ night.

1. Biology lab meets _____ three hours _____ Wednesday afternoon.

2. Business 210 is offered _____ the spring and _____ the fall.

3. English 225 starts _____ noon and goes _____ an hour and a half.

4. The biology lab is not open _____ August.

5. Most biology labs are held _____ the evening.

6. The language lab has open hours _____ 6:00 _____

    10:00 P.M. _____ the week and _____ 8:00 _____

    12:00 P.M. _____ Saturday morning.

J. Exercise: Use the catalog from Exercise I to make complete sentences about the following. Use negatives when necessary.

Example: Biology 100 / T TH →
   Biology 100 meets on Tuesday(s) and Thursday(s).

1. Biology 100 / 1:20
2. Chemistry 210 / M W / 7–9
3. Chemistry 210 / two hours
4. English 101 / M–F / 9:20
5. English 225 / 90 minutes
6. language lab / Sunday

K. Activity: **Comparing Schedules.** In pairs, take turns asking and answering questions about your schedules. Be sure to include questions about your English classes, other classes, language lab, work (if you have jobs), your free time, and so on. Use the following calendar to help you, and include specific days and times in your answers.

Example: S1: **When do you usually go to the language lab?**
   S2: **I usually go to the lab on Monday and Wednesday at 3:00.**

	Monday	Tuesday	Wednesday	Thursday	Friday	Saturday	Sunday
8:00 9:00 10:00 11:00 12:00 1:00 2:00 3:00 4:00 5:00 Evening							

L. **Exercise**: In pairs, use the map below to help you correct these false statements. You may correct the statements in several different ways.

Example: s1:   The administration building is at the corner of Bridge Road and Bradford Avenue.

  s2:   **Wrong! The administration building is at the corner of College Boulevard and Bradford Avenue.**

1. Smith Library is on Bridge Road.
2. The language lab is behind the computer science building.
3. The administration building is next to the theater.
4. The boathouse is near the music hall.
5. The student union is across the street from the lake.

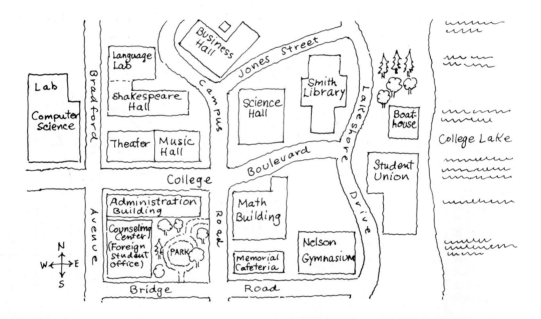

M. **Exercise**: Complete the following with appropriate prepositions of place or direction. Use the map to help you.

Example: "Excuse me. Where is the administration building?"

  "It's ___*at*___ 200 College Boulevard."

1. "Excuse me. Where is the computer science building?"

   "It's _____ the corner _____ College Boulevard and Bradford Avenue. It's _____ the street _____ the theater."

2. "Excuse me. Could you tell me where the foreign student office is?"

    "It's _____ the counseling center. That's _____ Bradford Ave-

    nue _____ the administration building."

3. "Excuse me. Do you know where the boathouse is?"

    "It's _____ Lakeshore Drive _____ the student union."

4. "Excuse me. How do I get _____ Smith Library _____

    here?" "Let's see. _____ We're _____ the counseling center

    now. First, go out the front door and turn _____ your right. Turn

    right again _____ College Boulevard and walk _____ the

    lake. Smith Library is _____ the corner _____ College Bou-

    levard and Lakeshore Drive. It's _____ the street _____ the

    boathouse."

**N. Exercise: Review of Tenses, Questions, and
Responses.** Miguel is visiting his foreign student advisor
again. Complete their conversation by circling the appropriate words. Be prepared to explain your choices.

ADVISOR: Hello, Miguel. Have a seat. How are you (do /(doing))? ((How)/ What kind)
are your classes? You are taking some difficult classes, (are / aren't)$_1$ you?

MIGUEL: Well, I (want / am wanting)$_2$ to talk to you about that. I (don't know / am
not knowing)$_3$ what to do about my calculus class. I (am not understanding / don't understand)$_4$ many things. (Neither / either)$_5$ do many of my
classmates.

ADVISOR: (Did / Were)$_6$ you talk to your professor about this?

MIGUEL: It's difficult to talk to him because he (is / is being)$_7$ very busy. He arrives
(at / on)$_8$ 9:20, exactly, and he (always leaves / leaves always)$_9$ (in / at)$_{10}$
the end of class.

ADVISOR: He has office hours, (doesn't / has)$_{11}$ he?

MIGUEL: Yes, he (does / do).$_{12}$ I (am going to / am going)$_{13}$ make an appointment
with him.

ADVISOR: That's good. Now tell me about your other classes.

MIGUEL: I (enjoy / enjoyed)$_{14}$ them very much. I have classes (from / for)$_{15}$ 9:20 (at /
until)$_{16}$ noon (on / in)$_{17}$ Monday, Wednesday, and Friday. Tuesdays, I have
a lab (for / to)$_{18}$ two hours (in / on)$_{19}$ the evening. I (usually go / go usually)$_{20}$ (at / to)$_{21}$ the library every night . . .

O. Activity: Asking for and Giving Directions. Work in pairs and take turns asking for and giving directions for the following locations on the map from Exercise L. Then take turns asking for and giving directions from your classroom to some places in your area: the library, the student union, your dorm, apartment, or house, your favorite place to study, or a nice place to take a walk. Finally, choose one conversation to role play for the class.

> *Example:* S1: **How do I get to the language lab from here?** *or*
> **Where is the language lab?**
> S2: **Just go up Campus Road. You'll pass the music hall on your left. . . .**

1. from the math building to the language lab
2. from Computer Science to the Student Union
3. from Shakespeare Hall to the park
4. from Nelson Gymnasium to Business Hall

FOR YOUR REFERENCE

Common Irregular Verbs

Simple	Past	Past Participle
be	was/were	been
become	became	become
begin	began	begun
bite	bit	bitten
blow	blew	blown
break	broke	broken
bring	brought	brought
build	built	built
buy	bought	bought
catch	caught	caught
choose	chose	chosen
come	came	come
cost	cost	cost
cut	cut	cut
do	did	done
draw	drew	drawn
drink	drank	drunk
drive	drove	driven
eat	ate	eaten
fall	fell	fallen
feel	felt	felt
fight	fought	fought

Simple	Past	Past Participle
find	found	found
fly	flew	flown
forget	forgot	forgotten
freeze	froze	frozen
get	got	got/gotten
give	gave	given
go	went	gone
grow	grew	grown
have	had	had
hear	heard	heard
hide	hid	hidden
hit	hit	hit
hold	held	held
hurt	hurt	hurt
keep	kept	kept
know	knew	known
lay	laid	laid
leave	left	left
lend	lent	lent
let	let	let
lie	lay	lain
light	lit	lit
	lighted	lighted
lose	lost	lost
make	made	made
mean	meant	meant
meet	met	met
pay	paid	paid
prove	proved	proven/proved
put	put	put
quit	quit	quit
read	read	read
ride	rode	ridden
ring	rang	rung
run	ran	run
say	said	said
sell	sold	sold
send	sent	sent
set	set	set
see	saw	seen
show	showed	shown/showed
shut	shut	shut
sing	sang	sung
sit	sat	sat
sleep	slept	slept
speak	spoke	spoken
spend	spent	spent
stand	stood	stood

Simple	Past	Past Participle
steal	stole	stolen
swim	swam	swum
take	took	taken
tear	tore	torn
tell	told	told
think	thought	thought
throw	threw	thrown
understand	understood	understood
wear	wore	worn
write	wrote	written

Spelling Rules for *-s, -ed, -er, -est,* and *-ing* Endings

This chart summarizes the basic spelling rules for endings with verbs, nouns, and adjectives. Chapter 2 gives more information on nouns, including irregular plural forms. Chapter 8 gives information on adjectives and adverbs, including irregular forms.

Rule	Verb	-s	-ed	-er	-est	-ing
For most words, simply add *-s, -ed, -er, -est,* or *-ing* without making any other changes.	clean cool	cleans cools	cleaned cooled	cleaner cooler	cleanest coolest	cleaning cooling

Spelling changes occur with the following:

Rule	Verb	-s	-ed	-er	-est	-ing
For words ending in a consonant + *y*, change the *y* to *i* before adding *-s, -ed, -er,* or *-est*.	carry happy lonely study worry	carries studies worries	carried studied worried	carrier happier lonelier worrier	happiest loneliest	
For most words ending in *e*, drop the *e* before adding *-ed, -er, -est,* or *-ing*.	dance late nice save write		danced saved	dancer later nicer saver writer	latest nicest	dancing saving writing
Exceptions:	.agree canoe					agreeing canoeing

Rule	Verb	-s	-ed	-er	-est	-ing
For most words ending in one vowel and one consonant, double the final consonant before adding *-ed, -er, -est,* or *-ing.*	begin			beginner		beginning
	hot			hotter	hottest	
	mad			madder	maddest	
	plan		planned	planner		planning
	run			runner		running
	win			winner		winning
Common exceptions*: happen, open, travel	bus	buses	bused			busing
	happen		happened	opener		happening
	open		opened	traveler		opening
	travel		traveled			traveling
words ending in *w, x,* or *y*	fix		fixed	fixer		fixing
	play		played	player		playing
	sew		sewed	sewer		sewing
For most words ending in *f* or *lf,* change the *f* to *v* and add *-es.*	half	halves	halved			
	load	loaves				
	shelf	shelves	shelved			
Exceptions:	belief	beliefs				
	chief	chiefs				
	proof	proofs				
	roof	roofs				
	safe	safes				
For words ending in *ch, sh, x, s, z,* and sometimes *o,* add *-es.*	church	churches				
	wash	washes				
	class	classes				
	fix	fixes				
	quiz	quizzes				
	tomato	tomatoes				
Exceptions:	dynamo	dynamos				
	ghetto	ghettos				
	piano	pianos				
	portfolio	portfolios				
	radio	radios				
	studio	studios				

* In words ending in one vowel and one consonant, do *not* double the final consonant if the last syllable is not stressed.

2

CITY LIFE

Nouns and Articles

COUNT NOUNS;
INDEFINITE ARTICLES: *A /AN*;
COUNT NOUNS WITH *THERE + BE*

Have you ever been to New York City? What have you seen or heard about it? Share your experiences while answering the following questions about the picture.

1. Describe the pictures. What is happening in each one?
2. What does *commuting* mean? What are some common methods of commuting?

© CHARLES HARBUT

© MARK ANTMAN/THE IMAGE WORKS

In Praise of New York City

When people talk about New York City, they usually mean Manhattan. Manhattan is a narrow rock island twelve miles long. Although two million men and women work on this little island, only half a million of those who work there live there. As a result, a million and a half commuters have to get on the island every morning and off it every night. Twenty-eight bridges and tunnels connect Manhattan to the rest of the country. Every day thousands of cars, trucks, buses, motorcycles, and bicycles carry residents, workers, and tourists to and from this financial and cultural center of the United States.

Adapted from "In Praise of New York City"
by Andy Rooney

Discussing the Passage

1. Compare the number of commuters and the number of residents in New York City. What other major U.S. cities with large numbers of commuters can you think of?
2. There are many problems with living in large cities. Traffic and parking are two common ones. Can you think of others?

Nouns

A noun can be a person, place, thing, idea, emotion, or quantity. There are two basic noun groups: those you can count (count nouns) and those you cannot count (noncount nouns). This section covers count nouns: Parts Two and Three cover noncount nouns.

Noncount Nouns	Count Nouns		Irregular Noun Plurals	
	Singular	*Plural**	*Singular*	*Plural*
air	book	books	child	children
furniture	box	boxes	foot	feet
love	city	cities	goose	geese
rice	class	classes	man	men
water	student	students	mouse	mice
			ox	oxen
			person	people
			tooth	teeth
			woman	women
			deer	deer
			fish	fish
			series	series
			sheep	sheep
			species	species

---

* See pages 50–51 for spelling rules for *-s* endings.

A. Exercise: Write the plural forms of these count nouns.

1. watch *watches*
2. bus _____
3. woman _____
4. shelf _____
5. person _____
6. thief _____
7. tooth _____
8. radio _____
9. child _____
10. mouse _____
11. ski _____
12. monkey _____
13. loaf _____
14. box _____
15. tree _____
16. tomato _____
17. city _____
18. piano _____
19. ghetto _____
20. subway _____
21. church _____
22. ferry _____

Indefinite Articles: *A/An*

A or *an* with a singular count noun means "one" or refers to a person or thing that is not specific. *A* and *an* do not appear with plural count nouns or non-count nouns.

	Examples	Notes
Singular Nouns	There is **a book** on the desk. We live in **a house** in the suburbs.	*A* comes before a singular count noun that begins with a consonant sound.
	There is **an apartment** above the store. It takes him **an hour** to commute to work.	*An* comes before a singular count noun that begins with a vowel sound.

B. Exercise: Add *a* or *an* or use *X* to indicate that no article is necessary.

1. ____*a*____ house
2. _____ apartment
3. _____ churches
4. _____ elevator
5. _____ tunnel
6. _____ commuter
7. _____ art gallery
8. _____ building
9. _____ offices
10. _____ island

C. Exercise: Complete the following conversation with the appropriate singular or plural forms of the nouns in parentheses. Include *a* or *an,* if an article is necessary.

AGENT: Could I help you?

ELLEN: Yes, I'm looking for ___*an apartment*___ (apartment). Is it possible to

find _____ (apartment) or _____
                            1   2

(studio) for under seven hundred dollars _____ (month)?
                                                                           3

AGENT: Well, I occasionally have _____ (apartment) that rents
                                                                    4

for less than seven hundred dollars _____ (month).
                                                            5

Right now I have _____ (townhouse) available on the
                                                    6

east side. It is renting for $635 a month plus _____
                                                                       7

(utility). And I often have _____ (studio) available.
                                                    8

In fact, right now there is _____ (studio) downtown for
                                                    9

five hundred and ninety dollars. It's in _____
                                                               10

(eight-story building) with good security. It's _____
                                                                    11

(very nice place) with _____ (large kitchen), and it's
                                                    12

in _____ (interesting neighborhood).
                               13

ELLEN: Let me think about it and call you tomorrow. Thanks.

Count Nouns with *There* + *Be*

You can form statements and questions with *there* + *be* (*there is/are, was/were, has been/have been*). When *there* begins a sentence, the verb agrees with the noun that follows it. In affirmative statements, *a* or *an* normally appears with a singular noun. *Some* often appears with plural nouns. *Any* appears in questions and negative statements.

	Affirmative Statements	**Negative Statements**
Long Forms (s. and pl.)	**There is** an island in the river. **There are** (some) islands in the river.	**There is** no tunnel to Connecticut. **There are** no tunnels to Connecticut.
Contracted Forms	**There's** an island. **There're** (some) islands.	There **isn't** a tunnel. There **aren't** (any) tunnels.

	Questions	**Affirmative Answers**	**Negative Answers**
Yes/No Questions and Short Answers	**Is there** a bridge across the East River?	Yes, **there is.**	No, **there isn't.**
	Are there (any) bridges across the East River?	Yes, **there are.**	No, **there aren't.**

D. Exercise: Form complete sentences by using *there is* + *a/an* or *there are* with the following. (Use the map to help you.)

Example: subway in New York City →
> **There is a subway**
> **in New York City.**

1. several tunnels to New York City
2. large park in Manhattan
3. museum in the park
4. two large airports
5. island in the East River
6. several bridges across the East River

E. Exercise: In pairs, ask and answer questions about the map. Use *any* in your questions and *some* or *not any* in your responses.

Example: ferries to Manhattan →
       S1: **Are there any ferries to Manhattan?**
       S2: **Yes, there are some.**

1. tunnels to New Jersey
2. bridges to New Jersey
3. ferries to Manhattan
4. airports in Manhattan
5. tunnels under the Hudson River
6. museums in Manhattan
7. rivers around Manhattan
8. islands in the Hudson River

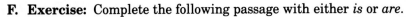

F. Exercise: Complete the following passage with either *is* or *are*.

ELLEN: Hello, I talked to you yesterday about rentals. *Is* there still a townhouse for rent?

AGENT: Yes, there ____₁. As I said yesterday, there ____₂ two bedrooms. The townhouse has two floors. Upstairs there ____₃ a full bath, and downstairs there ____₄ a half bath. There ____₅ four closets, but there ____₆ a very small kitchen. In the kitchen, there ____₇ only two cupboards and one large cabinet. The rent ____₈ six hundred thirty-five dollars a month. Utilities ____₉ not included. Would you like to see it?

ELLEN: Yes, I think that I would. ____₁₀ there a chance I could see it this afternoon?

G. Activity: Complaining. You have just rented a furnished apartment. The rental agent gave you a full description of the apartment, but you did not go in to see it because the renters were still there. When you go to the apartment for the first time, you find that it is a mess! You return to the rental agent with a list of your complaints. In pairs or in groups of three, role-play a scene complaining to the rental agent. You can begin with "When I rented my apartment, you told me there was (were) . . . , but there isn't (aren't). . . ."

PART TWO

NONCOUNT VERSUS COUNT NOUNS (1); *HOW MUCH* VERSUS *HOW MANY;* UNITS OF MEASUREMENT

Have you ever fixed up a house or an apartment? What are some of the things you often have to do when you move into a new place? Share your experiences while answering the following questions about the picture below.

1. Where are the young women? What are they doing?
2. What do they still need to do?
3. Do they have a lot of food in the apartment?

Setting Up a New Apartment

ELLEN: May, after we clean the kitchen, let's go shopping. There's no food to eat at all, and we need a little more paint and a few more cleaning supplies.

MAY: And some furniture! So let's make a list. How much paint do we need and how much food should we buy?

ELLEN: We need another gallon of white paint for the living room and a quart of blue paint to finish the bathroom. As for food, let's get a few necessities today and wait to do the rest.

MAY: Okay. Let's see . . . A dozen eggs. A pound of butter. Two loaves of bread. A jar of peanut butter. Some orange juice. A few bars of soap. A tube of toothpaste. A few rolls of paper towels. Anything else?

ELLEN: Are those what you call necessities? What about milk, cheese, . . .

MAY: Well, just add them to the list.

Discussing the Passage

1. Which items are the necessities for May? What items does Ellen add to the list?
2. Imagine that you are buying food and household items for a new home. Name ten to fifteen items that you think are necessities.

Noncount Versus Count Nouns (1)

Noncount nouns include ideas (*history*), emotions (*love*), activities (*tennis*), or mass nouns, things that you can measure (*gasoline*) or group together (*furniture*). The most common mass nouns are names of foods.

	Examples	Notes
Noncount Nouns	food, bread, butter, cheese, chicken, chocolate, coffee, cream, fruit, fish, meat, milk, salt We need **bread**. There isn't **any food** to eat.	Noncount nouns are singular and take singular verbs. Do not use *a* or *an* with noncount nouns, however. Instead, you can use adjectives such as *some* and *any*.
Count or Noncount Nouns	glass (for the window) a glass (of water) business (as a study or an activity) a business (a store) We're having **chicken** for dinner. Have you ever held a **chicken?**	Some nouns are either count or noncount, depending on their meaning in context. *A* or *an* normally comes before these nouns when they are count nouns.

A. Exercise: Write C in front of the count nouns and N in front of the noncount nouns.

1. _____ egg   6. _____ cheese   11. _____ grapefruit

2. _____ apple   7. _____ spoon   12. _____ salt

3. _____ rice   8. _____ fork   13. _____ sandwich

4. _____ sugar   9. _____ milk   14. _____ potato

5. _____ chocolate 10. _____ flour   15. _____ cereal

B. Exercise: The following sentences contain nouns that can be count or noncount. Complete them with *a* or *X* to indicate that no article is necessary.

Examples: This morning, my mother made __*a*__ pie.

Generally, I like __X__ pie for dessert.

1. I like tea with _____ lemon.

   Did you remember to buy _____ lemon?

2. I smell _____ gas.

   Neon is _____ gas.

3. Real estate is _____ good business.

   _____ business is good this year.

4. All animals are afraid of _____ fire.

   There was _____ fire in our kitchen this morning.

5. I caught _____ fish yesterday.

   Many people prefer _____ fish to beef.

6. He doesn't like _____ chocolate cake.

   For her birthday, her mother baked her _____ cake.

7. _____ fruit is healthy.

   Is an avocado _____ fruit?

How Much Versus *How Many*

How much is used to ask questions with noncount nouns. *How many* is used to ask questions with count nouns. Answers to these questions often include indefinite pronouns or adjectives. They may also include units of measurement, such as *a pound of . . .* or *a bottle of . . .*

	Examples	**Notes**
Noncount Nouns	**How much bread** do we have? We have **a little** bread. We don't have **any** bread.	Answers to questions with noncount nouns may include a variety of indefinite adjectives such as *a lot (of), lots of, some, much, (a) little* or *not . . . any.*
Count Nouns	**How many loaves** of bread should I buy? Don't buy very **many loaves.** Buy **a few loaves** of bread.	Answers to questions with count nouns may include a variety of indefinite adjectives such as *a lot (of), lots of, some, many, (a) few,* or *not . . . any.*

Note: The expressions *some, (not) any, a lot of,* and *lots of* may be used with both count and noncount nouns. The expressions *(a) little, (a) few, (not) much,* and *(not) many* are covered in Part Three.

Common Units of Measurement

To give specific amounts of either count or noncount nouns, use the following units of measurement. *Of* follows all the expressions except *dozen*.

bag	sugar, potato chips, potatoes
bar	candy, hand soap
bottle	detergent, ketchup, juice, soda, other liquids
box	cereal, detergent
bunch	bananas, carrots, grapes, green onions, flowers
can	soup, beans, tuna, soda
carton	eggs, milk
cup, tablespoon, teaspoon	all liquid and dry recipe ingredients
dozen*	eggs, bakery products, fruit and vegetables
gallon, quart, pint	all liquids, ice cream
head	lettuce, cabbage
jar	mayonnaise, peanut butter, jam, mustard, other foods that are spread
loaf	bread
package	potato chips, spaghetti
piece	cake, bread, pie, meat, etc.
pound, ounce	meat, poultry, fruit, vegetables, cheese
roll	paper towels, toilet paper
six-pack, twelve-pack, case	beer, soda
stick	butter
tube	toothpaste

---

* *Dozen* does not use *of*. Compare: *I bought a dozen eggs. I bought a carton of eggs.*

C. Exercise: Use the picture to complete the list of things that May and Ellen bought at the grocery store.

Example: *one bunch* of grapes

1. _____ of ketchup
2. _____ of eggs
3. _____ of milk
4. _____ of lettuce
5. _____ of green onions
6. _____ of mayonnaise
7. _____ of potatoes
8. _____ of laundry detergent
9. _____ of toothpaste
10. _____ of paper towels
11. _____ of hand soap
12. _____ of soda

D. Exercise: Look at the following advertisements for "specials" at local supermarkets. In pairs, take turns asking and answering questions with *how many,* using the cues.

Example: pounds of bananas / less than \$1 →
             S1: **How many pounds of bananas can you buy for less than a dollar?**
             S2: **You can buy three pounds.**

1. gallons of milk / less than \$5
2. boxes of crackers / less than \$3
3. heads of lettuce / less than \$2
4. pounds of Swiss cheese / less than \$7
5. tubes of toothpaste / less than \$4
6. bottles of ketchup / less than \$2
7. quarts of ice cream / less than \$3
8. jars of mayonnaise / less than \$3
9. bags of potato chips / \$2
10. six-packs of soda / less than \$5

DAIRY SPECIAL!
milk 1^{89} / gallon
ice cream 2^{29} / quart
Swiss cheese 3^{49} / lb

MUNCHIES!
crackers 1^{39} / 1-lb. box
potato chips 1^{26} / 8 oz.

Superwhite toothpaste	1^{89}	mayonnaise	1^{19}
daisies	2^{50} / bunch	ketchup	1^{29}
soda	2^{19} / six-pack	lettuce	79¢ / head
hand soap	3 bars / 1.00	bananas	39¢ / lb.
SPECIAL! eggs	1^{19} / carton		

E. Exercise: In pairs, practice making questions with *how much*. Take turns asking and answering questions about the ingredients in the recipe.

Example: salt →
    S1: **How much salt do you need to make chocolate fudge?**
    S2: **You need an eighth of a teaspoon of salt.**

1. sugar   4. butter
2. cocoa   5. vanilla
3. milk

⊙⊙⊙⊙⊙Chocolate Fudge⊙⊙⊙⊙⊙⊙	
cocoa :	6 tablespoons
sugar:	2 cups
butter:	3½ tablespoons
salt :	1/8 teaspoon
milk:	3/4 cup
vanilla.:	1 teaspoon

F. Activity: Giving Recipes. Do you know how to make an omelette? Do you know how to make a hamburger or a chocolate milkshake? Think of a simple recipe and list the ingredients that you need to make it.

G. Exercise: In pairs, take turns asking and answering questions. Following the examples, make short conversations about the items.

Examples: S1: **I bought some new albums today.**   (*albums* = count noun)
             S2: **How many albums did you buy?**
             S1: **I bought three.**

             S1: **I bought some Swiss cheese today.**   (*cheese* = noncount noun)
             S2: **How much did you buy?**
             S1: **I bought two pounds.**

1. Costa Rican coffee
2. gas for the car
3. tickets for the jazz concert
4. detergent
5. fresh fruit
6. strawberry ice cream for dessert
7. carrots
8. wine glasses
9. chicken
10. bananas

H. Activity: Describing Purchases. Think about the last time you went shopping. Following the examples in Exercise G, tell your partner about the items you bought.

I. Exercise: Use the following chart to convert the items below from British units of measurement to metric units of measurement.

Example: two gallons of gas →
Two gallons of gas is approximately equal to seven liters of gas.

Basic Units

Length	meter = about 1.1 yards
	centimeter = .01 meter = about .4 inch
	kilometer = 1,000 meters = about .6 mile
Volume	liter = about 1.06 quarts
	milliliter = 0.001 liter
	5 milliliters = 1 teaspoon
Weight	30 grams = 1.1 ounces
	kilogram = 1,000 grams = 2.2 pounds
Temperature	Celsius: 0°C = 32°F
	37°F = 98.6°F

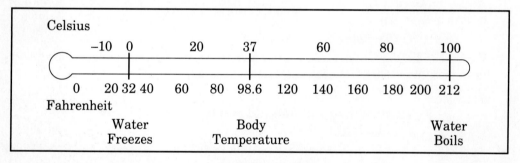

1. one quart of milk
2. five pounds of cheese
3. 72 degrees Fahrenheit
4. five yards of rope
5. one cup (eight ounces) of sugar
6. thirty miles

J. Activity: Playing a Memory Game. All members of the class should sit in a circle. One student will begin the game by saying, "I went to the supermarket, and I bought *a bottle of ketchup.*" The next student must repeat the first student's item and add one; for example: "I went to the supermarket, and I bought *a bottle of ketchup and a jar of peanut butter.*" The third student will repeat the first two items and add one. You may not write anything, and you are "out" if you forget any of the items *or* if you make a mistake in grammar!

PART THREE

NONCOUNT NOUNS VERSUS COUNT NOUNS (2); NONCOUNT NOUNS WITH *THERE + BE*; (*A*) *LITTLE* VERSUS (*A*) *FEW*; *NOT MUCH* VERSUS *NOT MANY*

What are some of the advantages of city living? What are some of the disadvantages? Share your experiences while answering the following questions about the picture.

1. Who is the man in front of the apartment building? What is his job?
2. Who is the man on the far right?
3. What things are easy to do in a big city? What are some things that are difficult to do?

City Life

Living in a big city has both advantages and disadvantages, but many people think of the disadvantages first. For example, it is often difficult to find good housing in a large city. Apartments are expensive, and there are very few houses available in safe locations. Employment is another problem. Jobs are hard to find in many cities. Transportation is also difficult. Bicycles can be dangerous, buses are not always on time, and parking is expensive.

City living also has advantages, however. Shopping is much better in a city. There are special stores for everything imaginable. There are restaurants, delicatessens, and grocery stores with food from every part of the world. And, of course, entertainment is one of the biggest advantages of city life. There are art galleries, museums, clubs, plays, concerts, and shows for everyone's taste.

Discussing the Passage

1. What are two advantages of life in a big city? What are two disadvantages?
2. Why is housing a problem in a big city?

Noncount Nouns Versus Count Nouns (2)

Abstract nouns are another common type of noncount noun. Abstract nouns may be ideas, activities, or emotions. They often refer to categories or groups that include count nouns. Compare:

Noncount Nouns	Count Nouns
employment	jobs
	occupations
	professions
homework	assignments
	exercises
information	facts
	statistics
love	dates
	feelings
news	broadcasts
	programs
violence	arguments
	fights
	wars
weather	climates
	storms
	tornadoes

A. Exercise: Ellen lives in a large Eastern city. Her family lives in the West. She teaches at a public elementary school. Using the following cues, form sentences about Ellen's opinions by adding *is important* or *are important*.

Examples: Friends **are important.**

Good transportation **is important.**

1. Free time . . .
2. Honesty . . .
3. Warm clothes . . .
4. Patience . . .
5. Money . . .
6. Neighbors . . .
7. Friends . . .
8. Letters . . .
9. Accurate information . . .
10. News from home . . .

B. Exercise: Fill in each blank with one word from the following list. Some blanks have more than one correct answer.

cities   parking   transportation   housing
area   homes   life   jobs

___*Life*___ in a big city has both advantages and disadvantages. There are usually many apartments for rent. However, _____ can be very expensive.
                                                                    1
For example, very few people can afford to buy _____. Additionally, it is
                                                        2
difficult to find housing in a safe _____.
                                        3
Employment is another problem. _____ are hard to find in many
                                    4
_____. _____ is also difficult. Bicycles can be dangerous, buses
    5   6
are not always on time, and _____ is expensive.
                                7

Noncount Nouns with *There + Be*

There + be is also used with noncount nouns. With noncount nouns, the verb *be* is always singular: *there is, there was, there has been.* Indefinite articles (*a, an*) are not used. Compare:

	Singular	**Plural**
Count Nouns	There **is** a good movie tonight.	There **are** good movies every night.
Noncount Nouns	There **is** always good entertainment in New York City.	

C. Exercise: In pairs, take turns making comments and contradicting them. Form complete sentences from the cues. Each set of cues includes one count and one noncount noun. Be sure to use the correct form of the verb with each.

Example: cars / heavy traffic →
     S1: **In big cities, there are always a lot of cars.**
     S2: **That's not true. There isn't always heavy traffic in a big city.**

1. buses / convenient transportation
2. cheap apartments for rent / inexpensive housing
3. shows and concerts / good entertainment
4. poor people / poverty
5. international restaurants / international food
6. unusual buildings / interesting architecture
7. dirty streets and dirty air / serious pollution

(A) *Little* Versus (a) *Few; Not Much* Versus *Not Many*

A few, few, and *not many* are used with count nouns. *A little, little,* and *not much* are used with noncount nouns. *A few* and *a little* mean "some" (but not a large amount). *Not many, few, not much,* and *little* mean "a small amount" (perhaps not enough). *Not many* and *not much* are more common in conversational English than *few* and *little*.

With Count Nouns		With Noncount Nouns	
a few	There are **a few** apples left. (There are some apples left.)	**a little**	There is **a little** milk left in the carton. (There is a small amount of milk left.)
few	**Few** apples are left. (There is a very small number of apples, probably not as many as we want or need.)	**little**	There is **little** milk left. (There is a very small amount of milk left, probably not enough.)
not many	There aren't **many** apples left.	**not much**	There isn't **much** milk left in the carton.

D. Exercise: Contrast of (a) *Few* and (a) *Little*. Add *a few* or *few* before count nouns and *a little* or *little* before noncount nouns.

ELLEN: What will we eat for breakfast tomorrow? Maybe we need to go shopping

and buy _____ things at the store.
                    1

MAY: We have very _____ money, but I think we have enough for grocer-
                            2

ies for tomorrow's breakfast.

ELLEN: Luckily, we have _____ apples, _____ eggs, and
                                3   4

_____ butter. All we need is _____ bread and
          5   6

_____ jelly for breakfast.
          7

MAY: But what about lunch and dinner? We have _____ needs, but we
                                                          8

do need to eat!

ELLEN: Well, there are _____ cans of soup and _____ peanut
                            9   10

butter in the cupboard. It's not much, but it will keep us going until I get

my check on Monday.

E. Exercise: In pairs, make short conversations with the following cues and *how much, how many, a few, a little,* and units of measurement. Use the example as a model.

Examples: sugar / three →

There is only a little sugar left. How much should we buy?

Let's get three bags.

onions / two →
S1: **There are only a few green onions left. How many should we buy?**
S2: **Let's get two bunches.**

1. ketchup / one
2. hand soap / five
3. mustard / one
4. eggs / one
5. lettuce / two

6. toothpaste / two
7. cheese / several
8. potato / three
9. laundry detergent / two
10. juice / several

F. Exercise: With a new partner, make new conversations using the cues in Exercise D. This time use *not many* and *not much* instead of *a few* and *a little.*

Examples: sugar / three →
S1: **There isn't much sugar left. How much should we buy?**
S2: **Let's get three bags.**

green onions / two →
S1: **There aren't many green onions left. How many should we buy?**
S2: **Let's get two bunches.**

G. Exercise: Review of Units of Measurement and Quantity Expressions. Circle the correct answer in each of the following sentences.

Example: How (much /(many)) apples do you need for the pie?

1. I always put (a few / a little) salt in my soup.
2. We don't have (many / much) potatoes in the house.
3. Is there (much / many) juice in the refrigerator?
4. She eats (lots of / many) candy.
5. We eat (few / little) beef, but we eat (many / a lot of) fish.
6. I bought a (dozen / carton) of eggs.
7. When you go to the store, please buy (some / few) butter.
8. How (much / many) milk should I buy?
9. Jack didn't catch (some / any) fish last night.
10. I forgot to buy a (tube / roll) of toothpaste.
11. There aren't (many / some) Chinese restaurants near here.
12. There isn't (a little / much) ice cream left.

H. Activity: Describing Places. What's your favorite city? What does it have to offer? Is there a lot of entertainment? Are there good restaurants? Is there public transportation? Are there interesting stores and boutiques? Does it have many problems, such as pollution, traffic, or crime? In a brief presentation, describe your favorite city to your classmates including both its good points and a few of its bad points.

PART FOUR

THE WITH LOCATIONS AND OTHER SPECIAL USES; REVIEW OF ARTICLES

Which major cities have you lived in or visited? Share your experiences while answering the following questions about the picture.

1.   What city is this? How do you know?
2.   Why are big cities often located near water?

© JAMES R. HOLLAND/STOCK, BOSTON

Cities of the World

Most of the greatest cities in the world are located near oceans, rivers, or lakes. New York City, Rio de Janeiro, and Buenos Aires are on the Atlantic Ocean, while San Francisco, Tokyo, and Santiago are on the Pacific Ocean. Singapore is located on an island in the South China Sea, and Venice is on an island in the Adriatic Sea. London is on the Thames River, Paris is on the Seine River, Cairo is on the Nile River, and Budapest is on the Danube River. Chicago, Cleveland, and Toronto are all on the Great Lakes—Chicago on Lake Michigan, Cleveland on Lake Erie, and Toronto on Lake Ontario.

Because of their locations, most of these cities have famous landmarks associated with water. New York City has the Statue of Liberty on Liberty Island, San Francisco has the Golden Gate Bridge, and Venice has the Grand Canal, to name only a few. The city in the picture on page 72 is Hong Kong.

Describing the Passage

1. What are some other cities that are located on the Atlantic Ocean? On the Pacific Ocean?
2. What are some other cities located on rivers? On lakes?
3. Can you think of other famous landmarks associated with water?

The with Locations

The appears with many proper names. The list at the end of the chapter gives you examples. Notice the common exceptions in the list.

A. Exercise: Complete the following passage with *the* or *X*.

The Old and the New

In cities in __X__ Asia and ____₁ Europe, the old and the new exist side by side. In ____₂ city of Paris, modern factories and department stores are just around the corner from famous landmarks such as ____₃ Louvre, ____₄ Champs-Elysées, or ____₅ University of Paris. Similarly, in ____₆ London, especially along the banks of ____₇ Thames River, historic buildings like ____₈ Houses of Parliament and ____₉ Tower of London are right in the middle of a busy city full of office buildings and apartments.

B. Exercise: Turn to the map of the United States and Canada on page 95. Use it to describe the locations of the following places. Be sure to use *the* when necessary.

Example: Los Angeles →
Los Angeles is in the West. It's in California. It's on the West Coast. It's on the Pacific Ocean.

1.	Washington, D.C.	5.	St. Louis
2.	Rocky Mountains	6.	Vancouver
3.	Miami	7.	Colorado River
4.	Hudson Bay	8.	Montreal

C. Activity: Describing the Town or Area You Live in. In pairs, take turns describing locations of some "landmarks" in the town or area you live in.

Examples: a pizza parlor →
S1: **Joe's Pizza Parlor.**
S2: **It's on Crest Street across from the public library.**

a bank →
S2: **The First National Bank.**
S1: **It's downtown. It's next to Sears.**

1.	a bridge	6.	a bank
2.	a lake	7.	a theater
3.	a hospital	8.	a river
4.	a museum	9.	a mountain range
5.	a church	10.	an ocean

The with the Verb *Go*

The use of *to* and *the* with *go* is idiomatic. Compare the following sentences.

I'm going	She's going	He's going
home.	to church.	to the beach.
downtown.	to class.	to the city.
there.	to New York City.	to the hospital.
swimming.	to school.	to the library.
shopping.	to town.	to the mountains.
	to work.	to the museum.
		to the post office.

D. Activity: Rapid Oral Practice. In pairs, take turns asking and answering questions based on the cues.

Example: store →
S1: **Where are you going?**
S2: **To the store.**

1.	home	4.	downtown	7.	church	10.	class
2.	store	5.	beach	8.	town	11.	there
3.	hospital	6.	Los Angeles	9.	city	12.	work

E. Exercise: Complete the following passage by using *to, to the,* or *X.*

"Good morning, ladies and gentlemen. Welcome to today's tour of Greater London. To start our tour, we're going ___*to*___ Windsor, a suburb of London, where we'll visit famous Windsor Castle. This should take about two hours.

"At 11:00 we'll board the bus again and go ___1___ downtown. There is no tour this afternoon, so you will have some free time to go ___2___ shopping, ___3___ post office, or ___4___ British Museum, perhaps. The British Museum is wonderful! Try to go ___5___ there sometime during your stay in London.

"Remember that tomorrow we are going ___6___ Brighton, ___7___ beach. Bring a bathing suit and a towel, and you can go ___8___ swimming in the English Channel."

The Houses of Parliament on the Thames River, London

F. Exercise: Review of Articles. Complete the following passage with *a, an,* or *X*. Remember: Noncount nouns do not normally take an article, but a word such as *a* or *an* must come before a singular count noun.

Chicago is *an* interesting city. It has ____₁ good museums, ____₂ beautiful skyline, ____₃ first-class entertainment, and ____₄ mixture of people. ____₅ Chicago's fine restaurants have an international flavor. You can find ____₆ Italian, ____₇ Japanese, or even ____₈ Armenian restaurant there.

Chicago is ____₉ important commercial and financial center. ____₁₀ skyscrapers fill its downtown area, and ____₁₁ enormous department stores are located throughout "the Loop," as ____₁₂ downtown Chicago is called. Its airport, O'Hare International, is the busiest in the world. ____₁₃ airplane lands and ____₁₄ airplane takes off every thirty seconds.

This busy city is located in ____₁₅ beautiful area by Lake Michigan. This huge lake plays ____₁₆ major role in Chicago's weather. The weather in the "Windy City" can be unpredictable at any time of year, and the winter can be especially cold. However, most tourists find Chicago ____₁₇ fun place to visit.

G. Exercise: Review of Articles. Fill in the blanks spaces with *a, an, the, some,* or *X*. In some cases there is more than one possible answer.

San Francisco is in _____ West, in _____ California. This lovely city is
                         1   2
located on _____ Pacific Coast, on _____ beautiful bay. _____ famous Golden
             3   4   5
Gate Bridge crosses this bay. Seven highways and two railroad bridges cross

_____ San Francisco Bay. _____ San Francisco is also _____ main seaport.
   6   7   8
Because of its location, there are _____ wonderful views from _____ city.
                                      9   10
_____ scenery is truly magnificent. In addition, _____ city has _____ good cli-
   11   12   13
mate. There is _____ little rain most of the year.
                 14

San Francisco is _____ city of many hills. _____ of the world's steepest
                    15   16
streets go up these hills. In _____ center of _____ city are _____ tall office
                                 17   18   19
buildings. Other important landmarks include _____ University of San Francisco
                                                 20
and _____ Palace of Fine Arts.
       21

H. Activity: Describing Places. What are some of the important places in your hometown or in the town where you are living now? Does it have any major landmarks? Does your region or country have major mountains? Is it along an ocean? Are there many rivers or lakes? Give examples of some of the important features. Using the example as a model, tell about some of the following.

In the city: churches, museums, bridges, libraries, other important buildings, important streets
In the region or country: forests, rivers, lakes, mountains, oceans, deserts, canals

Example: **I live in Boston, a city on the East Coast. It's in New England. It has many historic landmarks, such as the Old North Church.**

I. Activity: Playing a Memory Game. Have you ever played the trivia game "Categories"? To begin, you choose a category: rivers, for example. Going around in a circle, each person must name a river. You can play the game in either of two ways. You can go in alphabetical order—*a,* the Amazon River; *b,* the Brule River, etc. The other way is to use the last letter in one to begin the name of the next—*a,* the Amazon River; *n* (the last letter of Amazon), the Nile River. If you can't think of a name, you are out of the game. The last person in the game wins. You can play as a class or you can divide into teams that will alternate naming rivers. You may use a time limit of thirty seconds or one minute for each answer. Choose a new category each time. Here are some suggestions:

rivers   mountains
lakes   capital cities
countries

Remember: For an answer to be correct, it must include *the,* if it is necessary.

FOR YOUR REFERENCE

The with Proper Nouns

The has specific uses with proper nouns, especially with geographical locations. Because proper nouns identify specific places, *the* is often used. There are few exceptions to the rules. Study the following chart and use it for reference.

Proper Nouns with *the*		Proper Nouns without *the*	
Use *the* when the class of noun (continent, country, etc.) comes before the name: *the* + *of* + name.	the continent of Asia the Union of Soviet Socialist Republics (the USSR) the city of Paris	Do not use *the* with names of continents, countries, states, provinces, cities, and streets.	Africa Russia Ohio Quebec Austin State Street
Exceptions:	the Netherlands the Sudan the Hague the Champs-Elysées		
Use *the* with most names of regions.	the West the Midwest	*Exceptions:*	New England southern (northern, etc.) Ontario
Use *the* with plural islands, lakes, and mountains. *Exceptions:*	the Hawaiian Islands the Great Lakes the Alps the Isle of Wight the Great Salt Lake the Matterhorn (and other mountains with German names that are used in English)	Do not use *the* with singular islands, lakes, and mountains.	Oahu Fiji Lake Superior Mt. Whitney Pike's Peak

Use *the* with oceans, seas, rivers, canals, deserts, forests, and bridges.	the Pacific Ocean the Persian Gulf the Mississippi River the Suez Canal the English Channel the Sahara Desert the Black Forest the Golden Gate Bridge		
Note: The class name is often omitted with well-known oceans, deserts, and rivers:	the Atlantic the Nile		
Use *the* when the word *college, university,* or *school* comes before the name (*the* + ... + *of* + name).	the University of California the Rhode Island School of Design	Do not use *the* when the name of a college or university comes before the word *college* or *university.*	Boston University Lawrence College
Use *the* with names of museums, libraries, and with most famous buildings.	the British Museum the Chicago Public Library the Louvre the Houses of Parliament the Palace of Fine Arts		

3

BUSINESS
AND MONEY

Modal Auxiliaries and Related Structures

PART ONE

MODAL AUXILIARIES OF REQUEST AND PERMISSION

Do you have a bank account? What services does your bank offer? Share your ideas by answering the following questions about the picture.

1. What are some of the services available for the customers of this bank?
2. What are the various customers probably doing?

Bank Accounts

MRS. NELSON: Good morning. May I help you?

ALI: Yes, thank you. I would like to open both a savings and a checking

account. Could you please tell me about the different kinds of accounts you have?

MRS. NELSON: Certainly. One type of checking account is the NOW account. A NOW account gives you 5-1/4 percent interest on the money in your account. And, if you keep a minimum balance of $300, there is no service charge.

ALI: The NOW account looks good. And would you explain a little about savings accounts, please?

MRS. NELSON: We offer several types. Will you need to make regular deposits and withdrawals?

ALI: Yes, I will.

MRS. NELSON: In that case, I recommend a regular savings account. Our other accounts pay higher interest, but you may not withdraw money without paying a penalty fee.

ALI: I think the regular account will be best. Could I open both a checking and a savings account?

MRS. NELSON: Of course. To begin, would you please fill out these applications?

Discussing the Passage

1. What would Ali like to do?
2. What is a NOW account? How is it different from a regular checking account?
3. Why is a regular savings account good for Ali?

Introduction to Modal Auxiliaries

The modal auxiliaries (*can, could, may, might, must, ought to, shall, should, will,* and *would*) form a special group because they do not use normal verb tense endings. Instead, they are used *with* verbs to create special meanings. Also, their meanings change according to the context of the sentence. This chapter focuses on simple forms; Chapter 12 includes information on perfect forms.

The simple form of a main verb follows a modal auxiliary. *Not* appears after the modal to form the negative. In a question, the modal appears before the subject. A modal may also be used alone as a short answer. Note that contractions of some modals are very common in conversation.

	Affirmative Statements	**Negative Statements**
Long Forms	I **should open** a savings account. You **can open** a bank account now.	I **should not spend** so much money. I **cannot deposit** very much money today.
Contracted Forms	would: **I'd, you'd, he'd, she'd, it'd, we'd, they'd**	**can't, couldn't, shouldn't, won't, wouldn't**

	Questions	**Possible Responses**
Yes/No Questions and Short Answers	**May** I **help** you? **Would** you **like** more information?	Yes, you **can.** No, I **wouldn't.**
Tag Questions and Short Answers	I **could open** an account tomorrow, **couldn't** I? There **won't be** a service charge, **will** there?	Yes, you **could (can).** No, there **won't.**
Information Questions and Short Answers	Where **could** I **get** some information? When **should** we **go** there? What **will happen?**	You **might try** over there. We **should go** soon. I **don't know.**

Modal Auxiliaries of Request and Permission

Requesting Action

		Examples	Notes
Would **Could**	Formal	**Would** you please help me? **Could** you help me, please?	*Could* and *would* are common in both informal and formal situations.
Can **Will**	Informal	**Can** you help me? **Will** you help me, please?	*Can* and *will* are informal; friends or people in the same age group use *can* and *will* in informal conversation. *Please* makes any request more polite.

Requesting and Giving Permission

		Examples	Notes
May	Formal	**May** we sit here? No, you **may not.** **May** I help you? Yes, I'd like a beer.	*May* is rather formal. People of different age groups and people who perform services, such as waiters or salespeople, often use it.
Could		**Could** I use your pencil? Yes, you **can.**	*Could* appears in formal or informal requests for permission, but not normally in answers.
Can	Informal	**Can** I take this chair? Sure. Help yourself.	*Can* is the least formal. It appears in questions and answers.

The following expressions, which do *not* contain modals, are very common both in responding to a request for action and in giving permission:

	Question: May I sit here? *Response:*
More formal	Of course. Certainly. Surely. I'm sorry, but . . . (my friend is sitting here).
Less formal	Sure. You bet. Okay. No problem. Sorry. No way. (very informal)

A. Exercise: Underline all modal auxiliaries in the passage "Bank Accounts" at the beginning of the chapter and discuss their meanings.

B. Exercise: Mrs. Nelson is helping Ali to open a checking account. Change the commands to polite requests for action.

Example: ALI: Help me. →
ALI: **Could you help me, please?** *or*
Would you help me, please?

1. ALI: Explain this form to me.
2. MRS. NELSON: Fill out this application.
3. MRS. NELSON: Complete this form.
4. MRS. NELSON: Print your name.
5. MRS. NELSON: Tell me your social security number.
6. MRS. NELSON: Write in ink.
7. ALI: Tell me about savings accounts.

C. Exercise: In pairs, ask for permission and respond using the following cues. Pay attention to the relationship between the speakers when you ask for permission.

Example: (two strangers in a cafeteria)
sit down / no / someone else is sitting there →
S1: **May I sit here?**
S2: **I'm sorry, but someone else is sitting there.**

1. (customer and a gas station attendant)
use your phone / no / the phone isn't working
2. (young man applying for a job, speaking to the receptionist)
speak to the manager / yes
3. (two strangers in a grocery store)
go ahead of you in line / no / I'm in a hurry
4. (teenager and parent)
borrow the car tonight / yes
5. (two friends)
copy your notes from history class / yes
6. (two professional people who meet at a conference)
have your business card / no / I don't have any right now

Requests with *Borrow* and *Lend*

Making requests and giving permission often involve borrowing and lending things. The verbs *borrow* and *lend* can be confusing. Compare:

	Examples	Notes
Borrow	May Could I **borrow** your pen? Can	You ask to borrow something from someone.
Lend	Would Could you **lend me** your pen? Will	You ask someone to lend you something (give it to you for a period of time).

D. Exercise: In pairs, form requests and responses by using either *borrow* or *lend* and the following cues. Pay attention to the relationship of the speakers when you form your requests. If the response is negative, add an explanation.

Examples: (two friends)
borrow $5 / yes →
s1: **Could I borrow $5 from you?**
s2: **Sure.**

lend $5 / no →
s1: **Could you lend me $5?**
s2: **I'm sorry, but I don't have any money right now.**

1. (two students)
    lend dictionary / yes
2. (two strangers in a supermarket line)
    borrow pen / yes
3. (teenager and parent)
    lend $10 / no
4. (student and professor)
    borrow calculator / yes
5. (two sisters or brothers)
    lend your library card / no

E. Activity: Borrowing and Lending Things. Make a "chain" of requests and responses. Ask *to borrow* something you need from your neighbor. Your neighbor will respond and then will ask his or her neighbor *to lend* something. Continue the chain until everyone has made a request and response. Remember: You must alternate use of *borrow* and *lend*. Here are some suggested items: watch, car, grammar, book, class schedule, a dollar, bike.

F. Exercise: You are at a bank. In pairs, take turns making requests with the following cues and responding to them. These will include both requests for permission and requests for action. Use a variety of modal auxiliaries.

Example: explain the charges on my monthly statement →
S1: **Could you explain the charges on my monthly statement?**
S2: **Certainly.**

1. cash a check for me
2. withdraw money from my account
3. explain this loan application
4. describe the bank's policy on bad checks
5. speak with the bank manager
6. take out a $1,000 loan
7. get into my safety deposit box
8. open a savings account with only $10

G. Exercise: Complete the following conversation with modals of request or permission. Then, in pairs, role-play the conversation. Be sure to ask about currency from your own country, though.

ALI: Excuse me. *May (Could)* I get

some British pounds here?

TELLER: Yes, you _____. We have
1

a supply of most major currencies.

ALI: _____ you give me
2

$500 worth?

TELLER: You _____ have up to
3

$1,000. Do you want the money

in cash or in traveler's checks?

ALI: _____ I have approx-
4

imately $200 in cash and $300

in traveler's checks?

TELLER: Certainly. _____ you wait for a few minutes until our international
5

clerk is free? She calculates the amount based on today's exchange rate.

ALI: Of course.

TELLER: In the meantime, _____ you please sign here?
6

H. Activity: Making and Responding to Requests. In pairs or groups of three, make up conversations for these situations. Then role-play your best conversation for the class. Use the vocabulary that follows to help you ask and answer questions as customers and bank officers.

1. You and your husband (wife) would like to open a joint savings account.
2. You would like to open a checking account.
3. You and your friend would like to find out about credit cards.

minimum balance	interest
service charge	cost for a check that "bounces"
cost per check	(goes back to the writer because
credit limit	there's not enough money in the
monthly statement	account)

PART TWO

MODAL AUXILIARIES AND RELATED STRUCTURES OF ABILITY, EXPECTATION, AND PREFERENCE

What financial services are available to you as a student? What can you do to economize? Share your ideas by answering the following questions about the picture.

1. Where are these students?
2. What services are available for students?

Cash and Credit

JACK: I hear you're almost out of money.

ALI: Well, I'm in a difficult spot. I can't expect much help from home. We have tight currency controls in my country.

JACK: You can get a credit card.

ALI: I don't think I can qualify. Besides, I'm not sure I'll be able to control myself with a credit card. I'd rather get a job and earn the money.

JACK: You're a permanent resident, aren't you? You should be able to get at least a part-time job. But everyone needs a credit card for emergencies. Why don't we go to the bank? The credit manager ought to be there now. We'll just ask for information.

ALI: Okay. There's nothing to lose.

Discussing the Passage

1. What is Ali's problem?
2. What are currency controls? Will Ali get help from his parents?
3. Do you have any credit cards? Who is able to get a major credit card?

Modal Auxiliaries and Related Structures of Ability, Expectation, and Preference

Expressing Ability

	Examples	**Notes**
Can	Most working people **can** get a credit card, but most high school students **can't (cannot)**. **Can** Ali get a credit card? Why **can't** Ali work?	*Can* expresses present ability. It is sometimes difficult to hear the difference between *can* and *can't* in rapid speech. Normally English speakers stress *can* weakly and *can't* more strongly.
Could	Last year, I **could** speak English. The year before, I **couldn't**.	*Could* has several meanings, depending on the context of the sentence. When *could* expresses ability, it refers to the past.
Be Able to + *Verb*	A permanent resident **is able to** work. Ali **wasn't able to** find a job. **Will I be able to** speak English perfectly?	*Be able to* + verb expresses ability in the past, present, or future. The infinitive (*to* + verb) must come after *be able*: *be able to find, be able to speak*, etc.

Expressing Expectations

	Examples	Notes
Ought to Should	We'll go to the station at 9:00. The train **should (ought to)** be in by then. How long **should** it take us to get to the station? It **shouldn't** take more than twenty minutes.	*Should* and *ought to* sometimes express expectations. They mean "expect to" or "will probably." *Ought to* seldom occurs in questions or negative statements.

Expressing Preferences

	Examples	Notes
Would Like	I'**d like** to visit New York City. I **wouldn't like** to live there, though. **Would** you **like** to go with me? **Would** you **like** me to help you?	*Would like* expresses desires for things that haven't happened yet. A (pro)noun and/or *to* + verb (infinitive) may follow *would like*.
Would Rather	I'**d rather** travel in the United States than spend a lot of money on clothes. **Would** he **rather** take English? He **would rather not** take history.	*Would rather* expresses preferences or choices. *Than* + verb often follows it. *Not* comes after *rather* in the negative.

A. Exercise: Underline all examples of modal auxiliaries in the passage "Cash and Credit" at the beginning of Part Two and then tell their uses (ability, etc.).

B. Exercise: Oral Practice. Your teacher will read the following sentences aloud, using either *can* or *can't*. Listen for the differences in pronunciation and circle the word that you hear.

1. He (can / can't) open a checking account.
2. She (can / can't) write you a check.
3. You (can / can't) cash a check.
4. (Can / Can't) I get a credit card?
5. I (can / can't) get a job.
6. We (can / can't) take out a loan.

C. Exercise: In pairs or small groups, give at least five suggestions for each of the following questions. Use *can* or *be able to* + verb. Use the picture for ideas.

1. How can students save money on necessities such as food, housing, and transportation?
2. What fun things can you do free of charge in your city?
3. How can students save money on education-related expenses?
4. How can you economize on entertainment (theater tickets, movies, concerts, etc.)?

D. Activity: Telling About Things You Can or Can't Do. Students generally do not have much money to spend. Did your financial situation change when you began studying here? List ten things that you could do before that you can't afford to do now.

Example: **Before, I could go to restaurants often. Now I can only afford hamburgers.**

Student life does have advantages, however. Often students have much more freedom than working people do. For example, students often have a flexible schedule and wear informal clothing. List ten things that you can do now that you couldn't do before.

Example: **Last year, I couldn't wear blue jeans every day. Now I can. Next year, I won't be able to wear jeans, though, because I'll be working.**

E. Exercise: The following sentences tell about Ali's expectations. Change each sentence to use *should* or *ought to* instead of the main verb. Then add five original sentences about your own expectations.

Example: I expect to find a job soon. →
I should find a job soon.

1. I expect to receive a letter from my parents soon.
2. I expect to get a check from my family this week.
3. I'll probably be able to save a little money this month.
4. I expect to have some extra money next month.
5. I'll probably be able to take a short trip.

F. Exercise: *Would like* refers to things we want or hope to do in the future. Form sentences from the following cues that tell about things you did and things you would like to do.

> *Example:* find a job / save some money →
> **I found a job. Now I'd like (would like) to save some money.**

I found a job! Now I'd like to save some money.

1. open a checking account / start a savings account
2. find an apartment / buy a car
3. learn to play tennis / try wind-surfing
4. visit New York City / travel to California
5. study a lot of English / take some other courses

G. Activity: Making Plans. Are you the type of person who makes lists of things to do? What does your list for this week look like? In groups, talk about things you did and then tell what you would like to do before the end of the week.

> *Example:* **I wrote to my family, and I did all my laundry. Before the end of the week, I'd like to finish the next composition for English class. I would also like to visit the art museum.**

H. Exercise: In pairs, take turns asking and responding to questions based on the following cues.

> *Example:* go to Las Vegas / not gamble →
> S1: **Would you like to go to Las Vegas?**
> S2: **Thanks, but I would rather not gamble.**

1. buy a new car / get a used car
2. eat out / cook at home
3. make some investments / keep my money in the bank
4. find a larger apartment / not pay higher rent
5. look at houses for sale / buy a condominium
6. go to the movies / not spend any money
7. use your credit card / pay in cash
8. open a charge account / not have any bills to pay

I. Exercise: Using the cues, form sentences with *would rather* + *than*. Use contractions wherever possible. Follow the example.

> *Example:* Ali / get a job / borrow money →
> **Ali would rather get a job than borrow money.**

1. many people / work for themselves / work for a big company
2. I / write a check / use a credit card
3. Kaori / rent an apartment / live in a dorm
4. we / see a movie / go dancing
5. they / cook dinner at home / eat out

J. Exercise: In the following passage, a real estate agent is telling a customer about a house. Circle the modal that best fits the context.

"You know, this is an excellent time to buy real estate. Interest rates are down. Until recently, few people (should / could)$_1$ afford the high monthly mortgage payments. But now, with the lower interest rates, more people (would like / are able to)$_2$ afford a house. If you're like most people, you (would rather / would like)$_3$ live in your own house than rent from someone else. So you really (should / can)$_4$ think about buying now.

"Now here is a lovely house. It's a real bargain. It has a lot of good features, and you (ought to / would rather)$_5$ be able to buy it for a good price. (Would / Could)$_6$ you (rather / like)$_7$ to see the inside? I have the key, so we (would like / can)$_8$ go in and look around.

"On the right we have a very big living room. You (should / will be able to)$_9$ entertain lots of guests here . . ."

K. Activity: Offering Suggestions and Making Excuses. In pairs, take the roles of two students: Student 1 is very rich and spends a lot of money. S1 is taking only one class, so he (she) doesn't have to study very much. Student 2 is on a scholarship and has very little money. S2 is taking five classes and has to study a lot. S2 is embarrassed about the situation. S2 tries to avoid going to expensive places. Use *can, could, should, would, would like,* and *would rather* to create a conversation between the two students.

Example: S1: **Could you join me for dinner? Let's go out to that elegant new French restaurant. We can go dancing afterwards or . . .**

          S2: **That sounds nice, but we can't go there in blue jeans. Wouldn't you rather have a pizza somewhere? Besides, I can't dance because I hurt my leg . . .**

PART THREE

MODAL AUXILIARIES AND RELATED STRUCTURES OF ADVICE AND NEED

How do you manage your money? Share your ideas by answering the following questions about the picture.

1. Describe Ali's room.
2. What is Ali planning? Do you have a budget? Does this look like your budget?

Making a Monthly Budget

Do you often run out of money before the end of the month? Then you'd better consider making a budget. To plan a monthly budget, first of all, you should list your fixed expenses. That is, list all the money you *must* spend each month for rent, utilities, phone, food, and so on. If you have to guess at some of your expenses, you should guess higher, rather than lower. Then list large expenses, such as tuition and insurance, and figure out their monthly costs. Subtract all of these from your total monthly income.

Now plan for emergencies, such as medical or dental care. To do this, you ought to add a small amount of your monthly income as fixed expenses for emergencies. The rest is your "spending money" for entertainment, clothing, travel, and so on.

By planning a budget and following it, you won't have to worry about being short of cash each month.

Discussing the Passage

1. What are *fixed expenses?* Why should you list all of your fixed expenses first?
2. If some costs change, why should you guess higher, rather than lower?
3. What is *spending money?*

Modal Auxiliaries and Related Structures of Advice and Need

Giving Advice

	Examples	**Notes**
Ought to **Should**	You **ought to** attend class regularly. You **should** not be absent.	Both *should* and *ought to* can give advice. *Ought to* is not common in questions or negatives, however.
Had Better	You**'d better** hurry or you'll be late to class. **Hadn't** you **better** hurry? You**'d better** not stay here any longer or you'll be late.	*Had better* is stronger than *should* or *ought to*. It does not appear in affirmative questions.

Expressing Need or Obligation

	Examples	**Notes**
Must	You **must** have a driver's license in order to drive.	In affirmative statements, **must** expresses need or obligation.
Must Not	You **must not** drive without a license.	In negative statements, **must not** expresses a strong need not to do something or a prohibition.*
Have to	You **have to** take a written test first. Does he **have to** take the test in English? Then you **will have to** pass a driving test.	To express present or future need, use *have/has to* or *will have to*.
Had to	I **had to** take the written test twice. I only **had to** take the driving test one time.	*Had to* expresses a past need or obligation. In most cases, it means that the speaker completed the action.†

*The opposite of *must not* is *may* or *can*, expressing permission. Compare: *You must not smoke here. You may smoke here.*
†See Chapter 12 for information on perfect modals that describe past needs that were not completed.

Expressing Lack of Need

	Examples	Notes
Not Have to	You **don't have to** take the English test if you don't want to. I **didn't have to** study very hard to pass. I **won't have to** study late tonight.	*Not have to* expresses the idea that something is, was, or will not be necessary. It is the opposite of *must* and *have to*.

A. **Exercise:** Reread the passage "Making a Monthly Budget" at the beginning of Part Three. Using *should* or *ought to,* give at least three good pieces of advice on making a budget.

Example: **You should make a list of all of your expenses.**

B. **Exercise:** How can you save money? Change the following commands to negative statements giving advice on how to save more. Use *so much* or *so many* in your sentences.

Examples: Make only a few long-distance phone calls. →
You shouldn't make so many long-distance phone calls.

Drink less coffee. →
You shouldn't drink so much coffee.

1. Leave fewer lights on.
2. Eat less junk food.
3. Buy fewer things with credit cards.
4. Spend less on groceries.
5. Buy fewer clothes.
6. Take fewer trips.

C. Exercise: In pairs, take turns making suggestions and responses based on the following cues. Use *had better* in your responses.

Example: go to the movies / study →

1. go to the football game / go job hunting
2. visit the art exhibit / clean my apartment
3. go shopping / save money
4. go out to dinner / do my homework
5. stop at the café for coffee / see my professor
6. play a game of tennis / go to the library

D. Exercise: Change partners and use the cues from Exercise C to make new questions and responses. Use the following example as a model and make any necessary changes.

Example: go to the movies / study →
    MICHAEL: **Why don't we go to the movies?**
        ALI: **Hadn't you better study?**
    MICHAEL: **Yes, but I would rather have some fun.**

E. Exercise: You are a student who wants to buy or find the following items. In pairs or small groups, take turns asking for and giving advice. Try to share as much information as possible. Use *ought to, should, shouldn't, had better,* and *had better not.*

Example: computer →
    S1: **What kind of computer should I look for?**
        How much should I spend?
        Where should I buy it?
    S2: **You should (shouldn't, had better, had better not) . . .**

1. a typewriter   3. inexpensive presents to send home
2. a good apartment   4. a used bike

F. Exercise: Complete the following sentences with *must not* or *don't have to.*

Example: You *must not* write a check for more money than you have in your account.

1. You _____ keep your money in a bank, but it's a good idea.

2. You _____ forget to pay your bills on time.

3. At many banks, you _____ pay for your checks if you also have money in a savings account.

4. Today, many banks have automatic teller machines, so you _____ go inside a bank at all if you don't want to.

5. You _____ write bad checks.

G. **Exercise:** Complete the following sentences with *must, must not,* or *don't have to.*

    Examples: If you carry a lot of cash you _must_____ be careful.

                If you keep your money in the bank, you _don't have to_ worry about losing it.

1. If you open a bank account, you _____ show identification.

2. If you want free checking, you _____ go under the minimum balance.

3. However, if you pay for each check, you _____ keep a minimum balance in your account.

4. If you have a lot of money in the bank, normally you _____ wait very long to get a credit card.

5. If you want to get a credit card, you _____ establish credit with a bank.

H. **Exercise:** Use *had to* to explain how you did the following tasks.

    Example: open a checking account →
              In order to open a checking account, I had to go to the bank and talk to a bank officer. I had to deposit some money and choose some checks . . .

1. get a driver's license   4. find housing in your area
2. get a passport   5. be accepted to your school
3. open a savings account

I. **Activity: Explaining Proverbs.** A proverb is a wise saying that teaches a lesson. The language of proverbs is often traditional. In small groups, rephrase the following proverbs, keeping the same meanings. Do similar proverbs exist in your language? If so, give your classmates a translation of some of them. After you have finished, choose one member of your group to give a brief report to the class.

    Example: Don't look a gift horse in the mouth. →
              Explanation: If someone gives you a gift or does you a favor, you should thank him. You shouldn't be critical.

1. Early to bed and early to rise makes a man healthy, wealthy, and wise.
2. A penny saved is a penny earned.
3. Neither a borrower nor a lender be.
4. Don't count your chickens before they hatch.
5. Don't put all your eggs in one basket.
6. A bird in the hand is worth two in the bush.

PART FOUR

MODAL AUXILIARIES OF POSSIBILITY AND PROBABILITY

What is the best thing to do with your savings? Share your ideas by answering the following questions about the picture.

1. What ways of investing are shown in the picture?
2. What are *stocks?*
3. What can you do at a brokerage office?

Investing

You may be one of the fortunate people with plenty of money. In that case, you can save your money or invest it to make more.

If you want a safe investment, banks might be your best choice because they insure your deposits up to $100,000. On the other hand, you could earn much more money by trying alternative investments: treasury bills, jewelry, art, real estate, or a common favorite, stocks.

Investing in the stock market may be either rewarding or disappointing. When a person makes a good investment, we often say, "She must be incredibly lucky!" Or when a person makes a bad investment, we will say, "He must have terrible luck." Yet, most people who successfully invest in the stock market rely on much more than luck. They have a variety of unusual qualities—patience, ability to think independently, flexibility, and self-confidence—in addition to good luck.

Discussing the Passage

1. What are some safe ways to invest? Which are the most unpredictable? Why?
2. What qualities do successful investors have? Which quality do you think is the most important?
3. Which ways of investing are the most common in your culture? Have you ever made any investments?

Modal Auxiliaries of Possibility, Impossibility, and Probability

Expressing Possibility

	Examples	Notes
May	He **may** have enough money to pay the bill.	In affirmative statements, *may, might,* and *could* are similar in meaning. They express the idea of "maybe," "perhaps" or "it's possible." *May* never appears in questions about possibilities.
Might	He **might** have to borrow some money.	*Might* rarely appears in questions.
Could	It **could** rain tomorrow.	*Could* appears less often than *may* or *might* to express possibility.
May Not **Might Not**	He **may not** arrive on time. I **might not** see you tomorrow.	*May not* and *might not* mean "maybe not."

%

Expressing Impossibility or Disbelief

	Examples	Notes
Can't **Couldn't**	It **can't** be five o'clock! That **couldn't** be Irene! She's out of town.	*Can't* and *couldn't* often express the idea of impossibility. They show surprise or shock.

no emphasis

Expressing Probability (Assumptions or Deductions)

	Examples	Notes
Must	John walks five miles a day. He **must** enjoy walking.	*Must* expresses the same idea as "probably."
Must Not	He **must not** have enough money to ride the bus.	*Must* does not appear in questions about probabilities.

A. Exercise: In the passage "Investing" at the beginning of Part Four, underline all uses of modals of possibility and circle all uses of modals of probability.

B. Exercise: You can use *could* or *might* to make suggestions to people. Using the following cues, tell what each person *could* or *might do*. For each situation, try to add one suggestion of your own.

Example: I'm having problems with my math course.
(talk to your professor)
(get a tutor) →
You could talk to your professor.
You might get a tutor.

1. I don't have enough money to finish school.
    (get a job)
    (apply for a loan)
2. My apartment is very expensive.
    (find a roommate)
    (look for a cheaper apartment)
3. I need to buy an unusual present for a special friend.
    (go to the art fair on Saturday)
    (try the new shopping mall)
4. I just won the lottery!
    (take a long vacation)
    (make some investments)

C. Exercise: The following sentences tell about plans and possibilities. Rephrase them with *may* or *might*. Then add your own ideas. Make three statements about things you are hoping or planning to do.

Example: It is possible that Ali will open a savings account. →
Ali may open a savings account.

1. It is possible that Ali will sell his Persian rug.
2. Perhaps Michael will take Finance 101.
3. Ali has the opportunity to buy a used bike.
4. Maybe Michael will look for a job.
5. It is possible that Michael will try working in real estate.
6. Ali has a chance to sell his car.

D. **Exercise:** In pairs, take turns responding to the following statements. Using the cues, tell what *may* or *might happen* as a result of each situation. Then add your own ideas or opinions in each case.

Example: There are problems in the Middle East.
(some oil countries / not be able to export oil)
(price of gas / go up) →
Some oil countries might not be able to export oil.
The price of gas may go up.

1. That factory is going bankrupt.
(many people / lose their jobs)
2. The banks have just raised interest rates.
(people / put more money in the bank)
(some people / not be able to afford new homes)
3. A new company is opening in town.
(there / be a lot of new jobs soon)
4. That airline always has delays and mechanical problems.
(the government / investigate the situation)
(people / not fly on that airline anymore)

E. **Activity:** In small groups, try to think of at least three possible solutions for the following problems. Discuss the advantages and disadvantages of each solution and then decide which one is best. Present your conclusion to the class.

1. An American family has invited you to dinner and you would like to take them a gift. What can you take?
2. Suppose that the public transportation system in your city stopped working tomorrow. How could you get to school?
3. Your family sends you money each month, but this month the money didn't arrive. How can you get money to pay your rent?

F. **Exercise:** Respond to the following situations with exclamations using *can't* or *couldn't*. Then explain why you are surprised.

Example: The thermometer outside your window says it's 80°F. →
That can't be right! It's the middle of winter!

1. The sign at your local gas station says that gas costs $6.85 a gallon.
2. You see a woman on the street who looks exactly like your mother.
3. Your digital clock says 2:00 P.M., but it's dark outside.
4. The bill at a hamburger place for you and a friend comes to $68.92.
5. The movie you are watching stops after twenty minutes.

G. Exercise: In pairs, take turns responding to the following statements. Use *must* and the verbs *be* or *feel* with the cue to form your responses.

Example: I just bought a new house. (broke) →
              You must be broke.

1. Prices on the stock market are falling. (nervous)
2. My bank is bankrupt. (worried)
3. I just inherited a lot of money. (thrilled)
4. I just lost $500 at the horse races. (upset)
5. My investments are doing extremely well. (rich)
6. Someone stole my son's wallet. (furious)
7. My wife just found a job. (relieved)
8. My friend didn't get a job with our company. (disappointed)

H. Activity: Responding to Good or Bad News. How did you do on the last test? Did you get an A (or an F)? Have you had an interesting date recently? In pairs, take turns telling your news and responding to your partner's news. Use your own ideas or choose some of the following.

get an A (F)	meet a new boyfriend
get a new apartment	(girlfriend)
break up with a boyfriend	lose your job
(girlfriend)	

I. Exercise: Read each sentence and then try to come to a conclusion about the reason for each decision or situation. Use *must* in your conclusions. Several conclusions may be possible for each sentence.

Example: Michael has decided to get a job. →
              He must need money.

1. Ali has decided to move closer to campus.
2. Michael has decided to drop Finance 101.
3. Ali has decided to wait for a while before he opens a savings account.
4. Michael has decided not to invest in the stock market.
5. Ali's father has decided not to come to visit Ali this year.

J. Exercise: Review of Modal Auxiliaries. In small groups, rewrite the following conversation by changing the words in italics. Add a modal or use a different modal but try to keep the same meaning.

Example: What *can* I do for you today? →
              What could (may) I do for you today? *or*
              May I help you?

Opening an Account

MR. SMITH: What *can*$_1$ I do for you today?

NELLA: I'd *like to*$_2$ open up a savings account and a checking account.

MR. SMITH: Will there be just one name on the accounts? You look very young. You *can't*$_3$ be married.

NELLA: Actually, I am married, but I *would prefer to*$_4$ have the accounts in my name only.

MR. SMITH: I see. *Could*$_5$ you please fill out these two applications? You *should*$_6$ fill in both the front and the back.

NELLA: *May*$_7$ I use your pen?

MR. SMITH: Certainly. We *prefer*$_8$ everything in ink. How much *do* you *want*$_9$ to deposit in the accounts?

NELLA: It will be $32,570 altogether.

MR. SMITH: *Could*$_{10}$ you repeat that? You *probably*$_{11}$ mean $3,257.

NELLA: No, I meant $32,570.

MR. SMITH: My goodness!

NELLA: *Please let me*$_{12}$ explain. We *might*$_{13}$ buy a condominium. We *should*$_{14}$ know more about it by the end of the month.

MR. SMITH: Please let us know if we *can*$_{15}$ be of help to you. We *may*$_{16}$ be able to give you a loan, for example.

NELLA: Thanks for your help.

K. Activity: Giving Advice. Congratulations! You have just won $2,500,000, the grand prize in the state lottery! What will you do with all that money?

The first thing is to contact an investment counselor who will give you advice on various possibilities: gold, precious gems, real estate, the stock market, savings banks, art, antiques, etc.

Because you've never been to an investment counselor before, you decide to get friends', as well as several counselors', advice before making your decisions.

One-third of the class can set up office as investment counselors with various specialties. The rest of the students are investors. Afterwards, take turns role-playing some of your conversations about investing.

FOR YOUR REFERENCE

Modal Auxiliaries and Related Structures

Modal Auxiliaries

	Meanings	**Examples**
Can	informal request present ability present impossibility	**Can** you help us? I **can** carry that for you. It **can't** be six o'clock.
Could	request past ability present impossibility	**Could** you put the box on the table? Five years ago I **could** lift heavy things, but I can't now. That **couldn't** be John! He's in Hawaii!
May	request or permission present possibility	**May** I leave early today? Yes, you **may.** I **may** be late for dinner because we have a meeting.
Might	present possibility	We **might** go to Chicago this weekend.
Must	present need present prohibition present probability	You **must** let us know if you won't be able to come to the concert. You **must not** be late. She **must** be upset because she missed the beginning of the show.
Ought to	present expectation present advice	They **ought to** arrive at any moment. You **ought to** call them to see if there is some problem.
Should	present expectation present advice	The mailman **should** be here soon. You **should** write your parents more often.
Would	request	**Would** you help me for a moment, please?
Would Like (to)	present desire or preference	**Would** you **like** to go to the movies?
Would Rather	present preference	I don't feel well. I **would rather** stay home.

Related Structures

Meanings	Examples	
Be Able to	present ability past ability	I **am** not **able to** run very far now. When I was younger, I **was able to** run at least five miles.
Had Better	present advice	You **had better** do your homework.
Have to	present need present lack of need past need past lack of need	I **have to** study. You **don't have to** read page 16 today. We **had to** read page 16 yesterday. He **didn't have to** take the test.

4

JOBS AND PROFESSIONS

The Perfect Tenses; *Would, Used to, Was/Were Going to*

THE PRESENT PERFECT TENSE (1); *EVER, NEVER, ALREADY, JUST RECENTLY, STILL,* AND *YET*

What is the best way to find a job? Share your experiences while answering the following questions about the picture.

1. Where are these people and what are they looking for?
2. What information is on the bulletin board?

106

Discussing the Passage

1. What kind of company is Headhunters Limited?
2. What types of people do they try to help?

The Present Perfect Tense (1)

The present perfect tense has different meanings. It can describe actions or situations that occurred at an *unspecified* time in the past. It also refers to *repeated past* actions. Time expressions such as the following often appear with this use of the present perfect tense: *already, just, recently, still, yet, so far, up to now, once, twice, three (four, etc.) times*. With specific past times (*yesterday, in 1985*), the simple past tense is used.

Actions or situations at an unspecified time in the past:	I've **been** to Madrid. My sister **has** just **returned** from there.
Repeated past actions at unspecified times:	I've **visited** Madrid five times. My sister **has traveled** to Spain many times.

	Affirmative Statements	Negative Statements
Long Forms	I We You **have worked** there. They He She **has worked** there. It	I We You **have not worked** there. They He She **has not worked** there. It
Contracted Forms	**I've (You've, We've, They've)** worked. **He's (She's, It's)** worked.	I (You, We, They) **haven't** worked. He (She, It) **hasn't** worked.

	Questions	Affirmative Answers	Negative Answers

Yes/No Questions and Short Answers	I
	Have we **gone** there?
	    you
	    they
	
	    he
	Has she **been** successful?
	    it
		I
		Yes, we **have.**
		    you
		    they
		
		    he
		Yes, she **has.**
		    it
			I
			No, we **haven't.**
			    you
			    they
			
			    he
			No, she **hasn't.**
			    it

Note: See pages 50–51 for spelling rules for the -*ed* ending of regular past participles. See pages 48–50 for a list of irregular past participles.

Tag Questions and Information Questions

Here are some examples of questions with the present perfect tense.

	Questions	**Expected Responses**
Tag Questions and Short Answers	You've called them, **haven't you?** He hasn't called them, **has he?**	Yes, I **have.** No, he **hasn't.**

	Questions	**Possible Responses**
Information Questions and Short Answers	**When** have you written them? **Why** has he written them? **Who** has called? **What** has happened?	Many times. Because there have been some problems. No one. Nothing important.

A. Exercise: Underline all uses of the present perfect tense in the advertisement at the beginning of the chapter.

B.   Exercise: The Present Perfect Tense with Regular Verbs. These people are interviewing for new jobs. Tell about their previous work experience by forming complete sentences with the present perfect tense.

Example: Applicant: Thomas Woo
Job title: Auto mechanic
Previous experience:
a. change tires →
Thomas has (he's) changed tires.

1. Applicant: Thomas Woo
Job title: Auto mechanic
Previous experience:

a.   change tires
b.   tune engines
c.   replace mufflers
d.   clean radiators
e.   repair brakes

2. Applicant: Christina Barragan
Job Title: Architect
Previous experience:

a.   design apartment buildings
b.   help with designs for offices
c.   plan a park

3. Applicant: Alex Gutierrez
Job title: Chef
Previous experience:

a.   work as assistant chef in a large restaurant
b.   manage a small restaurant
c.   prepare special parties
d.   create several new recipes

4. Applicant: Sara Albrecht
Job title: Clothing store manager
Previous experience:

a.   manage a small clothing store
b.   hire new employees
c.   place orders
d.   organize special sales

Special: 50% OFF

C. **Exercise: The Present Perfect Tense with Irregular Verbs.** Complete the following with the present perfect form of the verbs in parentheses. Use contractions when possible.

1. I *'ve had* _____ (have) a bad day. So far, I

    _____ (bring) several customers the wrong

    food, I _____ (break) a lot of dishes, and no

    one _____ (leave) me tips!

2. What a terrible day! So far, I _____ (give)

    the wrong change three times, I _____

    (make) a $1,000 error, and someone _____

    (steal) my keys.

3. I quit! So far today, I _____ (lose) three

    brushes, I _____ (fall) off the ladder, and I

    _____ (put) my foot in a paint can.

4. What else can go wrong? Tonight so far, I

    _____ (sleep) through the alarm twice,

    and the guard dog _____ (bite) me.

5. Things _____ (not go) very well today . . . So

    far, I _____ (not sell) any daisies, I

    _____ (send) customers the wrong flowers,

    and I _____ (freeze) the roses.

6. I'm the worst driving instructor in town! So far, I

    _____ (run) a red light, I _____

    (hit) a tree, I _____ (drive) down a one-way

    street, and a policeman _____ (give) me a

    ticket.

D. Exercise: The Present Perfect Tense with Regular and Irregular Verbs.
Imagine that you are finishing work for the day. Your boss is checking to see that
you have completed everything. In pairs, take turns asking and answering questions. You may give short or long answers.

Example: count the cash →
           S1: **Have you counted the cash?**
           S2: **Yes, I have.** *or*
                 No, I haven't.

1. Your job: bank teller
     count the cash
     make a list of checks
     separate the coins
2. Your job: janitor
     wash the windows
     sweep the floor
     empty the wastebaskets
     polish the furniture
     clean the bathrooms
3. Your job: secretary
     type the reports
     answer today's mail
     file all the important papers

**E. Exercise: The Present Perfect Tense—Statements, Tag Questions, and
Short Answers.** Work in pairs. One of you is an office manager, and the other is
an applicant for an office job. The office manager should ask questions based on the
following cues. The applicant should reply with short answers.

Example: work in an office →
           S1: **You've worked in an office, haven't you?**
           S2: **Yes, I have.** *or*
                 No, I haven't.

1. type reports
2. take dictation
3. file letters
4. use an adding machine
5. do bookkeeping
6. work on a word processor
7. study data processing

Ever, Never, Already, Just, Recently, Still, and Yet

These adverbs are frequently used with the present perfect tense. Questions and affirmative statements with *already, just,* and *recently* refer to actions or situations at an unspecified time in the past. *Ever, never, still,* and *yet* refer to past actions or situations that also include the present.

	Examples	**Notes**
Questions	Have you **ever** had a job?	*Ever* means "at any time." It must come before the past participle.
	Have you **already** started work? Have you started work **already?**	*Already* means "before now." It may come before the past participle or at the end of a question.
	Have you started work **yet?**	*Yet* means "up to now." It is normally at the end of a question.
Affirmative Statements	Yes, I've **just** started work.	*Just* refers to the recent past—a few minutes, hours, or days ago. It must come before the past participle.
	Yes, I've **already** started work. Yes, I've **recently** started work. Yes, I've started work **recently.**	*Already* and *recently* normally come before the past participle or at the end of a statement.
Negative Statements	No, I have **never** worked. *or* No, I haven**'t ever** worked. No, I haven't started work **yet.** No, I **still** haven't started work.	*Never* and *not ever* mean "not at any time." They must come before the past participle. *Yet* normally comes at the end of a negative statement. *Still* also means "up to now." It emphasizes the continuous nature of the situation. *Still* must come before *has* or *have.*

F. Exercise: Questions and Statements with *Ever/Never.* Imagine that you are looking for a job. In pairs, use the following model and cues to make short conversations. Use *ever* in your questions and *never* in your answers.

Example: auto mechanic / rebuild an engine
            tune →
            S1: **So, you would like a job as an auto mechanic. Have you ever rebuilt an engine?**
            S2: **No, I've never rebuilt an engine, but I've tuned quite a few.**

1. data processor / write a program
    work with
2. travel agent / refund tickets
    write
3. electrician / put in new lights
    replace
4. photographer / enlarge pictures
    take
5. nurse / assist during an operation
    watch
6. plumber / install new pipes
    repair
7. carpenter / build a new house
    remodel
8. office manager / fire a secretary
    hire

G. Activity: Talking About Work Experience. In small groups, play a guessing game. Choose one person who has had a job. That person will answer questions from the rest of the group. The rest of the group will try to guess the job. You may ask the person about places he or she has worked and about job duties, but you may not ask about the job title. You must guess the job title.

Examples: **Have you ever worked in a restaurant?** Answer: **Yes.**
            Have you ever waited on tables? Answer: **No.**
            Have you ever washed dishes? Answer: **Yes.**
            Guess: **You've worked as a dishwasher.**

H. Exercise: Questions and Answers with *Yet/Already*. John is having a hard time finding a job. He is telling Caroline about his job search. Use the example as a model to form short conversations.

Example: try all the big companies →
>CAROLINE: **Have you tried all the big companies yet?**
>JOHN: **Yes, I've already tried all the big companies.** *or*
>**Yes, I've tried all the big companies already.**

1. look in the want ads
2. put an ad on the bulletin board
3. talk to the manager at the insurance company
4. apply for jobs at the phone company
5. check all the banks

I. Exercise: Negative Statements with *Still*. Caroline is suggesting some possibilities to John. In pairs, form questions with *again*. Give answers with *still*.

Examples: look for jobs at the phone company
>they / not offer me anything →
>CAROLINE: **Have you looked for jobs at the phone company again?**
>JOHN: **Yes, but they still haven't offered me anything.**

1. put an ad in the newspaper
>I / not get any responses
2. write the university a letter
>they / not answer
3. telephone the factory manager
>he / not return my call
4. check the hospital employment office
>there / not be any job openings
5. apply for jobs at the electric company
>they / not call me for an interview

J. Exercise: With a new partner, repeat Exercise I. This time use *yet* in John's answers, but not in Caroline's questions.

Example: CAROLINE: **Have you looked for jobs at the phone company again?**
>JOHN: **Yes, but they haven't offered me anything yet.**

K. Exercise: Questions and Answers with *Yet/Just.* Use the cues to complete the conversation between an impatient boss and her quick secretary.

Example: finish the report →
S1: **Have you finished the report yet?**
S2: **Yes, I've just finished it.**

1. open the mail
2. type the letter to the New York office
3. call the insurance agent
4. make copies of the notes from yesterday's meeting
5. take a break

L. Exercise: Review of Adverbs. Petros has just gotten work at University Hospital, and you're discussing the job. In pairs, use the present perfect tense with the following cues to ask and answer questions. Use *yet* in each question and make any other necessary changes.

Example: learn all of the laboratory procedures (no / yet) →
S1: **Petros, have you learned all of the laboratory procedures yet?**
S2: **No, I haven't learned all of them yet.**

1. make any mistakes (no / yet)
2. get your first paycheck (yes / just)
3. spend your paycheck (no / yet)
4. break any equipment (no / never)
5. have a day off (yes / just)
6. begin to enjoy the job (yes / already)
7. ask for more hours of work (no / still)
8. meet the chief of research (no / ever)

M. Activity: Making Suggestions. In small groups, role-play the following situation. One student in the group needs a job badly. He or she has already tried many things, but hasn't had any luck finding work. The other members of the group should make five or six suggestions about possible employers and jobs in the community. Try to use the present perfect tense with time words in both questions and answers.

Example: S1: I really have to find a job. I'm desperate! Do you have any helpful suggestions?
S2: Well, have you tried A & B Market? They're always looking for people.
S1: I've already applied there. They don't need anybody now.
S3: How about the student bookstore?
S1: I thought about that, but I've never used a cash register before.
S4: I know! The Globe Cinema! They're looking for ticket takers.
S1: That's a good idea. I've never done that, but I'm sure I can learn.

PART TWO

THE PRESENT PERFECT CONTINUOUS TENSE; THE PRESENT PERFECT TENSE (2)

What is it like to work in a restaurant? Have you ever worked in one? Share your experiences, while answering the following questions about the picture.

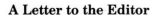

1. Where are these young people working?
2. What job is each of the employees doing?

A Letter to the Editor

Editor
Morning News
Martin, Ohio

Dear Editor:

My 21-year-old son, Bill, is mentally handicapped. Earlier this year, a pizza parlor hired him, and he has worked there since March. According to his boss, he has been doing very well. The management has made a special effort to help Bill feel comfortable. Because of this, Bill has learned to fit in with the other employees. In fact, everyone at the pizza parlor has been trying to help.

This is the first chance that Bill has had to earn his own living. It has made a strong impression on him. He has seemed so happy during this time. Above all, he is proud of himself because he feels useful, and he is financially independent.

The public school special education program prepared Bill for this job. When he was in school, he had several training jobs. These taught him the skills for his work.

I would like to say thank you to the pizza parlor and the Martin Public Schools! We appreciate your help so much!

Sincerely,

Mickey Duke

Discussing the Passage

1. What are several reasons Bill has been successful at this job?
2. What is a *special education program*?

The Present Perfect Continuous Tense

The present perfect continuous tense describes actions or situations that began in the past and have continued to the present or are still true in the present. This tense emphasizes the continuous nature of the activity. It does not normally occur with repeated actions. Time expressions such as these often appear with this tense: *so far, up to now, to date, for* (+ a period of time), or *since* (+ a beginning time).

<table>
<tr>
<td>Actions that began in the past and have continued to the present:</td>
<td>I have been working for the company since 1982.
My boss has been working here for ten years.
This week we've been training some new employees.</td>
</tr>
</table>

	Affirmative Statements	**Negative Statements**
Long Forms	I We You **have been working** hard. They He She **has been working** hard. It	I We You **have not been working** hard. They He She **has not been working** hard. It
Contracted Forms	**I've (You've, We've, They've)** been working too much. **He's (She's, It's)** been working.	I (You, We, They) **haven't** been working too much. He (She, It) **hasn't** been working.

	Questions	Affirmative Answers	Negative Answers
Yes/No Questions and Short Answers	I **Have** we you they **been making** mistakes? he **Has** she **been causing** it problems?	I Yes, we you they **have.** he Yes, she **has.** it	I No, we you they **haven't.** he No, she **hasn't.** it

Note: See pages 50–51 for spelling rules for the *-ing* ending of present participles. See page 15 for a list of verbs that do not normally appear in the continuous tenses; remember that the verbs *hear, mean, need, see,* and *want* sometimes do appear in the present perfect continuous.

Tag Questions and Information Questions

Here are some examples of these questions with the present perfect continuous tense.

	Questions	Expected Responses
Tag Questions and Short Answers	You've been working a lot, **haven't you?** He hasn't been coming late, **has he?**	Yes, I **have.** No, he **hasn't.**

	Questions	Possible Responses
Information Questions and Short Answers	**Where** **How long** have you has she been working? **Why** **Who** has been doing her work? **What** has been going on here?	At the bank. For two months. Because she needs money. Mary has. Nothing new.

A. **Exercise:** These people have been working all day, and they are tired. Tell why by forming complete sentences with the present perfect continuous tense.

Example: bank teller / count money →
He's a bank teller, and he's tired. He's been counting money all day.

1. cab driver / drive a taxi
2. airplane pilot / fly
3. mechanic / tune engines
4. gym teacher / run
5. secretary / file papers
6. dentist / fill cavities

B. **Exercise:** Imagine that you are telling a friend about your work this week. In pairs, take turns asking and answering questions using the cues that follow.

Example: office / fun / learn to use the new computer →
S1: **How has work at the office been going?**
S2: **It's been fun this week. We've been learning to use the new computer.**

1. travel agency / exciting / plan a tour to China
2. restaurant / busy / prepare for a large party
3. laboratory / interesting / experiment with different chemicals
4. law office / difficult / work on a new case
5. newspaper / enjoyable / write some good stories
6. hospital / confusing / try out a new schedule

C. **Exercise: Contrast of the Simple Present and Present Perfect Continuous Tenses.** Use the following cues to make statements. Use the simple present tense with *normally* or *usually* and contrast it with the present perfect continuous tense.

Example: leave work early / stay late →
Caroline usually leaves work early, but this week she has been staying late.

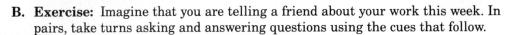

1. do very little work / work very hard
2. make a lot of mistakes / do everything perfectly
3. come to work late / come on time
4. refuse to make coffee / make coffee for everyone
5. spread rumors about everyone / not gossip
6. complain a lot / keep quiet

D. **Activity: Talking about Recent Changes.** Has your usual routine changed lately? Has it changed since you began taking classes? Think of some changes that have taken place and discuss them in small groups, following the model in Exercise C. Use time expressions such as *usually, normally, most of the time, almost always, lately, recently,* and *since.*

The Present Perfect Tense (2): The Present Perfect Versus the Present Perfect Continuous

The present perfect continuous tense describes actions or situations that began in the past and have continued to the present or are still true in the present. To express the same meaning with a nonaction verb, use the present perfect tense. Time expressions such as *for* + period of time and *since* + beginning time usually appear in these sentences to give the past-to-present meaning. A few verbs, such as *live, work,* and *study,* are used with the present perfect continuous or the present perfect with little difference in meaning when a time expression is used. Compare:

	Examples with Action Verbs	**Examples with Nonaction Verbs**
Actions or Situations Still True in the Present	**I've worked** at IBM for five years. *or* **I've been working** at IBM for five years. **We've lived** here since 1981. *or* **We've been living** here since 1981.	**I've known** John for five years. **We haven't heard** any news since yesterday.
Actions or Situations at an Unspecified Time in the Past	**I've worked** at IBM. **I've lived** in Boston.	**I've owned** several cars.

Note: See page 15 for a list of verbs that do not normally appear in the continuous tenses. Remember that *mean, need, want, hear,* and *see* sometimes appear in the present perfect continuous.

E. Exercise: Reread the opening passage. Underline all the verbs in the present perfect or present perfect continuous tenses. Discuss which verbs could appear in either tense.

F. Exercise: The following sentences use the present perfect tense. Tell which actions or situations are still true now and which occurred at an unspecified time in the past.

Examples: I've worked at that bank. → **unspecified time in the past**

I've worked at that bank for five years. → **still true now**

1. Lately I've felt bored with my job.
2. So I've applied for a job at another company.
3. I've wanted to work there ever since I finished school.
4. I've had a job interview there.
5. I've called the manager several times.
6. She's been on vacation since the first of the month.

G. Exercise: Form complete sentences from the following cues by adding *for* or *since*.

Example: Bill has had a job / several months →
Bill has had a job for several months.

1. Bill has worked at the pizza parlor / last spring
2. Bill has been at work / 7:30
3. Jane has been working here / seven years
4. She has been supporting herself / six months
5. Mr. Johnson has been unemployed / March
6. He has been searching for a job / a long time
7. Margaret has had four interviews / the beginning of the month
8. She's gotten two jobs offers / Monday

H. Exercise: Contrast of the Present Perfect and Present Perfect Continuous Tenses. Petros is telling about his lab job. Complete the passage with the present perfect or present perfect continuous form of the verbs in parentheses. Give both forms when possible and explain any difference in meaning.

"I *'ve wanted (have been wanting)* _____ (want) to work in a

lab for a long time, and finally I *'ve gotten* ___ (get) the opportunity to try. I

_____ (start / just) working, and so far it _____ (be) a very
$\quad$ 1 $\qquad\qquad\qquad\quad$ 2

interesting experience. My employer _____ (own) the lab since 1972. He
$\qquad\qquad\qquad$ 3

_____ (have) a lot of different employees since then. One person
$\quad$ 4

_____ (work) for him for fifteen years, but most of the employees now
$\quad$ 5

_____ (not work) there for very long.
$\qquad$ 6

"So far, the work _____ (not seem) very difficult. Of course, I
$\qquad\qquad\qquad$ 7

_____ (not understand) everything, but I _____ (learn) a
$\quad$ 8 $\qquad\qquad\qquad\qquad$ 9

lot. At night, I _____ (study) some of the manuals at home, and everyone
$\qquad$ 10

at the lab _____ (help) me during the day. I _____ (appreci-
                11   12

ate / really) their help."

I. **Activity: Complaining.** Is there anything that you would like to complain about?
    Has your landlord been promising to fix the kitchen sink for weeks but still hasn't
    done it? Have your roomates been promising to clean the apartment but still
    haven't cleaned it? Take this opportunity to practice complaining! Each person
    should make at least one complaint.

Example: **My roommate has been promising to clean out the refrigerator since
            Christmas. Here it's February and he still hasn't done it!**

J. **Exercise: Contrast of the Present Perfect and Simple Past Tenses.** In pairs,
    take turns asking and answering questions about Sandy's work schedule. Use the
    following cues.

> Sandy's work schedule at General Hospital:
>
> | | |
> |---|---|
> | 6:30 | take temperatures |
> | 7:30 | check vital signs (pulses, blood pressure) |
> | 7:45 | serve breakfast |
> | 8:00 | give the patients medicine |
> | 9:00 | help with bathing |
> | 9:30 | make beds |
> | 10:00 | write notes on the charts |
> | 10:30 | have a conference with doctors |
> | 11:00 | explain procedures to patients |

Examples: 8:00 / check the patients' pulses →
          S1: **Has Sandy checked the patients' pulses yet?**
          S2: **Yes, she has. She checked them a half hour ago.**

              7:00 / check the patients' pulses →
          S1: **Has Sandy checked the patients' pulses yet?**
          S2: **No, she hasn't checked them yet.**

1. 10:00 / help with bathing the patients
2. 9:00 / make beds
3. 7:00 / take temperatures
4. 11:00 / have a conference with the doctor
5. 9:30 / write notes on the chart
6. 7:30 / give the patients medicine
7. 11:30 / finish her morning work

K. Exercise: Contrast of Tenses. Complete the following with the simple present, simple past, present perfect, or present perfect continuous form of the verbs in parentheses. In some cases, more than one form is correct. Try to explain those cases.

Bill *started* ___ (start) working at the pizza parlor in March. He

_____ (work) there successfully for several months. Since the beginning,
          1

the owners of the pizza parlor _____ (make) a special effort to help Bill
                                           2

feel comfortable. Because of this, Bill _____ (learn) to get along well with
                                                   3

the other employees and the customers. In fact, everyone at the pizza parlor

_____ (help) Bill in every way they can.
          4

For the first time in his life, Bill _____ (be) able to earn his own liv-
                                              5

ing. This _____ (make) a strong impression on him. He _____
                 6

(receive / already) several paychecks, and he _____ (open / just) his own
                                                         7

savings account. But paychecks _____ (not be) the most important part of
                                        8

the job. Most importantly, Bill _____ (be) proud of himself because he
                                         9

_____ (feel) useful. Now he _____ (have) a good reason to get
          10   11

up in the morning.

Last year, the public school special education program _____ (train)
                                                                  12

Bill for this job. It _____ (teach) him the skills he _____ (need)
                        13   14

to find and keep a job. Both Bill and his parents _____ (be) hopeful about
                                                            15

his future.

L. Activity: Interviewing. Have you ever applied for a job? Have you ever had a job interview? In pairs, role-play interviews for a variety of jobs, using the following format as a guide.

INTERVIEWER	INTERVIEWEE
Good morning (afternoon).	. . .
To begin, what is your name?	My name is . . .
And . . . ?	I live . . .
Have you finished high school (university) studies?	. . .
Why are you applying for this job? Have you ever . . . ?	Well, I haven't . . . , but I have . . .
Oh, really? When was that?	. . .
Since then, how long (often, many times) have you . . . ?	. . .
Is there anything else you would like to tell me about yourself?	

PART THREE

WOULD, USED TO,
WAS/WERE GOING TO

Has the medical profession changed much in the last hundred years? Share your ideas and experiences while answering the following questions about the picture, which shows a scene from the 1800s.

1. What is happening in the picture?
2. What are these men's professions?

Changes in Jobs

In North America many professionals, particularly those in health care, practice differently from the way they used to. As an example, doctors used to take care of everyone in a family, and they would often go to a patient's home when there was a problem. Now doctors are specialists; they practice in large clinics, and technicians do many of the doctors' former duties.

Strange as it may seem now, barbers used to be surgeons. They would cut hair *and* perform operations. They did not do operations in the stomach or the chest, however. Most people used to avoid those operations, anyway.

People also used to avoid dentists if at all possible. A person who was going to see the dentist was an unhappy person. In the days before anesthesia, those visits would often be extremely painful. Dentists had one solution to almost every tooth problem: pull the tooth.

Fortunately, much has changed. Health care today is often quite painless—except when the bill arrives.

Discussing the Passage

1. How has health care changed in North America? Around the world?
2. What did barbers do in the past that they no longer do?

The Habitual Past

Would + simple form and *used to* + simple form can describe actions in the past that happened repeatedly or on a regular basis. *Used to* also refers to situations in the past that no longer exist.

	Examples	**Notes**
Repeated Actions in the Past	We **would visit** our grandparents every summer. They **used to come** to our house each Christmas.	Both *would* and *used to* describe repeated past actions.
Continuous Actions or Situations in the Past	He **used to work** in Detroit. He **used to be** an electrician.	For continuous actions, use *used to,* not *would.*
	There **used to be** a lot of factories in Detroit. My father **used to have** a job in a factory, but he **doesn't** work there **anymore.**	For past situations that no longer exist, use *used to,* not *would.* *Used to* and *not . . . anymore* are common in sentences that compare past and present situations.

A. Exercise: Underline all uses of *would* and *used to* in the passage "Changes in Jobs" at the beginning of Part Three. Can you substitute *would* for *used to* in all cases? Are there cases where only *used to* is possible?

B. Exercise: Caroline got a promotion. She has new responsibilities, so she doesn't do most of her old duties anymore. Tell about the changes by making sentences from the following cues. Use the example as a model.

Example: answer the telephone / hire new employees →
Caroline used to answer the telephone. Now Christina answers it, and Caroline hires new employees.

1. run the photocopier / order supplies
2. type letters / edit the company newsletter
3. take dictation / write business letters
4. schedule appointments / manage the office
5. take messages / leave messages
6. file memos / make calls to customers

C. Exercise: In pairs, use the following cues to make statements with *would* and *used to*.

Example: icemen / deliver ice →
GRANDPA: **In my day, icemen would deliver ice every day.**
CHILD: **They used to deliver ice, but they don't anymore.**

1. doctors / make housecalls
2. dentists / clean patients' teeth
3. gas station attendants / clean windshields
4. milkmen / deliver milk
5. businessmen / travel by train
6. pharmacists / make their own medicine

D. Exercise: Indicate whether *would* can be used with the following cues. (*Used to* is correct with all of them.)

Example: My family *used to* live in Chicago.

We *would* visit my grandparents every weekend.

1. My father _____ work in a factory from 1943–1946.

2. He _____ leave for work at 6:30 every morning.

3. My brother _____ be a good student.

4. He _____ have a part-time job after school, also.

5. We _____ eat dinner at 8:00 every night.

6. We _____ do our homework after dinner.

7. On weekends, we _____ help around the house.

8. Housework _____ be more difficult than it is now.

E. Exercise: Complete the following passage with combinations of *would, used to,* and the simple past tense. Do not overuse *would* or *used to.* Then write your own second paragraph. Continue the ideas in the passage by telling about changes in daily life in your area or country. Be sure to include some household jobs that are done differently now (or are done by different people in the house now).

Fifty years ago, life in the United States _was (used to be)_ (be) quite different. There _used to be_ (be) many daily or weekly chores that we no longer have to do. And there _____ (be) fewer machines. For example, we
1
_____ (not have) a refrigerator. We _____ (have) an icebox, and
2   3
the iceman _____ (deliver) ice to the houses on our street every day. He
4
_____ (drive) a horse-drawn wagon. The milkman _____ (come)
5   6
to the house daily. People _____ (shop) for food each day, too. Women
7
_____ (wash) clothes by hand with a scrubbing board and _____
8   9
(hang) them outside to dry on the clothesline. In the past, a household in the
United States _____ (be) much more difficult to manage than it is now.
10
In my area (country), . . .

F. Activity: Telling Stories. How did you spend your childhood? Would you play outside often? Did you like to play games? Did you use to read a lot? Were you well behaved? Did you get into trouble a lot? As a class or in small groups, share stories about some of the things you used to do (would do) when you were a child.

The Future in the Past

The expression *was/were going to* + simple form describes past plans or intentions. In most cases, these plans did not take place.

	Affirmative	Negative
Statements	I **was going to** help, but I couldn't.	He **wasn't going to** help, but finally he did.
Yes/No Questions	**Were** you **going to** help?	**Wasn't** he **going to** help?
Information Questions	Why **were** you **going to** help?	Why **wasn't** he **going to** help?

G. Exercise: In pairs, use the following cues to make short conversations: *was/were going to* + simple verb form.

Example: write the report / yesterday →
        S1: **Have you written that report yet?**
        S2: **I was going to write it yesterday, but something came up.**

1. mail the package / this morning
2. call the repairman / earlier
3. change the date of the meeting / yesterday
4. get the paychecks ready / this morning
5. check the supplies / last week
6. count the money in the cash drawer / this morning

H. Activity: Making Excuses. In pairs, take turns asking and answering questions of your own based on the model in Exercise G. Ask about schoolwork, household responsibilities, plans for trips, and so forth.

Example: S1: **Have you read the assignment yet?**
        S2: **I was going to read it last night, but something came up (but I didn't have time; I went to the movies; etc.).**

You might want to use some of the following cues:

proofread your paper	do the shopping
copy the lecture notes	wash the dishes
return the library book	make the plane reservations
pick up the dry cleaning	call the travel agent

I. Activity: Discussing Changes. Have there been important changes in the economic life of your country or city? How has the economy changed? Why have these changes taken place? Did the economy of your country rely on one crop like coffee? Did your city have one major industry like the auto industry in Detroit?

In small groups, choose a country, a city, an industry, or a profession and compare the past situation with the present situation. Discuss what changes have taken place and the reasons for them. Make notes about the most interesting changes and report them to the class.

PART FOUR

THE PAST PERFECT TENSE

Have you looked through the want ads in your local paper? Share your information while answering the following questions about the newspaper ads.

1. What kind of newspaper is this (for example, a city daily or a student newspaper)?
2. What kinds of jobs are available for students?

Finding a Job

MANUEL: I lost my job two weeks ago, and it's been very difficult to find a new one. I've spent the last few days job hunting. Before this, I had always spent my free time with my girlfriend, Sandy. She must think that I'm not interested in her anymore.

JOHN: Job hunting has been very difficult for me, too. I need a job, but like most students, I haven't ever had one. I don't have the work experience most employers want.

MANUEL: Last week I found out that a friend of mine had just quit her job in the physics lab. Why don't you apply for it?

JOHN: That sounds great! I'll do that right away. I did well in my science courses last year. You know, I'd considered being a dishwasher, but this sounds much better!

MANUEL: Well, I think I've just taken care of your employment problem! Now I've got to concentrate on mine.

Discussing the Passage

1. How had Manuel spent his free time before he lost his job?
2. What did Manuel find out last week?
3. What had John considered doing?

Employment

POSITION AVAILABLE—Childcare: providing care to children from families in crisis. Requirements: Three credits in early childhood education, six months experience in childcare. Hours: 20-40 hours/week; $5.80/hour. Call The Respite Center: 555-2350

POSITION AVAILABLE—Family Service Worker: To work with parents and families in crisis. Duties: Take incoming calls, assess needs, provide counseling, arrange childcare, provide information to parents. Requirements: B.A. Social Work plus relevant experience. Master's candidates preferred. Hours: 20 hours/week; $8.25/hour. Call The Respite Center: 555-2350

WORK IN COLORADO: If you would like to work at a ski resort this winter, Telluride, Colorado might be the place for you. See our slide presentation, May 8 at 7 p.m. in the Union. Watch for our recruiters on campus May 9 & 10. For more information about Telluride Ski Corp., contact the office of Financial Aid.

RENTAL AGENTS: Must be personable and dedicated. Full- and part-time positions available. Offering opportunities for advancement. Must have transportation. Send resume and salary requirements to P.O. Box 7214, Milwaukee, WI 53202.

SUMMER WORK: Time is running out. Have you got your summer job lined up? We still have openings. Write Summer Opportunities, P.O. Box 421, Madison, WI 53701.

JOB: SEEKING aggressive graduate skier, salesperson with car, to market travel programs in an interstate area. Immediate need. Salary with commission. European travel and work within 1 year. Call Sue at Adventure Travel, Milwaukee, WI (414) 555-1448.

The Past Perfect Tense

The past perfect tense refers to an activity or situation completed *before* another event or time in the past. It is more common in written English than in spoken English. Time expressions such as the following often appear with the past perfect: *before (1950), by (May 1), by then, by that time, ever, never, already, still, yet*. Note that placement of adverbs is the same as with the present perfect tense. Chapter 7 covers other time expressions and sentence types that often occur with this tense.

Activities completed before another time in the past:	John **had arrived** at work long before 8:30. By 9:15, his boss still **had not arrived.** **Had** his boss **arrived** by 9:30? It was the first time that his boss **had** ever **been** late.

	Affirmative Statements	Negative Statements
Long Forms	I You He She **had arrived** by noon. It We They	I You He She **had not arrived** by noon. It We They
Contracted Forms	**I'd (You'd, He'd, She'd, It'd, We'd, They'd)** arrived.	I (You, He, She, It, We, They) **hadn't** arrived.

	Questions	Affirmative Answers	Negative Answers
Yes/No Questions and Short Answers	**Had** I you he she **arrived?** it we they	Yes, I you he she **had.** it we they	No, I you he she **hadn't.** it we they

Note: See pages 50–51 for spelling rules for the *-ed* ending of regular past participles. See pages 48–50 for a list of irregular past participles.

Tag Questions and Information Questions

Here are some examples of questions with the past perfect tense.

	Questions	**Expected Responses**
Tag Questions and Short Answers	You had gone there, **hadn't you?** She hadn't already left, **had she?**	Yes, I **had.** No, she **hadn't.**

	Questions	**Possible Responses**
Information Questions and Short Answers	**When** had you last seen Mary? **Where** had he	Two weeks before the accident. At school.
	Who had last seen her? **What** had happened to her?	John. We don't know.

For more information on forms and meanings of these questions, see Chapter 1, Part Four.

A. **Exercise:** Underline all past perfect verbs in the conversation "Finding a Job" at the beginning of Part Four. Can you explain why that tense was used in each case?

B. **Exercise:** John finally got a job, and he began work on Monday. Before then, he'd made a lot of preparations. Use the following cues and the past perfect tense to tell about his preparations. See his calendar at the top of the next page.

Example: Friday / buy new work clothes →
             By Friday, he had bought new work clothes.

1. Thursday / call his girlfriend
2. Saturday / get a haircut
3. Sunday / do laundry
4. Monday / write his parents
5. the following weekend / receive his first paycheck
6. the end of the month / pay all of his bills
7. Christmas / ask Emily to marry him
8. the end of the year / give Emily a ring

Monday	
22	*Interview*

Tuesday	
23	

Wednesday	
24 ●	*Got a job! Call Emily.*
New Moon	

Thursday	
25	*Buy work clothes / new shoes*

Friday	
26	*haircut / bus pass*

Saturday	
27	*do laundry / movies*

Sunday	
28	*write parents*

Monday	
29	*Start working !!!!*

Tuesday	
30	

Wednesday	
31 ●	Last Quarter

Thursday	
1	

Friday	
2	

Saturday	
3	

Sunday	
4	

C. Exercise: In pairs, take turns asking and answering questions about John. To check your answers, refer to the calendar above.

Example: get a haircut / Thursday →
　　　　　S1: **Had John gotten a haircut by Thursday?**
　　　　　S2: **No, he hadn't. He got a haircut Friday.**

1. find a job / before Wednesday
2. buy work clothes / before the weekend
3. buy a bus pass / by Sunday
4. get new shoes / before Thursday
5. start his new job / by the weekend
6. write his parents / before he began working

D. Exercise: Use the simple past and past perfect tenses with the following cues to give short descriptions of these people's job search.

Example: John / get a job in a physics lab / want to work in the hospital →
　　　　　John finally got a job in a physics lab. He had wanted to work at the hospital, but there weren't any jobs.

1. Gary / find work as a taxi driver / want to be a physics teacher
2. Denise / get a job as a cook / hope to be an auto worker
3. Melanie / enroll in a computer class / try to work as an architect in Chicago
4. Miki / write a book / dream of being a newspaper reporter in California
5. Jim / join the army / hope to become an astronaut
6. Susan / get a job as a clerk / look for work as a decorator

E. **Exercise:** Using the following cues, form sentences with the past perfect and *ever*.

Example: as a taxi driver / drive a taxi →
When I got a job as a taxi driver, it was the first time that I had ever driven a taxi.

1. as a bank teller / wear a suit
2. in an office / carry a briefcase
3. in a hospital / see an operation
4. in a bank / use a computer
5. as a secretary / take dictation
6. in a gas station / repair an engine

F. **Exercise: Contrast of Tenses.** First, read the following passage for meaning. Then complete the passage with appropriate tenses of the verbs in parentheses. Choose from the simple past, past continuous, past perfect, simple present, and future tenses.

Elephant Wins in Court

Rampyari ____*is*____ (be) an unusual female. Since her childhood, she ____*had been*____ (be) a working woman, but in 1981 she _____(lose) the
1
ability to make money. Until that time, she _____(work) loyally for her
2
employer, without bonuses or overtime pay. Then, in 1983, she _____(go)
3
to court about her job.

During her trial in 1983, Rampyari _____(come / never) to the
4
courtroom. Because of her large stomach, she _____(not be) able to climb
5
the stairs to the courthouse. Also, she _____(be) very upset and emotional
6

because she _____ (not work) anymore. She _____ (retire)
                        7   8
early, long before the normal age, but it _____ (not be) by choice.
                                                      9

Finally, after two years in court, Rampyari _____ (receive) $2,300 in
                                                            10
damages. She _____ (become) wealthy. And she _____ (become)
                        11   12
the first elephant in Indian history to win in the courtroom!

Before 1981, this lovable circus performer _____ (entertain)
                                                            13
audiences for sixteen years. Then one winter night, she _____ (walk) down
                                                                        14
an Indian highway when a truck _____ (hit) her. Because of the injury,
                                              15
now she _____ (walk) with difficulty. She _____ (be) still young
                    16   17
for an elephant, and perhaps she _____ (go) back to work sometime in the
                                              18
future, but not in the circus. That would be too difficult for her now.

If she goes back to work in the future, the defense lawyers will ask for a retrial.
No one _____ (want) to pay $2,300 to a working elephant.
                    19

Adapted from *The Christian Science Monitor*
November 1983

G. Activity: Discussing Employment Possibilities. In pairs or in small groups, discuss one or more of the following. Then give a summary of your discussion to the entire class.

1. Have your career plans changed? Were you going to study something different? Why did your plans change?
2. Is unemployment a major problem in your area or country? What has caused it? Has your government tried to improve the situation? Which jobs have the best future? Which jobs have no future?
3. Do you think jobs in the field you have chosen will change very much in the future? Have they changed very much in the last twenty years? What has caused these changes? What may cause future changes?

5

LIFESTYLES

Phrasal Verbs and Related Structures

INSEPARABLE PHRASAL VERBS

What was a typical North American family like thirty years ago? Share your ideas and opinions while answering the following questions about the picture.

1. Who are the people in this picture? What is each person doing?
2. What time of day is it? How do you know?
3. Were most families like this in the past? Are they like this now?

The "Typical" American Family

In the 1950s, according to popular television shows, the American family (let's call them the Smiths) consisted of a mother, a father, and two or three children. The Smiths were a very happy family. Their problems were not serious; the children got along with each other, and Mr. and Mrs. Smith obviously cared about each other very much.

Mr. Smith (Dick) was a businessman, and Mrs. Smith (Susie) was a housewife. She spent most of her time at home, where she took care of the house and the children (Billy and Mary). In the morning, she usually got up before the rest of the family, went into the kitchen, and made breakfast. Soon Dick, Billy, and Mary sat down to eat. The children talked about their plans for the rest of the day while Dick looked at the newspaper and thought about his day's work. Susie, of course, cheerfully served everybody.

When breakfast was over, the children left for school and Dick went to work. Then Susie Smith sat down with a cup of coffee and the morning newspaper. She had the whole day to herself, until the children came back from school. At that time, she listened to them patiently as they talked about their day at school, and she helped them with their homework.

According to television, this was the "typical" scene in family after family, all across the United States. Nowadays, we laugh when we look at those old 1950s television programs, because we know how very much they differed from real life.

Discussing the Passage

1. What did each person in the "typical" American family use to do in the mornings?
2. Do you think this family was really typical? Why or why not?
3. Can you describe the "typical" American family of today?

Inseparable Phrasal Verbs (1)

Certain prepositions customarily follow certain verbs. These prepositions are sometimes called *particles*. The following is a short list of some common verb + particle combinations in English. These phrasal verbs are "inseparable" because the particle has only one possible position in the sentence. In most cases, it immediately follows the verb. With the phrasal verbs in this group, the particle does not change the basic meaning of the verb.

Verbs	Examples
agree (disagree) with	Mary doesn't **agree with** her mother.
belong to	That toy **belongs to** Billy.
care about	Mrs. Smith **cares about** her children.
consist of	The family **consists of** four people.
depend on	Children **depend on** their parents.
differ from	Your opinion **differs from** mine.
dream about (of)	Mary **dreams about** getting married someday.
laugh at	Everybody **laughed at** the dog's tricks.
leave for	The children **leave for** school at 7:45 A.M.
listen to	The mother **listened to** the child's story.
live with	She **lives with** her daughter.
look at	Last night we **looked at** old photographs.
look for	She **looked for** her keys for an hour.
sit down	Everyone **sat down** at the table.
talk about	We **talked about** our plans for the summer.
talk to	My teacher **talked to** me about my homework.
think about (of)	Mr. Smith **is thinking about** his work.
wait for	Mrs. Smith **waited for** Mary at the bus stop.

Some phrasal verbs can have a noun or pronoun between the verb and the particle. Here are some examples.

Verbs	Examples
ask (someone) **about**	Mrs. Smith **asked** the children **about** their day.
ask (someone) **for**	Dick **asked** Susie **for** a second cup of coffee.
help (someone) **with**	Dick **helped** Susie **with** the dishes.
borrow something **from** someone	Susie **borrowed** some milk **from** her neighbor.
lend something **to** someone	The neighbor **lent** some milk **to** Susie.
remind someone **about** **remind** someone **of**	Billy **reminded** his mother **about** the football game. You **remind** me **of** your grandmother.

A. **Exercise:** Underline all the verb + particle combinations in the passage "The 'Typical' American Family" at the beginning of this chapter. Discuss the meanings of the verbs with your classmates.

B. **Exercise:** Fill in the blanks with the correct particle.

Example: During breakfast, Mrs. Smith reminded her husband __*about*__ the parents' meeting that evening.

1.   Billy spent fifteen minutes looking _____ his geography book.

2.   During the day, Susie Smith listened _____ the radio while she worked in the house.

3.   She borrowed some sugar _____ her neighbor.

4.   At school, the children laughed _____ a funny story.

5.   Mary lent her red pencil _____ a classmate.

6.   During class, Billy dreamed _____ going outside and playing.

7.   This reading book belongs _____ Mary.

8.   At work, Dick Smith asked his boss _____ a raise.

9.   Susie waited _____ the children to come home from school.

10.   Then Susie helped them _____ their homework.

11.   During dinner, the family members talked _____ their day.

12.   Mrs. Smith almost always agrees _____ Mr. Smith.

C. Exercise: In pairs, ask and answer the following questions about your life as a high school student. Use the phrasal verbs in italics in your answers.

Example: S1: Was it easy for you to *talk about* your problems with your teachers?
    S2: **No, it wasn't easy for me to talk about my problems with my teachers.**

1. At what time did you use to *leave for* school?
2. Did someone *help you with* your homework?
3. Did you ever *disagree with* your teachers?
4. Did your teachers *care about* your opinions?
5. What did you sometimes *dream about* while you were sitting in class?
6. When you were a teenager, whom did you *talk to* about your future?

Inseparable Phrasal Verbs (2)

There are many verb + particle combinations in which the particle changes the meaning of the verb. That is, the meaning of the two words together is different from the meanings of the verb and the preposition by themselves. These verb + particle combinations have an *idiomatic* meaning. They are different from sentences with prepositional phrases. Compare:

	Examples	**Notes**
Verb + prepositional phrase	Jim lives **on Middleton Street.** (The house where Jim lives is located on Middleton Street.) Jim ran **into his house.** (Jim entered his house, running.)	In these sentences the verb keeps its basic meaning.
Verb + particle (phrasal verb)	Jim **lives on** $500 a month. (Jim spends $500 a month.) Jim **ran into** an old friend. (Jim met an old friend by chance.)	In these sentences, the verb has an idiomatic meaning.

The following is a short list of inseparable phrasal verbs with idiomatic meanings.

Verbs	Examples	Meanings
come back	Are you going to **come back** early?	return
drop (stop) by	My neighbor **dropped by** this afternoon.	visit
get along with	The Smiths **get along with** their neighbors.	be friendly with
get together with	Let's **get together with** the Nelsons this weekend.	meet socially
get up	On weekends, everybody **gets up** late.	leave one's bed after sleeping
go over	Let's **go over** the homework.	review; correct
grow up	I **grew up** in Wisconsin.	become an adult
live on	Can you **live on** $500 a month?	exist; support oneself financially
look after	Will you **look after** the boys while I'm out?	supervise; watch
look like	You **look like** your father.	resemble
move out of (move into)	When are you **moving out of** your apartment? When are you **moving into** your new house?	leave; relocate
run into	I **ran into** an old friend yesterday.	meet accidentally
stay up	How late did you **stay up** last night?	remain awake
take care of	Will you **take care of** my plants while I'm gone?	watch; supervise

D. Exercise: In pairs, ask and answer the following questions about your life with your family. Use the phrasal verbs in italics in your answers.

Example: S1: **Do you ever *run into* friends when you are shopping?**
S2: **Yes, sometimes I run into friends when I am shopping.**

1. Where did you *grow up?*
2. When you were very small, who *looked after* you?
3. When you were a child in school, did you *come back* home for lunch?
4. Did someone *go over* your homework with you?
5. How late did you *stay up* on school nights?
6. Do you *look like* your father or your mother?
7. Do you *get along with* everyone in your family?
8. In your family, who usually *gets up* first?
9. Who *takes care of* the house?
10. Do relatives and neighbors *drop by* your house very often?

E. Exercise: Replace the verbs in italics with phrasal verbs from the Inseparable Phrasal Verbs (2) chart on page 141.

Example: When Susie and Dick go out in the evening, a babysitter *watches* the children. →
When Susie and Dick go out in the evening, a babysitter *looks after* the children.

1. That child doesn't *resemble* either of her parents.
2. When are you going to *return*?
3. I *meet* my best friend for dinner once a week.
4. Yesterday, I *accidentally met* my college roommate on the street.
5. I need to *review* my notes before the test tomorrow.
6. Please feel free to *visit us* any time you're in the area.
7. I have only a part-time job, so it's hard for me to *exist on* my salary.
8. We are going to *leave* this apartment next month.

F. Exercise: The following letter from Susie Smith to her friend Nancy contains many particle errors. Cross out the errors and correct them. Use the lists on pages 138, 139, and 141 to help you. Note the date!

March 18, 1957

Dear Nancy,

    I have been thinking ~~over~~ *about (of)* you a lot lately. I'm sorry for not writing sooner, but I've been so busy with the children.

    I ran ~~through~~ *into* your mother at the market the other day, and we talked with your life in the BIG CITY! It's interesting how much your life differs in your mother's— and mine.

    You asked me for my life as a "typical American housewife." My life consists in my children, my husband, and my home. As you know, we recently moved on this big, expensive new house, so we don't have much money these days. I thought in trying to find a part-time job because it's not easy to live with Dick's salary. Dick doesn't want me to work, though, and I think it's more important for me to take care to the house and kids. Anyway, I know I can depend for Dick to support us all.

    The kids are wonderful. They are growing in so fast! Every afternoon, when they come to from school, we talk with their day, and I go under their homework with them. I really enjoy listening on them.

    What else can I tell you, Nancy? Sometimes I get together from other mothers in my neighborhood and we talk on our kids and husbands. I think I'm lucky because Dick helps me for the housework more than most other husbands do. Occasionally, I go to my neighbor Julie's house and ask her about some advice, or I borrow some sugar or something of her. Now and then I run around some old friends from high school.

    And that's my life, Nancy. Sure, sometimes I dream for doing something different and exciting, and I think on you in the city. But really—I am very happy.

Love,

Susie

G. Activity: Describing a Traditional Family. In small groups, discuss the following questions. Then use this information as the basis for a brief presentation to the class.

1. In your culture, how many people does a traditional family consist of ? How many people work outside the home?
2. Who usually takes care of small children?
3. Do young couples in your culture live with their parents, or do they live by themselves?
4. The "typical" American family has changed a lot in the last thirty years. Has the "typical" family in your culture also changed? In what ways?

PART TWO

SEPARABLE PHRASAL VERBS

Do you know the meaning of the terms *nuclear family* and *extended family?* In American society, which one is more important these days? How about in your culture? Share your opinions while answering the following questions about the picture on page 145.

1. Who are the people in the picture? What is the relationship between them?
2. What does the picture tell about their lifestyles?

Family Photograph

Last week my oldest son, Bob, called me up. He said, "Mom, Jean and I had a great idea: For your birthday, we'd like to take a family photograph. What do you think?" I thought it over and decided it would be nice to have a photograph of all my children and grandchildren together.

The photo was ready yesterday, so Bob picked it up. And here it is! I must say, it's beautiful. That's me, sitting in the center. Over on the left are Jean and Bob and their teenage son, Alan. Next to Bob, the woman with the baby is my daughter Dawn. She and her husband separated recently; I had hoped that they would work out their differences, but it didn't happen that way. Now Dawn is trying to bring up two children by herself. It's not easy, so I help her out whenever I can.

Behind me in the picture are my daughter Patty, her husband Steve, and their two kids. Such a happy family; they enjoy doing things together, and they always talk over their problems without arguing.

And on the right you see my youngest son, Michael. He always wears such strange clothes . . . I really can't figure him out. But he's young; he's still trying out different ideas and lifestyles. He'll be all right.

My husband and I worked hard to bring our kids up well. They're very different from one another, but they're fine people and I love them all. They make me very happy.

Discussing the Passage

1. Using the information in the passage, can you identify each person in the photograph?
2. How do the woman's four children differ from one another?
3. Is this a "typical" North American extended family? In what ways?

Separable Phrasal Verbs

With *inseparable* verbs, the verb and particle are a unit; they must be together. However, English also has *separable* phrasal verbs. With these verb + particle combinations, *noun* objects may come after the verb and particle or between them. *Pronoun* objects must come between the verb and particle. Compare:

	Examples	Meanings
Inseparable	*noun* My mother **ran into** Laurie.	My mother saw Laurie.
	pronoun My mother **ran into** her.	My mother saw her.
Separable	*noun* I **called up** my mother.	I telephoned my mother.
	noun I **called** my mother **up**.	I telephoned my mother.
	pronoun I **called** her **up**.	I telephoned her.

Common Separable Phrasal Verbs

Verbs	Examples	Meanings
bring up	Dawn **is bringing** her kids **up** by herself.	raise (a family)
call up	Yesterday my son **called** me **up**.	telephone (verb)
drop off	Could you **drop** me **off** downtown?	take someone or something (on the way somewhere, often by car)
figure out	I can't **figure out** this problem.	understand, solve (a problem), decide
find out	Did you **find out** her phone number?	learn, discover
help out	My mother often **helps** me **out** with the kids.	assist, help
look over	Please **look over** your paper before you give it to me.	read quickly; review

pick out	Did you **pick out** a present?	choose, select
pick up	I **picked** her **up** after class.	go (often by car) to get someone
take out	Please **take out** the garbage.	take outside
talk over	We **talked** the situation **over.**	discuss
think over	I'll **think over** your advice.	think about something carefully
throw away	Did you **throw** yesterday's paper **away?**	discard; put in the garbage
try out	Let's **try out** these new skis.	test, experiment with
wake up	The phone **woke** me **up.**	cause someone to stop sleeping
work out	I hope we can **work** it **out.**	find a solution, resolve

A. **Exercise:** Underline all the separable phrasal verbs in the passage "Family Photograph" at the beginning of this section and circle the noun or pronoun object of the verb. In each case, change the word order of the verb, particle, and object *if possible.*

Example: My son called (me) up. → **no change possible**

I had hoped that they would work out (their differences.) → **work their differences out**

B. **Exercise:** Fill in the blanks with the correct particle.

Example: I would like to find *out* that girl's name.

1. I threw _____ my mother's letter by accident.

2. Please think my suggestion _____ and give me your opinion.

3. I can't figure _____ the answer to this math problem.

4. These days it's really hard to bring kids _____ .

5. I need to drop _____ a package at the post office.

6. Every day, Mrs. Smith picks her children _____ at the bus stop.

7. We tried _____ a new computer system, but we didn't like it.

8. I call my mother _____ every Sunday.

9. The noise from the birds woke Mr. Smith _____ at 5:00 A.M.

10. Let's talk _____ your idea with the boss.

C. **Exercise:** Change all the noun objects in Exercise B to pronouns. Pay attention to word order.

Example: I would like to find out that woman's name. → I would like to **find it out.**

Families of Separable Phrasal Verbs

Phrasal Verbs Related to Clothing, Cleaning, and Household Items

There are a few groups of related phrasal verbs in English. Some examples follow.

Verbs	Examples	Meanings
have on **put on** **try on**	She **has on** a new hat. I always **put** my socks **on** first. Did you **try** it **on** before you bought it?	*Have on* means "wear"; *on* means "on one's body."
take off	Please **take off** your coat.	
clean off **dust off** **wash off**	**Clean off** the table, please. I **dusted off** the bookshelves. I **washed** the grease **off** my hands.	*Off* means "remove from the surface of something."
clean out **sweep out**	We need to **clean out** this closet. Please **sweep out** the garage.	*Out* means "remove from the inside of something."
clean up **pick up** **sweep up** **wash up**	Don't go into the kitchen until I **clean** it **up.** Please **pick up** your toys. I have to **sweep up** the floor. It's time to **wash up** for dinner.	*Up* means "lift or remove something that dropped or fell." It also means "completely."
turn off	Could you **turn** the T.V. **off?**	*Off* means "stop something" such as water or an electric appliance.
turn on	Please **turn** the light **on.**	*On* means "start something" such as water or an electric appliance.
turn down **turn up**	**Turn down** that stereo! Could you **turn** the T.V. **up?**	*Down* and *up* refer to sound levels.

D. Exercise: First, complete the following phrases with appropriate particles. Then substitute a pronoun for the noun. Some phrases may have more than one correct answer.

Example: turn *down (up, on, off)* the stereo
        turn it down (up, on, off)

1. sweep _____ the closet

2. clean _____ the bathroom

3. turn _____ the lights

4. clean _____ the table

5. turn _____ the sound

6. clean _____ the house

7. dust _____ the lamp

8. take _____ your hat

E. Exercise: Patty, Steve, and their two children are a happy family. In pairs, take turns asking and answering questions about them, using the separable phrasal verbs in this section. Use the example as a model.

Example: drop off the children at school / Steve →
        S1: **Who drops the children off at school?**
        S2: **Steve drops them off at school.**

1. clean up the kitchen / Steve
2. pick up the kids' toys / the kids
3. take out the garbage / the son
4. wake up the children / Patty
5. help the kids out with homework / Patty and Steve
6. sweep out the garage / Patty
7. clean off the table before dinner / the daughter
8. call up Grandma on Saturdays / the kids
9. pick out new living room furniture / Patty and Steve
10. help out around the house sometimes / Patty's mother

Patty and Steve share everything....

F. Exercise: Complete the following sentences with the correct verb, pronoun, and particle. Some will have more than one correct answer.

Example: Oh, no! I've just spilled orange juice on the floor. I'd better

   clean it up   .

1. Before you pay for a new shirt in a department store, you should

    _____ .

2. The music in the restaurant was so loud that we couldn't talk to each other. We

    asked the manager to _____ .

3. This sweater is too hot; I'm going to _____ .

4. My car is full of papers, bottles, and other junk. It's time to

    _____ .

5. Mary's toys were all over the floor. Her mother asked her to

    _____ .

6. Yesterday I noticed that our bookshelves are covered with dust. Today I'm going

    to _____ .

7. Sometimes Mr. Jones cannot find his reading glasses. He forgets that he

    already _____ .

8. The T.V. wasn't loud enough, so I _____ .

9. We don't need that light over there; please _____ .

10. The table is covered with newspapers and letters. Please

    _____ so that we can eat dinner.

Phrasal Verbs Related to School or Studies

Verbs	Examples	Meanings
add up	Your answer is wrong because you forgot to **add up** the last group of numbers.	total
finish up	Class is over; please **finish up** your tests.	*Up* can mean "completely" or "thoroughly." In some cases it does not change the basic meaning of the verb.
write up	Please **write up** this report for Monday.	
check in	A librarian **checks** books **in.**	receive
check out	I **checked out** three books.	take (books or movies from the library, etc.)
do over	You did this assignment incorrectly; please **do** it **over.**	repeat, do again
look over	I have to **look over** my notes before the next class.	read or look at quickly.
fill in	Please **fill in** all the answers.	give (information on a form)
fill out	You need to **fill out** this application.	complete (a form)
hand in, turn in	I **handed in** my composition late.	give (for example, to the teacher)
hand out	The teacher **handed out** some exercises.	give (for example, to the students)
hand back	The teacher **handed back** our essays.	return (for example, to students, after correction)

G. **Exercise:** In pairs, take turns asking and answering questions based on the following cues. Use the pronoun form in your answer. Pay attention to verb tenses.

Example: finish up your homework / Yes, an hour ago →
        S1: **Have you finished up your homework?**
        S2: **Yes, I finished it up an hour ago.**

1. check the books out of the library yet / Yes, two days ago
2. write up your lab report / No, tomorrow
3. look over your report to check for mistakes / Yes, before I typed it
4. turn in the final copy yet / Yes, the day before yesterday
5. your teacher hand back the tests / Yes, yesterday afternoon
6. fill out the scholarship application yet / No, later
7. add up the monthly expenses yet / No, this evening
8. do your chemistry assignment over / Yes, this morning

H. Exercise: Interviewing. Using the following cues, ask your partner about his or her activities this week. Indicate your partner's answer in the chart. Use the examples as models.

Examples: sweep up the kitchen →
S1: **Have you swept up the kitchen yet (this week)?**
S2: **Yes, I swept it up on Sunday.**

hand in your composition →
S1: **Have you handed in your composition yet (this week)?**
S2: **No, I haven't.**

Activity	Yes, when?	No

sweep up the kitchen
hand in your composition
call up your parents
take out the garbage
clean up your room (apartment, house)
throw away yesterday's newspaper
think over your plans for the summer
   (winter, etc.)
finish up your homework for tomorrow
clean out your car
pick out a birthday present for your
   friend (sister, mother, etc.)
	Sunday	
		X

PART THREE

SEPARABLE AND INSEPARABLE PHRASAL VERBS

What choices do young people in this country have after they finish high school? Share your ideas and opinions while answering the following questions about the pictures.

1.   What is this young man doing in each picture?
2.   Why do you think the young man worked before he went to college?

Going Back to School

    I was a terrible student in high school. Studying and learning were hard for me. I had to do many assignments over. I couldn't keep up with my classmates. Naturally, I didn't have a very good attitude; I wanted to get through with school as quickly as possible and get a job. And that's exactly what I did. As soon as I graduated, I moved out of

my parents' house. I spent the next five years working as a carpenter and living on $300 a month. It was hard.

I went through a lot during those five years, and my experiences really helped me to grow up. Finally, at age twenty-four, I felt ready to go back to school. After looking into lots of professional possibilities, I decided to study accounting. Math had always been pretty easy for me; I could add up numbers in my head.

I thought I'd be the oldest person in all my classes, but I've come across lots of people who took a few years off before starting college. Most of us are glad that we waited until now to begin our studies.

Discussing the Passage

1. What kind of student was the young man in high school? How has he changed?
2. Do young people in your country ever take time off between high school and college? What do they do with this time?
3. In your opinion, is it a good idea to work for a few years before starting college?

More Separable Phrasal Verbs

Verbs	Examples	Meanings
call back	Did Charles **call** you **back?**	telephone again
cut out	Save the newspaper. I want to **cut** an article **out.**	cut, remove
get back	Did you **get** your stolen wallet **back?**	receive
give back	Did you **give** the money **back?**	return
look up	I **looked** the word **up** in the dictionary.	search for information (in a book)
point out	He **pointed out** several problems.	mention, indicate
put away	He **put away** his toys at bedtime.	put something in its proper place
start over	Let's **start** the song **over** from the beginning.	begin again
take off	Yesterday I **took** a day **off.***	take vacation

* *Take off* has several meanings. In addition to "take a vacation" it can mean "leave," but with this meaning it is inseparable: *The plane took off on time.*

More Inseparable Phrasal Verbs

Verbs	Examples	Meanings
check into (check out of)	We **checked into** a first-class motel.	enter, register; leave
come across	Did you **come across** that letter?	find (something); meet (someone)
get through with	I want to **get through with** this job as quickly as possible.	finish
go over to	Let's **go over to** Miki's house.	go to visit
go through	I don't want to **go through** that again!	experience
keep up with	I can't **keep up with** the class.	stay equal to (in time, distance, money, work, etc.)
look into	We should **look into** the cost before we rent that house.	get information on
put up with	How do you **put up with** all this noise?	tolerate, live with

A. Exercise: Underline all the separable and inseparable phrasal verbs in the passage "Going Back to School" at the beginning of this section. Discuss the meanings of the verbs.

B. Exercise: Separable and Inseparable Phrasal Verbs. Replace the verbs in italics with phrasal verbs from the preceding lists. Pay attention to the placement of noun and pronoun objects.

Example: After I used my neighbor's camera, I ~~returned it~~ *gave it back* to him.

1. Yesterday I *found* some old photographs while I was cleaning.
2. I have to *finish* this assignment before I can go out.
3. We *registered* at the most expensive hotel in town.
4. I am tired of your rude behavior. I'm not going to *tolerate* it anymore.
5. I *searched for* information about India in an encyclopedia.
6. This composition is no good. I'll have to *begin* it *again*.

C. Exercise: Oral Practice. In pairs, ask and answer the following questions.

1. Is it difficult for you to *keep up with* the other students in this class?
2. Did you *look into* other English classes before you decided to take this one?
3. When was the last time you *took* a day *off* from work or school? What did you do?
4. Has your teacher ever told you to *do* a composition *over?* Did you do it?
5. Are you planning to *go over to* a friend's house tonight?
6. Have you *come across* any good restaurants lately?
7. Would you like to *start* your education *over* again? What would you like to study?
8. What is the worst experience that you have *gone through* since you have been in this city?

D. Exercise: Review of Separable and Inseparable Phrasal Verbs. Replace the italicized verbs with phrasal verbs. Choose from the following list and pay attention to word order in your sentences.

add up	live on
call up	look for
drop by	look into
figure out	move out of
get along with	run into
help out	work out

MIKE: Boy, it's great to be finished with school. What are your plans now?

JOHN: I'm trying to *decide*$_1$ where to live. I have to *leave*$_2$ the dorm this weekend.

MIKE: You know, I *met*$_3$ my friend Bruce on campus yesterday. He has a big apartment near the lake, and he's *trying to find*$_4$ some roommates. He's a nice guy. I think you would *be on good terms with*$_5$ him.

JOHN: Do you know if it's expensive? I don't have much money to *exist on.*$_6$ Whenever I *total*$_7$ my bills, I realize how poor I am.

MIKE: I'll *get information about*$_8$ it. I'll *telephone*$_9$ him this evening. Maybe we can *visit*$_{10}$ there tomorrow to see it.

JOHN: It's really nice of you to *assist*$_{11}$ me this way.

MIKE: I'm happy to do it. I'm sure we can *resolve*$_{12}$ your problem.

E. Exercise: Review of Separable and Inseparable Phrasal Verbs. Replace the italicized verbs with phrasal verbs. Choose from the following list, and pay attention to word order in your sentences.

figure out	put away	talk over
get up	put up with	think over
give back	start over	throw away
look like	take care of	work out
move out	take out	

LINDA: You know, Marge, I can't *understand*[1] how you can live this way. Look at this place! It *resembles*[2] a disaster area. Your papers are all over the floor. Why don't you ever *return* them *to their proper place?*[3] And why is the kitchen full of trash? Why don't you *put* anything *in the garbage?*[4] I'm telling you, I don't think I can *tolerate*[5] this mess much longer! I'm thinking about *leaving this apartment!*[6]

MARGE: Let's *discuss*[7] the situation. Maybe we can *find a solution to*[8] the problems. What else is bothering you?

LINDA: Lots of things. You never *take* the garbage *outside.*[9] You borrow my things and then you forget to *return*[10] them. You never *take responsibility for*[11] the plants. And that's not all . . .

MARGE: Okay, okay. Look, I'll try to be neater. I'll *get out of bed*[12] a little earlier in the morning and do some housework before I go to work. Let's *begin again,*[13] okay? I don't want you to *leave.*[14]

LINDA: Well, I'll *think about* it *carefully.*[15]

F. Exercise: Review of Separable and Inseparable Phrasal Verbs. Circle the correct answer in each sentence below.

1. When I'm at the beach, I enjoy looking (over / at / like) the birds and the waves.

2. I don't know the answer to your question. However, I will look (at / into / after) it and give you an answer tomorrow.

3. The bathtub is full. Turn (off / down / up) the water.

4. I made a lot of mistakes on my composition. I need to go (through / over to / over) them with my teacher.

5. My sister and I are good friends. I get (along with / together with / through with) her very well.

6. After Mr. Smith washes the dishes, he puts (them away / them on / up with them).

7. When Mr. and Mrs. Broder go out for the evening, their neighbor takes (out / off / care of) their baby girl.

8. Suzy's toys are all over the floor. Now she has to pick them (out / up / on).

9. Last week Joe was sick, so he had to take a couple of days (out / off / in) from work.

10. Last year I had a bad car accident, and I spent two weeks in the hospital. It was a terrible experience, and I hope I never go (over / through / for) anything like it again.

G. Activity: Role-playing. Pretend that you are one of the following persons. While shopping at the supermarket, you are very surprised to meet an old high school classmate whom you haven't seen in ten years. Naturally, you stop and talk to each other for a few minutes. Tell your old friend about your lifestyle: your marital status, social life, job, etc. Use as many phrasal verbs as possible in your role play.

1. You are thirty years old and still in college because you love to learn. You tried out five majors and finished two. Then you got a master's degree, and now you are beginning a Ph.D. program. You are happy being a "professional student."

2. You have recently gotten married, and you are staying at home while your husband/wife works. You like housework and enjoy being at home.

3. You are beginning a business and don't have much money. You are single, but you have little time to go out or meet people because you are always working.

PART FOUR

PARTICIPLES AND ADJECTIVES FOLLOWED BY PREPOSITIONS

Is adventure something that only young people look for? Share your ideas and opinions while answering the following questions about the picture.

1. Describe the picture. Where do you think this is?
2. Does this woman have a traditional lifestyle? What kind of person is she, probably?
3. Do you know people like her? Describe them.

The Elderly

The elderly is a phrase that used to cause a lot of negative feelings in older people. It made them feel that they were finished with the best part of their lives; their days of discovery and excitement were over.

No longer. The elderly today are often very healthy and adventurous. Many of them continue working well into their seventies or even eighties. Those who quit working are excited about their hobbies and interests. Retirement is not boring or frightening for them.

Helen Broomell of Minocqua, Wisconsin, is a perfect example. For forty-three years, she had been accustomed to the traditional life of a housewife and mother. During that time, she brought up six children.

When her last child moved out, she was not sad about it. On the contrary, she was thrilled about the opportunity to be completely on her own. Helen began to make preparations for the adventure of a lifetime. "And then," she says simply, "I took off."

Discussing the Passage

1. How are the elderly today different from older people in the past?
2. Describe Helen Broomell. What do you think she means when she says, "I took off"?

Participles Followed by Prepositions

Many present and past participles may be used as adjectives to describe feelings. As an adjective, the *present* participle (the *-ing* form) appears alone or is followed by a phrase with *to* or *for*. The *past* participle may be followed by a variety of prepositions, however. Chapter 8 includes more information on the uses of participles.

	Examples	Notes
Verb	Traveling **interests me.** Wild animals **frighten** me. Hiking **tires** me.	Below is a list of common verbs of emotion that follow these patterns.
Present Participle	Traveling is **interesting** (**to** me). Wild animals are **frightening** (**to** me).	The present participle as an adjective describes the effect of someone or something on someone.
Past Participle	I am **interested in** traveling. I am **frightened by** wild animals. I am **tired of** hiking.	The past participle as an adjective describes someone's feelings, opinions, or reactions. In addition to other prepositions, *by* can follow many participles.

Common Participles Used as Adjectives of Emotion

Be is used with all of the following past participles of emotion. They may also appear after the verbs *get (become), feel,* and *seem.*

> You **seem** tired.
> I **am (feel)** tired.
> I **get** tired easily when I don't eat well.

If you use a verb after one of these participle + preposition combinations, it must be in the *-ing* form. Compare:

> I'm tired of **school.**
> I'm tired of **studying.**

Past Participles	Examples
amazed at (by)	We were **amazed at** the beauty of Alaska.
annoyed at (with, by) something; annoyed with a person	We became **annoyed by** the travel delays. We became **annoyed with** the bus driver.
bored with (by)	I got **bored with** the tour guide's descriptions.
confused about (with, by)	We were **confused about** the schedule.
excited about (by)	Everyone got **excited about** the boat trip.
frightened of (by)	Jim seemed **frightened of** the animals.
inspired by	We were **inspired by** the scenery.
interested in	I was **interested in** everything I saw.
pleased about (with, by)	We were **pleased about** our decision to go to Alaska.
satisfied with (by)	We felt **satisfied with** most of the arrangements.
thrilled about an action; thrilled with a person or thing	We were **thrilled about** seeing a glacier. I was **thrilled with** the pictures I took.
tired of	By the end of the trip, we were **tired of** traveling.
worried about	Now, I'm **worried about** paying the bills.

A. Exercise: Underline all the present and past participles that act as adjectives in the passage "The Elderly" at the beginning of this section. Circle the prepositions used with the participles.

Example: Those who quit working are <u>excited</u> (about) their hobbies and interests.

B. Exercise: Complete the following passage with the missing prepositions. In some cases more than one preposition may be correct.

Helen Broomell had always been interested _____ Alaska's great
                                                    1
wilderness. Although she had been satisfied _____ her life as a housewife,
                                                            2
she was thrilled _____ the opportunity to take off by herself. At age 66,
                        3
she traveled 600 miles of the Yukon River alone by canoe.

There were many problems and inconveniences during Helen's trip, but they
were not annoying _____ her. On the contrary, she was so excited
                            4
_____ her experiences that the following summer, at age 67, she canoed
        5
another 700 miles.

On her trip, Helen came across a few Eskimos, but for the most part, she was
by herself. Helen never got bored _____ traveling alone, but occasionally
                                            6
she was frightened _____ the dangers of the wilderness (a bear once
                            7
joined her for dinner!).

Some older people (and many younger ones), who are worried _____
                                                                        8
the problems of daily living, are amazed _____ Helen's story. Yet her expe-
                                                    9
riences can be inspiring _____ people who never want to get tired
                                10
_____ life.
        11

C. Exercise: Choosing from the following verbs, make sentences with past participles.

bore   confuse   frighten   inspire   tire   worry

Example: At first Helen's family was *confused* by her decision to leave; they didn't understand it.

1. Helen's family was _____ about her plan to travel alone.

2. She told them she wasn't _____ with her life as a housewife, but she did want a change.

3. She didn't get _____ of her life on the road; she loved every minute of it.

4. Helen was _____ by the beautiful, high mountains of Alaska; she plans to return.

5. She was _____ by a bear once, though.

Adjectives Followed by Prepositions

Many adjectives are customarily followed by certain prepositions. The following is a short list of some common combinations in English.

Adjectives + Prepositions	Examples
absent from	Joanne is **absent from** her first class several times a week.
accustomed (used) to	She is not **accustomed to** getting up early.
afraid of	She's **afraid of** her teacher.
angry about something; angry at (with) someone	Joanne was **angry about** waking up late. The teacher was **angry at** Joanne.
different from	This new clock is **different from** my old one.
nervous about	I am **nervous about** the exam.
responsible for	I felt **responsible for** the problem.
sad about	We all felt **sad about** her decision to leave.
sorry about a thing; sorry for a person or thing	She felt **sorry about** her rude remark. I felt **sorry for** the lost dog.
sure about (of)	Are you **sure about** your decision?

D. Exercise: Imagine that you are eighty years old. Complete the following sentences using participles and adjective + preposition combinations. Remember, if you use a verb after these expressions, it must be in the *-ing* form.

Example: At eighty years old, I'm accustomed . . . **to a slow pace.**
to lots of sleep.
to forgetting some things.

At eighty years old . . .

1. I'm not used . . .
2. At times I am afraid . . .
3. And I get worried . . .
4. But I'm still excited . . .
5. I rarely get angry . . .
6. Sometimes I feel sad . . .
7. I get tired . . .
8. Some days I'm not sure . . .
9. I get nervous . . .
10. I am not sorry . . .

E. Activity: Expressing Feelings and Opinions. How do you feel about living in a new culture? Are you still excited about it, or do you get sad or homesick? First, write ten questions to ask a classmate about his or her feelings. Use preposition combinations from the lists in this section. After your teacher has checked your questions, separate into pairs or small groups. Take turns asking and answering your questions.

F. Exercise: Review of Phrasal Combinations. Complete the passage with one of these prepositions.

about	on	to
for	out	up
of	over	with

At 84, Nathan Saperstein is accustomed __*to*__ living with lots of people. He's the oldest resident in "The Shared Living House" in Boston. Saperstein lives _____ fifteen others, aged 23 to 84. Everyone has a private bedroom, but the
1
five bathrooms and the kitchen belong _____ everyone.
2

Everyone helps take care _____ the house. Each person is responsible
3
_____ certain jobs. Saperstein's job is "security guard." He explains, "At 11:00,
4
I turn the lights _____ and make sure that everything is okay." Others take
5
_____ the garbage, clean _____ the kitchen and bathrooms, or figure
6   7
_____ the bills. Although the jobs are divided, the housemates help each
8
other _____ whenever possible. The success of the house depends
9
_____ cooperation.
10

Saperstein is very satisfied _____ his situation. He gets along well
11
_____ all of his housemates. In other places, he says, a person might never find
12
_____ his neighbor's name. "Here I am part of a family. I know people care
13
_____ me." Saperstein is pleased _____ the atmosphere of the house.
14   15
The housemates always make time to talk _____ each other.
16

Of course, living with a large group means that everyone sometimes has to put
_____ _____ some inconveniences. When there is a problem, the house-
17   18
mates have a meeting to talk it _____. In this way, they are usually able to
19
work the problem _____.
20

A few people are unable to get used _____ living with such a large group,
21
and they move _____ of the house. But most of the housemates are thrilled
22
_____ the opportunity to have such a home. As Saperstein's 65-year-old house-
23
mate Christine Spurgeon says, "This isn't housing; it's *living.*"

G. **Exercise: Oral Review.** In pairs, take turns quizzing each other on phrasal combinations. Using the clues that follow, form true sentences based on your knowledge and experiences. If the combination is separable, also give the separated form.

Example: S1: **Bring . . . a family.**
S2: **It's expensive to bring up a family.** *or*
It's expensive to bring a family up.

1. call . . . a friend
2. be excited . . . a trip
3. get accustomed . . . speaking English
4. check . . . a hotel
5. clean . . . the house
6. feel nervous . . . a test
7. get together . . . friends
8. go . . . a bad experience
9. hand . . . a composition late
10. stay . . . late studying
11. put . . . your coat
12. pick . . . a friend at his or her apartment
13. do . . . a grammar exercise
14. be interested . . . sports
15. talk . . . a problem with your parents
16. dust . . . the bookshelves
17. add . . . your monthly expenses
18. think . . . a decision
19. take . . . your shoes
20. run . . . an old friend
21. have . . . a new shirt
22. look . . . a friend's cat while he or she is on vacation
23. borrow five dollars . . . a friend
24. grow . . . in California
25. try . . . a new grammar book

H. **Activity: Describing People.** What is it like to grow old in your culture? How are the elderly treated? Where do older people live? What is their role in family life? Do many older people keep on working?

Individually or in small groups, prepare a brief presentation on the elderly in your society. As you prepare your presentation, try to include as many phrasal verbs or other preposition constructions as possible.

6

TRAVEL AND TRANSPORTATION

Compound and Complex Sentences

COORDINATING CONJUNCTIONS AND COMPOUND SENTENCES

Have you done a great deal of traveling? Share your experiences while answering the following questions about the picture.

1. Where are these two women and what are they talking about?
2. What do you think they might do?

Creative Traveling

LAUREL: You know, I like to travel more than anything in the world!

NADIA: So do I, but money is always my problem. It's expensive to travel.

LAUREL: That's true, but you can usually find inexpensive ways to travel. Two girl-

166

friends of mine don't have much money, yet they travel everywhere. A few years ago, they took a seven-hundred-mile bicycle trip! They camped and cooked out, so the entire three-week trip cost them less than fifty dollars.

NADIA: That's great, but I'd like a little more comfort!

LAUREL: Well, the same friends once took a wonderful trip to Colorado. They wanted to ski, and they had a place to stay near the ski resort. As usual, though, they didn't have very much money, nor did they have a car. They couldn't fly to Colorado, and they couldn't drive either. Well, they really wanted to go, so they found someone to give them a ride for twenty-five dollars.

NADIA: Oh, I'd love to do that, too. Obviously, there are ways to travel cheaply, but you have to be creative to find them!

Discussing the Passage

1. What inexpensive ways to travel are mentioned in the conversation?
2. Have you ever tried any of them?
3. What are some other inexpensive ways to travel?

Compound Sentences

A compound sentence is two simple sentences joined together by a comma and a coordinating conjunction. The coordinating conjunctions are *and, but, or, nor, for, yet,* and *so.* A semicolon (;) may sometimes be used *instead of* one of these conjunctions.

	Examples	**Notes**
Simple Sentence	Alfonso has to travel often. He enjoys traveling.	A simple sentence has one subject/verb combination.
Compound Sentence	Alfonso travels often, **and** he enjoys it.	A compound sentence has at least two subject/verb combinations. A comma normally appears before the conjunction.
	He stays in hotels, **or** he visits friends.	*Or* shows a choice between two possibilities.
	He would rather drive, **but (yet)** he usually has to fly.	Both *but* and *yet* show contrast. *But* is more common in spoken English.
	He doesn't have much time, **so** he usually flies.	As a conjunction, *so* means "as a result" or "therefore."
	He usually flies, **for** he doesn't have much time.	As a conjunction, *for* means "because." *For* is formal; it is more common in writing than in speaking.
	He doesn't have much time, **nor** does he have much money.	*Nor* joins two negative statements. The word order of the clause with *nor* changes: The appropriate auxiliary verb must come *before* the subject.
	Alfonso travels as often as possible; he enjoys it	A semicolon can join two sentences *if* the relationship between them is clear.

A. **Exercise:** Underline all the compound sentences in the conversation at the beginning of this chapter. Circle the commas and the conjunctions.

B. Exercise: Combine the following sentences with *and, but, or, so, yet,* or *nor.* If a noun is repeated, change it to a pronoun in the second clause. Use each conjunction at least once. Pay attention to punctuation as you write your new sentences.

Example: Some people like to spend their vacations at home.
Others would rather take trips to faraway places. →
Some people like to spend their vacations at home, but others would rather take trips to faraway places.

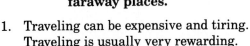

1. Traveling can be expensive and tiring.
   Traveling is usually very rewarding.
2. Hotels can be very expensive.
   Many travelers try to stay with family or friends.
3. To save money, you can try camping.
   You can stay in youth hostels.
4. Joe Van Gemert wanted to travel.
   Joe Van Gemert had very little money.
5. Joe had very little money.
   Joe had a lot of time.
6. Joe bought a bicycle.
   Joe has made trips on his bicycle all over the United States.
7. A bicycle doesn't need gasoline.
   A bicycle doesn't need much maintenance.

C. Exercise: Complete the following sentences. If possible, form *true* statements about your own traveling preferences and experiences.

1. I enjoy traveling by plane, but . . .
2. I have never visited Australia, nor . . .
3. For my next vacation, I will stay home and relax, or . . .
4. Luxury cruises are terribly expensive, yet . . .
5. I have heard that the Northwest Territories of Canada are very beautiful, so . . .
6. During the summer, many campgrounds are crowded and noisy, yet . . .
7. In the winter, the weather is usually terrible here, so . . .
8. Someday, I'll have enough money, and then . . .

D. Exercise: Write six original compound sentences about places you have visited or would like to visit. Use a different conjunction in each sentence: *and, or, but, so, yet, nor.*

Coordinating Conjunctions with Words and Phrases

Coordinating conjunctions can also join words or phrases within one sentence. *And, but, yet,* and *or* are often used to join two or more verbs, nouns, adjectives, and so on. No commas are used with two words or phrases.

Verbs:	Alfonso **missed** his plane **and had** to wait for another one.
Nouns:	He sometimes takes **a train or a bus.**
	Alfonso and his friend once traveled across South America by bus.
Adjectives:	Long trips are **interesting but** very **tiring.**
Adverbs:	On buses, you can travel **inexpensively yet comfortably.**
Phrases:	Do you plan to go **by bus or by car?**
	Do you plan **to look for a hotel or (to) stay with friends?**

E. Exercise: Eliminate the unnecessary words from the following sentences. Eliminate commas when necessary.

Example: Many people would like to travel often, but they can't afford hotels. →
            Many people would like to travel often but can't afford hotels.

1. John Fruth loved the outdoors, and he dreamed of living in the mountains.

2. He wanted to live in the mountains, but he needed to work at the same time.

3. So, he looked for jobs in resorts, and he looked for jobs in children's camps.

4. Most jobs in resorts and most jobs in camps include meals, or they include a place to live.

5. In this way, John could live cheaply, yet he could live comfortably.

But with Connected Statements

Two sentences with the same verb (one affirmative and one negative) may be joined with *but* without repeating the verb. Instead, a subject and auxiliary verb can follow *but*.

SIMPLE SENTENCES	CONNECTED STATEMENTS
Some people enjoy traveling. Other people don't enjoy traveling.	Some people enjoy traveling, **but** others **don't.**
My brother went to Alaska last year. I didn't go to Alaska last year.	My brother went to Alaska last year, **but** I **didn't.**
I haven't traveled a lot. My brother has traveled a lot.	I haven't traveled a lot, **but** my brother **has.**
Next year, I'll take a long trip. Next year, my brother won't take a long trip.	Next year, I'll take a long trip, **but** he **won't.**

F. **Exercise:** Complete the following sentences with the appropriate auxiliary verb.

1. My brother loves to travel alone, but I . . .
2. He has visited all fifty states in the United States, but I . . .
3. On the other hand, I have visited Canada, but he . . .
4. He doesn't like to camp out, but I . . .
5. I can't afford to take an expensive vacation this year, but he . . .
6. I will probably spend my vacation at home, but he . . .

G. **Exercise: Review of *Too/Either*.** Complete the following sentences with the appropriate auxiliary verb and *too* or *either*.

Example: My sister hates flying, and I ____*do*____ ____*too*____ .

She can never sleep on planes, and I ____*can't*____ ____*either*____ .

1. My sister always gets seasick, and I _____ _____ .

2. I have visited Africa, and my sister _____ _____ .

3. I haven't been on a safari, and she _____ _____ .

4. I'm planning to take a cruise next year, and she _____ .

5. I will write postcards to all of my friends, and she _____

_____ .

6. I can't wait to go, and she _____ _____ .

H. Exercise: Review of *So/Neither*. Use the words in parentheses to add informa-tion to the following sentences. Use *so* or *neither* in your new sentences. Pay atten-tion to the order of the subject and verb in each.

Examples: Airplanes are expensive. (trains) →
    Airplanes are expensive, and so are trains.

    Bicycling doesn't cost much. (hitchhiking) →
    Bicycling doesn't cost much, and neither does hitchhiking.

1.   Hitchhiking can be dangerous. (traveling alone at night)
2.   Bicycles are not always convenient. (buses)
3.   Hotels vary a lot in price. (motels)
4.   The United States doesn't have many youth hostels. (Canada)
5.   Plane reservations are not hard to make. (hotel reservations)
6.   Travel books do not always give you enough information. (travel agents)

I. Activity: Taking a Survey. Find out about the travel experiences of your class-mates by taking a survey. In small groups, write at least five questions to ask your classmates. Here are some examples, but be sure to add your own.

1.   Have you ever hitchhiked?
2.   Have you ever taken a bicycle trip?
3.   What is the longest distance you've traveled by train?
4.   What is the longest distance you've traveled alone?

After your group has finished choosing the questions, survey all of your classmates. Then, in your groups, tabulate the results of your survey and choose one member to report on your findings.

Examples: **Keiko has been to Yugoslavia, and so has Mario. Keiko traveled by train, but Mario bicycled through the entire country.**

    Isabelle and Pierre have visited the Amazon briefly, but Rosalina spent four months there!

PART TWO

INTRODUCTION TO COMPLEX SENTENCES; CLAUSES OF CONTRAST, PURPOSE, AND REASON

Have you ever bought a car? Share your experiences while answering the following questions about the picture.

1. Who is this man?
2. What is he advertising?

Why does WESTERN WHEELS sell more new and used cars than anyone else?

We sell more cars because we offer *high quality* and *excellent service* at the *lowest prices in town.* We take care of the paperwork so that you can get reasonable financing on your new or used car. Although other dealers may promise you a lot, we *guarantee* the best deal in town! Stop by our showroom today and take a look at the selection.

WESTERN WHEELS
74 7th Street

Discussing the Passage

1. What kinds of cars does Western Wheels sell?
2. According to the ad, why should you visit Western Wheels?

Introduction to Complex Sentences

Complex sentences are sentences that have a main (independent) clause and at least one dependent clause. A main clause has a subject and verb and can stand alone. It is a complete sentence. A dependent clause also has a subject and verb, but alone, it is *not* complete: it depends on the main clause.

main clause	*dependent clause*

Example: I am saving money because I want to take a trip.

	Examples	Notes
Simple Sentences	I ride a bicycle. Bicycles are inexpensive.	These are simple sentences; they have one subject/verb combination. They can also be main clauses of complex sentences.
Complex Sentences	I ride a bicycle **because** it is inexpensive. **Because** bicycles are inexpensive, most people can afford them.	Complex sentences have at least two subject/verb combinations. In many cases, a dependent clause can either begin or end a sentence. If a dependent clause begins a sentence, a comma normally follows it. No comma precedes the clause if it ends the sentence.
Incomplete Sentences (Dependent Clauses)	Because it is expensive. Because bicycles are inexpensive.	These dependent clauses are called *sentence fragments*. They are grammatically incomplete. To be complete, a sentence must have a main clause.

Types of Dependent Clauses

In a complex sentence, the dependent clause is connected to the main clause by a subordinating conjunction, such as *when, because, although, if*. English has numerous subordinating conjunctions; each shows a different relationship between the two clauses. In this chapter, you will study some clauses of condition, contrast, purpose, reason, and time. In Chapter 7, you will study more clauses of time.

Types of Dependent Clauses	Common Subordinating Conjunctions	Examples
Condition	if unless	**If** you want to save money on transportation, ride a bicycle.
Contrast (Concession)	although even though	Some people ride bikes in winter **even though** that can be dangerous.
Purpose	so that	Many people ride bicycles **so that** they can save money on transportation.
Reason	because	Many people ride bicycles **because** they want to get exercise.
Time	after, before, until since when, whenever while	Perhaps I'll buy a new bicycle **after** I start working. **When** I have enough money, I will buy a new bicycle.

A. Exercise: Circle all the subordinating conjunctions in the advertisement at the beginning of this section. What does each one express (condition, contrast, purpose, reason, result, time)?

B. Exercise: Tell whether the following are complete (C) or incomplete (I) sentences.

Example: __I__ If I have time.

1. _____ If I have time, I'll go to the travel agent.

2. _____ When I go to the travel agent.

3. _____ I'll get information for our trip while I'm at the travel agency.

4. _____ We should make reservations soon because many people will be traveling during the holiday.

5. _____ Even though we haven't decided the exact dates.

6. _____ It's better to make a reservation now so that we don't have problems later.

C. **Exercise:** The following are complex sentences. Circle the subordinating conjunctions and underline the dependent clauses. Finally, explain the relationship between the two clauses (condition, contrast, purpose, etc.).

Example: (When) I travel, I like to visit small towns. **(time)**

1. We have visited many small towns since we took our first trip in 1968.

2. Although small towns don't often have museums, theaters, or shopping centers, they can be very interesting.

3. Whenever I visit a small town, I stop at a local restaurant to have a meal and chat.

4. If I have time, I talk to many different people.

5. We try to plan our trips so that we can travel leisurely.

6. Some travelers are always in a hurry because they plan busy schedules.

7. We planned to have lots of free time while we were traveling in Europe.

8. We enjoyed ourselves very much even though we didn't visit every country.

Clauses of Contrast (Concession) and Reason

Clauses of contrast (with *although* or *even though*) and clauses of reason (with *because*) can begin or end sentences. A comma is normally used after a dependent clause that begins a sentence.

	Conjunctions	Examples
Contrast	although	**Although** I would like a car, I am happy with my bicycle.
	even though	I enjoy my bicycle **even though** a car would be more convenient.
Reason	because	I don't have a car **because** I can't afford one.

Clauses of Purpose

Clauses of purpose are formed with *so that,* meaning "in order to" or "for the purpose of." Clauses with *so that* do not normally begin sentences. A modal auxiliary must follow *so that (can, may, will* in a present or future time frame or *could, might, would* in a past time frame). Note: Do not confuse *so that* with the coordinating conjunction *so,* meaning "therefore."

	Conjunction	Examples
Purpose	so that	I use a bicycle **so that** I can save money. We saved money for months **so that** we would have enough for the trip.

D. **Exercise:** Use *so that* to combine the following pairs of sentences. Remember that you must use a modal auxiliary (*can, could, will,* or *would*) in the dependent clause. Make other necessary changes in the dependent clause.

Example: I applied for a loan at the bank. I wanted to buy a new car. →
   I applied for a loan at the bank so that I could buy a new car.

1.   Some people buy large, expensive cars. They want to ride in luxury.
2.   Other people buy small, economical cars. They don't want to spend a lot of money on gasoline.
3.   I worked at two different jobs. I wanted to have enough money to buy a car.
4.   I saved all my money. I wanted to be able to get a new car.
5.   In the end, I bought a bicycle. I wanted to have some money for a vacation.

E. **Exercise:** Complete the following sentences with *because, although,* or *so that.*

Example: Bicycles are very economical *because* they don't use gasoline.

1.   Many students use bicycles _____ they can save money.

2.   Bicycles are very convenient _____ you are able to take them almost anywhere.

3.   _____ many students use bicycles, it is easy to buy a used bicycle at any university.

4.   _____ cars are expensive, they are more comfortable than bicycles.

5.   I would like to take an automobile maintenance class _____ I can repair my car myself.

F. **Exercise:** Complete the following sentences. If possible, form *true* statements about your own preferences.

1.   I would like to buy a bicycle because . . .
2.   Many people ride bicycles so that . . .
3.   Some people would rather have a car because . . .
4.   Although new cars are expensive, . . .
5.   I'm saving my money so that . . .

G. Activity: Planning Trips. Have you ever made travel arrangements in English? If not, take this opportunity to do so. Choose a place that you have always wanted to visit. Call or visit a travel agent (if you don't know a travel agent, pick one from the phone book) and inquire about the following:

1. ways of traveling to your destination (plane, train, boat, car, etc.)
2. hotels, motels, guest houses, etc.
3. car rentals
4. tours around the area
5. places to visit, to shop, and to eat

Then prepare a report for your classmates about your "dream vacation" and your conversation with the travel agent.

PART THREE

CLAUSES OF TIME AND CONDITION: PRESENT OR UNSPECIFIED TIME

What is the best way to travel? Share your ideas and experiences while answering the following questions about the picture on the next page.

1. Describe the different types of transportation in the picture (exciting, dangerous, etc.). What are some of the advantages and disadvantages of each?
2. Have you traveled in any or all of these ways?

Mobility and Long-distance Travel

In the past, it took months or even years to travel long distances. However, if anything characterizes the twentieth century, it's mobility. Today, most countries have cheap, reliable transportation—trains, buses, planes, boats, and bicycles, in addition to cars. In fact, you can go almost anywhere quickly if you have the money. When you take a jet from New York to London, you arrive in six hours. If you ride on the *Concorde,* you can travel the same distance in three hours and twenty-seven minutes.

Because we are mobile, life has changed tremendously. Although places like Lima, Hong Kong, or Timbuktu may seem very far away, we can reach them just by buying a plane ticket. For better or for worse, the world has become much smaller during the twentieth century.

Discussing the Passage

1. What ways of traveling rapidly are mentioned in the passage? Can you think of any others?
2. How has transportation changed during the twentieth century? How has this affected our lives?

Introduction to Clauses of Time and Condition

There are a variety of connecting words to express time relationships in English. These include *when, whenever, after, before,* and *until.* Some describe things that happen at different times; others describe things that happen at the same time. You will study several uses of these connecting words in this chapter and others in Chapter 7.

Clauses of condition, with *if* and *unless,* can be similar to clauses of time, but they also express cause and effect. You will study some of these clauses in this chapter. You will study other clauses of condition in Chapter 12.

Clauses of Time: Present or Unspecified Time

When and *whenever* can relate two actions or situations that exist at the same time or that immediately follow one another. The simple present tense is normally used in both clauses in these sentences. Modal auxiliaries may also be used.

	Examples	**Notes**
when	**When I plan** a trip, I always **get** as much information as possible. I **ask** a lot of questions **when I visit** the travel agent.	Time clauses may begin or end a sentence. A comma follows a beginning time clause.
whenever	**Whenever I plan** a trip, I **get** very excited.	*Whenever* is similar to *when.* It means "any time" or "every time" and is used for emphasis.

Clauses of Condition: Present or Unspecified Time

If may relate two actions or situations by time and by cause and effect. Sentences with *if* are similar to sentences with *when* or *whenever,* but *if* gives added meaning: The main clause is the effect or result of the *if* clause. The simple present tense is normally used in both clauses in these sentences. It shows that the information is true or that the speaker or writer believes the information to be true in general. Modal auxiliaries are also used in some cases.

	Examples	**Note**
if	**If it's** possible, we **make** our travel plans in advance. You **should plan** in advance **if you want** to get discount prices.	The *if* clause may begin or end a sentence. Use a comma after a beginning clause.

A. Exercise: Use the map below to help you form complete sentences from the following cues. Use the example as a model. (To convert Greenwich Mean Time—GMT—to local time, add or subtract the value at the top of the chart.)

Example: 6:00 A.M.—Chicago / Honolulu →
   When it's 6:00 in Chicago, it's 2:00 in Honolulu.

1. 6:00 A.M.—Chicago / Paris
2. 7:00 A.M.—New York / Teheran
3. 6:00 A.M.—Los Angeles / Tokyo
4. noon—Los Angeles / Rio de Janeiro
5. 7:00 A.M.—Vancouver / Jakarta
6. 6:00 A.M.—Chicago / Buenos Aires

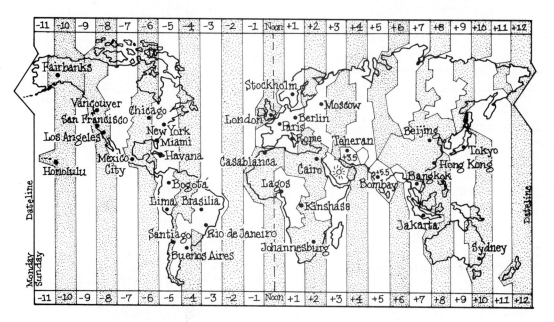

B. Activity: Comparing Time Differences. Use the map in Exercise A to figure the time difference between your hometown and the town you live in now. Then compare time differences between your hometown and those of your classmates.

C. Exercise: Use the map again to help you answer the following questions.

Examples: **If you travel from Paris to Moscow, you lose time.**
   If you travel from Stockholm to New York, you cross six time lines.

1. If you travel between the following cities, do you gain time or lose time?

   a. from Paris to Moscow
   b. from Rome to Mexico City
   c. from Honolulu to Tokyo
   d. from San Francisco to Buenos Aires

2. If you travel between the following cities, how many time lines do you cross?

   a. from Berlin to New York
   b. from Rio de Janeiro to Chicago
   c. from Bangkok to Los Angeles
   d. from Cairo to Miami

D. Exercise: The following information gives you the steps in making a plane reservation. Combine the sentences with *when*. Add pronouns and commas when necessary.

> *Example:* A customer talks to a travel agent. The customer gives the points of departure and destination. →
> **When a customer talks to a travel agent, he or she gives the points of departure and destination.**

1. The travel agent enters the information in the computer.
   The computer checks all flights between the two places.
2. The computer checks availability and prices.
   The computer gives the travel agent possible flights.
3. The agent tells the customer the alternatives.
   The customer chooses a flight.
4. The travel agent enters the reservation in the computer.
   The computer issues a ticket.

E. Exercise: Complete the following sentences in your own words.

> *Example:* Whenever I telephone my parents (friends, girlfriend, or boyfriend), . . . →
> **I forget about the time difference!**

1. Whenever I call my parents
   (friends, etc.), . . .
2. I call them if . . .
3. When we talk, . . .
4. I try to call whenever . . .
5. If I forget to call, . . .
6. When I get the telephone bill, . . .

F. Exercise: Answer the following questions in your own words.

1. What happens when you try to read in a moving car?
2. Do you get seasick if you travel by boat?
3. What is *jet lag?* When do people get jet lag? (Do people get jet lag when they travel north-south? East-west?)
4. Many people recommend special diets or exercises before long-distance travel. How should you prepare yourself (physically) if you plan to take a very long trip by plane?
5. Many people have a terrible fear of flying. How do you feel whenever you get on an airplane? What do you think about when you are on a plane?

G. Exercise: Review of Connecting Words. Complete the following passage about energy and movement by circling the appropriate connecting words. Be prepared to explain your choices.

ENERGY CONSUMED TO TRAVEL ONE KILOMETER
(in calories of energy per gram)

bicyclist	0.15	car	0.75–0.85
horse	0.50–0.70	cow	0.82
jet aircraft	0.60	pigeon	0.92
person, walking	0.75	dog	1.40

(Although / Because) cars seem necessary to many people, bicycles are still one of the best means of transportation. Cars are convenient, (because / but)$_1$ bicycles are more efficient. (Although / When)$_2$ people ride bicycles, they move using the least amount of energy possible.

According to a Duke University study, (when / yet)$_3$ a mouse walks one kilometer, it uses more than 50 calories of energy per gram of body weight. A rabbit uses only 5 calories. (When / Because)$_4$ the average cyclist travels one kilometer on a good bicycle, he or she uses much less energy. In fact, a normal bicyclist is almost three times more energy-efficient than any other traveler.

Bicycles are very efficient (because / so)$_5$ they use the leg muscles perfectly. (If / Although)$_6$ you study the leg muscles, you can see that the bicycle is designed (so that / when)$_7$ you can pedal very easily. This is unfortunate for some people, who ride bicycles (or / so that)$_8$ they can get in shape. (Because / Although)$_9$ bicycling takes very little energy, it does not help most people lose weight. You must bicycle long distances or very fast (so that / if)$_{10}$ you want to burn energy.

H. Activity: Explaining a Process. Do you have any good ideas for a nonpolluting, energy-saving device? Draw up plans for your invention. It may be a new device to make bicycles, motorcycles, or automobiles more efficient, less expensive, more comfortable, or easier to use. Or it may be a multipurpose household gadget such as an automatic refrigerator, food preparer/server, and dishwasher all in one. Don't worry about the device being practical or possible! Just use your imagination. In the process, you may want to draw a sketch of your invention. Then, in pairs or in small groups, give directions on how your great invention works. Explain it step by step using *if* and *when* throughout the explanation.

Example: If you want to lower your energy costs at school and get more work out of the students, you can use my "student generator." Every morning when the students arrive, they sit on bicycles instead of at desks. During the class, each student pedals and produces energy for the electricity and heat. If a student doesn't do the homework, he or she has to pedal an extra hour. . . .

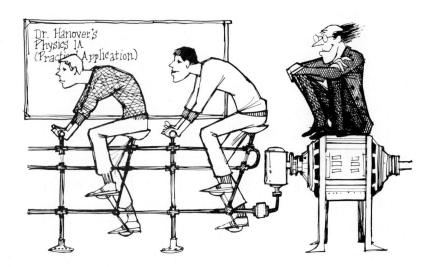

PART FOUR

CLAUSES OF TIME AND CONDITION: FUTURE TIME

Do you know anything about future possibilities for transportation? Share your information and ideas while answering the following questions about the picture.

1. What is the woman at the front of the room probably speaking about?
2. How do you think the cars of tomorrow will be different from today's cars?

Cars of the Future

"Today, we will see a film about cars of the future. In the film, you'll notice that people won't own cars in the twenty-first century; they will rent them when they need them. Now, let's watch the film . . .

"When she walks to the kitchen, Mary Carlson is going to push the 'CAR' button on the computer. Before she has finished her breakfast, a rented Supercar will be waiting for her at the door.

"When she gets into the car, Mary will use her Supercredit card to start the car and to record the mileage. When the Supercredit card starts the car, it is also going to charge her account for the use of the car and of the Superway.

"A short drive will bring her to the electronic highway. Before she reaches the entrance, she will enter her destination into the computer on the dashboard. The car's computer will automatically send this information to the highway control computer. Unless traffic is heavy, she will immediately put the car into automatic to enter the Superway. If traffic on the Superway is too heavy, Mary will turn into the waiting station. She'll wait there until the Superway computer has given her permission to enter. At the waiting station, one of the Superservice robots will serve her coffee and doughnuts. . . ."

Discussing the Passage

1. How does the "Superway" work? Can you describe this process?
2. Do you know of any kinds of electronic transportation that exist today?

Clauses of Time: Future Time

Time clauses can relate statements about future plans or possibilities. These sentences refer to the future, but the verb in the dependent clause is in the present or present perfect tense. The dependent clause may begin or end the sentence. A comma normally follows a beginning time clause.

	Examples	Notes
when	**When** we **finish** our work, we **will have** dinner. We **are going to have** dinner **when** we **finish** our work.	The verb in the dependent clause is normally in the simple present tense. It may *not* be in a future tense.
after	**After** we **complete** this project, we **will** all **need** a vacation!	The verb in the main clause is usually in a future tense, but a modal auxiliary may also be used.
before	The others **may arrive before** we **eat (have eaten).**	Note that in some cases the present perfect tense may be used in the dependent clause. Use of the present perfect stresses that the action in the dependent clause has been completed.
until	We **will not take** a break until we **finish (have finished).**	

Note: After, before, and *until* can be used as prepositions of time, as well as subordinating conjunctions. Compare the following.

Subordinating conjunction: I will finish **before I have dinner.**
                                              After I have dinner, I'll take a break.
           Preposition of time: I will finish **before dinner.**
                                              After dinner, I'll take a break.

A. Exercise: In the passage "Cars of the Future" at the beginning of Part Four, find all the complex sentences with *when, before, until,* and *after.* Underline the dependent clause in each. Note the tense of the verb in each clause of each sentence.

B. Exercise: Complete the following sentences with appropriate present, present perfect, or future forms of the verbs in parentheses.

Example: Before we *reach (have reached)* (reach)

the year 2050, Americans

will have (have) many

new forms of public transportation.

1. Before the next century _____

    (begin), more public transportation

    _____ (be) available.

2. When you _____ (leave) your house in the morning, you

    _____ (not take) your own car to work. In the future, you

    _____ (not have) one.

3. When you _____ (need) a car, you _____

    (rent) one from the Supercar fleet.

4. When you _____ (plan) to use a car, you _____

    (request) one on your computer.

5. The Supercomputer _____ (look) for other people with the

    same destination before it _____ (assign) you a car

    individually.

6. After the Supercomputer _____ (complete) its search, it

    _____ (plan) your route.

7. Then the Supercomputer _____ (deliver) a car to your door

    before you _____ (be) ready to leave.

8. After cities _____ (change) to this system, today's cars

    _____ (start) to disappear.

9. Until we _____ (begin) using this new technology, we

    _____ (continue) to have traffic jams, air pollution, and

high bills for car maintenance and insurance.

C. Exercise: Cars are still here today, though, and Nadia's going to buy her first used car. She's a little nervous about it, so she's making careful plans. These are some of the things she is going to do. Using *before, after,* and *until,* form complete sentences from the following cues. Use each subordinating conjunction at least once.

Examples: take the car to an auto mechanic →
   Before she buys her car, she's going to take the car to an auto mechanic.

   get insurance →
   After she has bought her car, she's going to get insurance.

1.   look at several different cars
2.   read about cars in consumer magazines
3.   compare prices
4.   borrow her parents' car
5.   test drive the car
6.   ask her friends for advice
7.   register the car at the Department of Motor Vehicles
8.   not use public transportation

D. Activity: Describing a Process. What things should you think about when you are making a major purchase, spending a large amount of money, or making any major decision? Choose one of the decisions below and write at least five sentences on things to consider about it. Use *before, after, when,* and *until* in your sentences.

   arranging a vacation   buying a major appliance (refrigerator, stove, etc.)
   choosing a school   buying a home
   finding a roommate   deciding to get married

Clauses of Condition: Future Time

Sentences with *if* or *unless* show a direct cause-effect relationship. The action or situation in the main clause is the effect or result of the action or situation in the *if/unless* clause.

	Examples	**Notes**
if	**If** the weather **is** nice, we **will go** to the beach. We **are going to stay** home **if** the weather **isn't** nice. We **may stay** home **if** the weather **isn't** nice.	The verb in the dependent clause is in a present tense. A future form (*will* or *be going to*) or modal auxiliary is used in the main clause.
unless	**Unless** the weather **is** bad, we **will go** to the beach. We **are going to stay** home **unless** the weather **is** nice. **Unless** it's a beautiful day, we **should stay** home and **work**.	*Unless* means "if . . . not." Sentences with *unless* are normally affirmative. Note that the dependent clause may begin or end the sentence. A comma normally follows a beginning dependent clause.

E. Exercise: In pairs, take turns making additional questions and answers based on the cues. Use *if* in your responses.

Example: Are you taking the car? (stop at a gas station) →
   S1: **Are you taking the car? Would you mind stopping at a gas station?**
   S2: **If I take the car, I'll stop at a gas station.**

1. Are you going near a gas station? (fill up the tank)
2. Are you planning to stop at a gas station? (add some oil)
3. Are you going to add oil? (check the water in the radiator, too)
4. Are you going to have extra time? (put air in the tires)
5. Are you going to have enough money? (buy new windshield wipers)
6. Are you planning to talk to the mechanic? (make an appointment for a tune-up)
7. Are you planning to go to a post office? (mail the payment for the car insurance)
8. Are you going near a police station? (pay this traffic ticket)

F. Exercise: A transportation expert is speaking about traffic and freeways. Complete her talk with the present or future forms of the verbs in parentheses.

"If you *visit* _____ (visit) Los Angeles, you *will find*

(find) hundreds of miles of freeways. You _____

                                                          1
(need) to take a freeway if you _____ (want) to go
                                          2
more than a few blocks in any direction. Unfortunately,

when you _____ (get) on a freeway, you _____ (see)
                   3   4
thousands of other individuals like you—trying to drive somewhere. If

you _____ (look) around, you _____ (notice) that most cars have
           5   6
only one person in them. And, if you _____ (open) the car window, you
                                                 7
_____ (feel / immediately) the effect of all these cars—your eyes
                 8
and nose _____ (burn) from the pollution.
                 9

"Regrettably, Los Angeles _____ (not be) unique. If you
                                              10
_____ (look) around the world, you _____ (see) similar problems
         11   12
in most major cities. If you _____ (travel) to Caracas, to Hong Kong, or to
                                        13
Cairo, you _____ (encounter) just as much traffic and pollution. These
                   14
_____ (be) global problems. If we _____ (want) to solve them, we
         15   16
_____ (have) to work together to find alternatives to private automobiles."
         17

G. Exercise: Change the appropriate clauses in the following sentences from *if* to *unless* or from *unless* to *if*.

Example: If people don't stop driving cars, traffic and pollution will be even greater problems in the future. →

   Unless people stop driving cars, traffic and pollution will be even greater problems in the future.

1. If people don't use mass transit more often, our streets and highways will become even more crowded.
2. If cities don't offer more mass transit, traffic will get even worse.
3. Unless everyone starts using smog control devices, cities like Los Angeles will become unsafe to live in.
4. If we don't develop a new kind of car, air pollution will become even more dangerous.
5. Unless we find an alternative to gasoline engines, we will add even more pollution to the air.
6. Unless we begin to make changes now, air pollution will cause more and more serious health problems.

© CHARLES HARBUTT

H. Exercise: Think about the next trip you will take. It may be a short trip or a long one. Think about how you will travel. Then complete the following sentences in your own words. Finally, try to add at least two original sentences.

Example: If I have enough money, I . . . →
           I'll go to Alaska.

1. I will go to . . . if . . .
2. I will stay there for . . . unless . . .
3. If I can . . . , . . .
4. Unless there is a problem, . . .
5. If I like . . . , . . .
6. If the exchange rates change . . .

I. Exercise: Error Analysis. Some of the following sentences have errors in verb tenses or in punctuation. Indicate which sentences have no errors. Correct any sentences with errors.

1. Unless I ~~don't~~ go to the party tonight, I'll see you tomorrow.

2. If we drive to Chicago next Tuesday, we visit the art museum.

3. Before we will return to Mexico, we will visit our cousins.

4. You should visit Toronto, when you are in Canada.

5. If you go to Canada you should also visit Montreal.

6. After we have visited Canada, we'll plan a trip to Europe.

7. We may go to Europe next year unless it's too expensive.

8. I am saving all of my money so that I would be able to travel next year.

9. I take trips whenever I will have enough money.

10. If we will be able to, we'll also go to China and Japan someday.

J. Exercise: Review of Complex Sentences. Combine the following sentences about air travel with *if, when, whenever, because, although,* or *so that.* Change verb tenses and change nouns to pronouns when necessary. Be sure to use correct punctuation when you form your new sentences.

Example: People think about long-distance travel. People think about planes. →
When (whenever) people think about long-distance travel, they think about planes.

1. Planes are fast and relatively economical.
   Long-distance travelers often choose planes over trains or boats.
2. Planes seem very much a part of our lives.
   Planes have been in existence for less than 100 years.

3. Companies are constantly doing research on planes.
   Companies want to develop faster and more efficient planes.*
4. Many of this century's greatest inventors have worked on planes.
   Tremendous advances have taken place in flight technology.
5. Engineers compare older planes with those of today.
   Engineers tell us that today's planes are safer.
6. Many airlines offer bargain fares to major cities.
   Airports today are full of vacationers and business people.
7. We will look into the future.
   We will find many new varieties of air transportation.
8. Inventors are working on new ideas.
   Inventors want to develop faster and cheaper methods of transportation.*
9. Inventors will probably develop faster and cheaper methods of transportation.
   New methods of air travel may replace airplanes.
10. We will enter the twenty-first century.
    We will have many different kinds of high-speed travel.

K. Activity: Paragraph Writing. Use your sentences from Exercise J as the basis for a short paragraph on air travel. You may want to add, change, or omit information.

L. Activity: Making Decisions. Making decisions is always a complicated process because we never know what may happen in the future. One way to make the choices clearer is to complete a decision tree. A decision tree helps you see the effects of each choice.

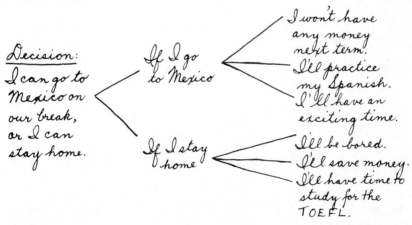

Decision:
I can go to Mexico on our break, or I can stay home.

If I go to Mexico
- I won't have any money next term.
- I'll practice my Spanish.
- I'll have an exciting time.

If I stay home
- I'll be bored.
- I'll save money.
- I'll have time to study for the TOEFL.

In pairs or in small groups, consider a decision that you are facing. It may be a general problem, such as how to study for an upcoming test or how to learn English faster, or it may be a specific problem you have now. Together work out a decision tree for each problem. Later, tell the class what you decided to do. Did the decision tree help you?

---

*Write 3 and 8 two ways, using two different connecting words.

7

NORTH AMERICA: THE LAND AND THE PEOPLE

Transitions; The Past Perfect Continuous Tense; Clauses of Time

COMPOUND SENTENCES AND TRANSITIONS

The term *North America* includes Mexico, Canada, and the United States, but this chapter focuses on Canada and the United States, where most people speak English. Look at the map of those two countries and think about what you know about the people and geography of this area. Share your information and experiences while answering the following questions about the map.

1. What is the capital of the United States? Of Canada?
2. What are the most important geographical features of Canada and the United States?

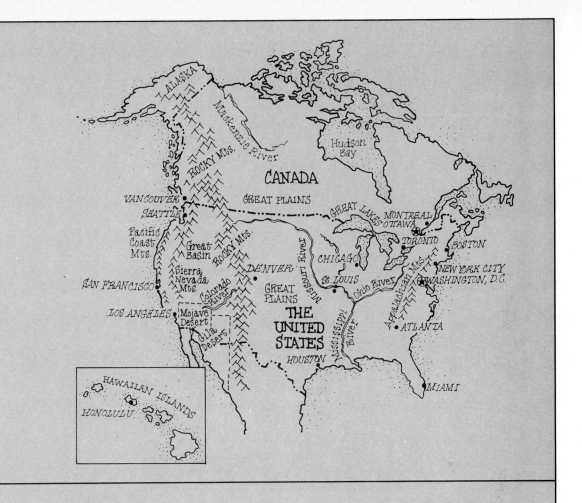

Land of Contrasts

Canada and the United States occupy a huge land area, and there are many differences from region to region. One difference lies in the climate, which varies from the extreme cold of Alaska and the Yukon to the lovely, warm climate of Hawaii. You can see the influence of the climate in the faces of the strong, tough Alaskan, on the one hand, and the relaxed, smiling Hawaiian on the other hand.

In addition to differences in geography and climate, the United States and Canada have many different types of people. For example, along the East Coast you will see the influence of British, Dutch, French, Italian, German, Scandinavian, and Hispanic culture—in the architecture, the food, the language, the customs, and the appearance of the people. The Midwest is a combination of Irish, German, Polish, and Scandinavian people, mainly. In contrast, the people of the Southwest have mixed Indian, Spanish, and northern European blood. In Canada, most immigrants were French or British; for this reason, Canada has two official languages: French and English.

© MARK ANTMAN/IMAGE WORKS

Quebec City, Canada

Each region of the United States has its unique geography, climate, and people; as a result, traveling across North America is almost like going through seven or eight different countries.

Discussing the Passage

1.   What three reasons are given for the regional differences in North America?
2.   How are the people different in the U.S. East, Midwest, and Southwest?

COURTESY SMITHSONIAN INSTITUTION

Sioux village with tipis in what is now Minnesota

A. Exercise: Review of Compound Sentences. Combine the following sentences with *and, but, or, so,* or *yet.* Use each conjunction at least once. Pay attention to punctuation. See page 168 for an explanation of compound sentences.

1. In the early days, clear water filled the Great Lakes.
   Clean air blew across the land.
2. North America was incredibly rich.
   There were huge areas of poor land.
3. In the early years, most of the West was almost empty.
   A few areas had large groups of Indians.
4. This open land was beautiful and inviting.
   Many newcomers decided to go west to find their fortunes.
5. New settlers could live near Indian lands.
   They could build their homes in areas where there were few Indians.
6. For centuries, millions of buffalo had lived on the plains.
   By 1885, hunters had killed almost all of the buffalo.

Transitions

Transitions are words or phrases that connect two related ideas. In written English, they often appear in compound sentences joined by a semicolon. In most cases, a comma follows the transition. Many transitions exist in English; the following list includes some of the most common ones.

	Transitions	Examples
Giving Examples	**for example** **for instance**	Canada is a land of diversity; **for example,** it has two national languages.
Adding Information	**in addition** **furthermore** **moreover** **besides**	Canada has large deposits of many valuable minerals such as gold, silver, and copper; **in addition,** it is very rich in farmland, fish, and lumber.
		Canada has some of the world's largest lakes; **moreover,** one third of the world's fresh water is in Canada.
Making Comparisons	**likewise** **similarly**	Canada produces many minerals; **likewise,** some parts of the United States are rich in mineral resources.
Showing Contrast **(Opposition)**	**in contrast** **on (the) one hand/** **on the other hand**	Quebec is a very old city with buildings from the 1700s; **in contrast,** Toronto is a newer city with highrises and skyscrapers.
Showing Contrast **(Concession)**	**however** **nevertheless** **still**	French is the main language in Quebec; **however,** many people there also speak English.
		The Canadian Arctic receives only ten inches of rain or snow each year; **nevertheless,** it has thousands of lakes and rivers.

	Transitions	**Examples**
Giving Reasons or Results	as a result consequently for this (that) reason therefore	South-central Canada has wide, flat, fertile plains; **as a result,** many farmers moved to this area to grow wheat.
Giving Sequences	now, next, then first, second, etc. earlier, later meanwhile finally	European settlers moved into Canada gradually. **First,** the English and French came to the eastern part of the country. **Later,** more English moved to the western coast. **Finally,** settlers began farming the central plains.

Note: Most transitions come at the beginning of a sentence. Except for transitions of sequence, transitions may also be used with a semicolon (;) in compound sentences. In both cases, a comma normally follows the transition.

However may also be used at other points within a sentence. Commas are almost always used at each point. Compare:

I enjoyed the dinner.   **However,** I did not like the dessert.
I did not, **however,** like the dessert.
I did not like the dessert, **however.**

B. Exercise: Rewrite the following sentences about Canada, using each of the following transitions once: *in addition, nevertheless, for example, however, in contrast, as a result.* Be sure to punctuate your new sentences correctly.

Example: Canada is rich in history and culture. It also has great natural resources. →
Canada is rich in history and culture; *in addition,* it has great natural resources.

1. Canada has ten provinces, and it has two territories—the Northwest Territories and the Yukon Territory.
2. Eastern Canada has many historical sites. Visitors can see walled cities, forts, and bridges from the early 1700s.
3. Central Canada has very fertile plains, so many farmers settled in the provinces of Manitoba, Sasketchewan, and Alberta.
4. Large prairies cover central Canada. Much of western Canada is mountainous.
5. Many people visit the mountains of western Canada, but there are few roads into these wilderness areas.
6. Northern Canada is a cold, treeless region, but many people consider it extremely beautiful.

C. Exercise: Use a transition and correct punctuation to combine these pairs of sentences about North America.

Example: New England has large wooded areas. The Great Lakes region has tremendous areas of forest land. (however / similarly / for example) →
    New England has large wooded areas; similarly, the Great Lakes region has tremendous areas of forest land.

1. The forests of North America have many varieties of the same tree. Over a hundred kinds of oak trees grow in America. (therefore / for example / likewise)
2. Wide, flat, rich plains cover much of the Midwest. Many farmers settled in this part of the United States. (for this reason / on the other hand / in addition)
3. The Rocky Mountains separate the plains from the Pacific Ocean. Strong, determined settlers found ways to reach the West Coast. (as a result / meanwhile / nevertheless)
4. Rivers on the east side of the Rockies flow to the Atlantic, and on the west side they flow to the Pacific. The Rocky Mountains are called the "Continental Divide." (for instance / moreover / for this reason)
5. Death Valley, California, receives less than 2 inches of rain per year. The Pacific Northwest gets up to 150 inches per year. (consequently / finally / on the other hand)

D. Exercise: First, look at the map of North and South America on the next page. Then complete the following paragraphs with appropriate transitions. Indicate where several choices are possible.

1. The Americas reach from the North Pole to the South Pole; ＿＿＿＿＿＿ ,

    they have every sort of climate. The area near the equator is closest to the sun;

    ＿＿＿＿＿＿ , it has very warm temperatures. ＿＿＿＿＿＿ , the areas

    near the poles are terribly cold all year. Between the poles and the equator,

    both continents have a range of temperatures; ＿＿＿＿＿＿ , South America

    has more areas with tropical climate.

2. Both North and South America resemble triangles; ＿＿＿＿＿＿ , the South

    American triangle is farther east. ＿＿＿＿＿＿ , it is farther from the South

    Pole than North America is from the North Pole.

3. Both continents have major north-south mountain ranges in their western

    areas. ＿＿＿＿＿＿ , both continents have smaller mountain ranges on their

    eastern sides. ＿＿＿＿＿＿ , the Andes in South America are much higher

    than the Rockies in North America. Seventeen mountains in the Andes are

    over 20,000 feet; ＿＿＿＿＿＿ , only one peak in North America, Mt.

    McKinley, reaches that height.

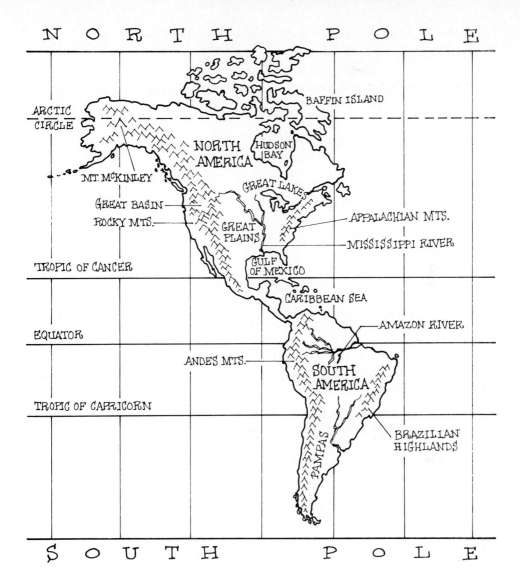

E. Exercise: In small groups, make statements using the following cues.

1. (The weather in) the United States (Canada) is . . .
    In contrast, my area (country) is . . .

2. The United States (Canada) has had immigrants from every part of the world.
    Therefore, it is . . .
    In addition, it is . . .

3. (Many) people in my culture (country) originally came from . . .
    As a result, . . .
    Moreover, . . .

4. When I came to this area, I had many feelings about living in a new culture.
    First, . . .
    Then, . . .
    Later, . . .
    Now, . . .

Now choose one set of sentences to use as the basis for a short composition.

F. Activity: Making Comparisons. Use information you have learned in this section and consult an encyclopedia to help you compare a region of the United States (Canada) to your own area or country. Or compare the region where you are living now to another region in the United States (Canada). In your description, use as many conjunctions and transitions as possible. You can talk about the climate, geography, industries, people, scenery, animals, resources, etc.

Examples: **My country is like Canada because we have a lot of forests. In addition, we have very cold winters.**

My city has a climate like New York's. However, we don't have as much rain.

PART TWO

THE PAST PERFECT CONTINUOUS TENSE; CLAUSES OF TIME: PAST TIME (1)

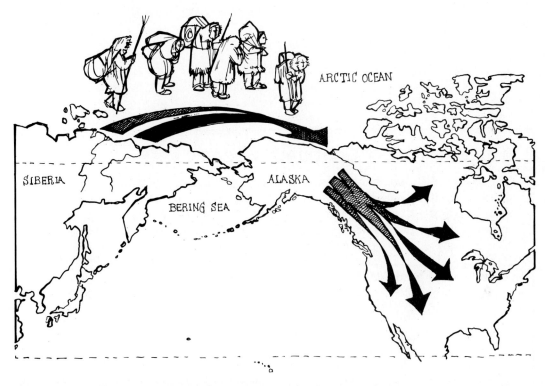

What do you know about the settling of the Americas? Share your information and ideas while answering the following questions about the picture.

1. Where did America's first immigrants come from?
2. When do you think these immigrants came to America?
3. Who are the descendants of these people today?

America's First Immigrants

Although we call American Indians "Native Americans," their ancestors actually came to America from Asia. A land bridge had developed between what is now the U.S.S.R. and Alaska thousands of years ago. Sometime before 13000 B.C., Asians who had been looking for new hunting and fishing places and warmer weather crossed the bridge from Asia to Alaska and continued southward. Many moved on to Central and South America to begin new societies and cultures. Approximately one million Native Americans were living in today's United States when the first Europeans arrived. Because the Europeans had been searching for a passage to India, they mistakenly called the Americans "Indians."

Discussing the Passage

1. Are there any "true" Native Americans?
2. How did American Indians reach North America?
3. Why did these immigrants come to North America?

The Past Perfect Continuous Tense

The past perfect continuous tense expresses a past activity in progress *before* another event or time in the past. Like the past perfect tense, it occurs more often in written English than in spoken English. These time expressions often appear with the past perfect continuous: *before 1492, by last week, by then, by that time, for* + a period of time.

	Examples	**Notes**
Statements	Long before 1492, Indians **had been living** in the Americas. Indians **had not been living** in all areas of North and South America though.	Use *had been* with the present participle of a main verb for all forms.
Yes/No Questions	**Had** Indians **been living** there for a long time?	Use *had* in short answers: "Yes, they had." "No, they hadn't."
Information Questions	**How long had** Indians **been living** there before 1492? **Who had been living** there?	*Had* comes before the subject in most information questions.

A. Exercise: Reread the opening passage at the beginning of this section. Underline the past perfect continuous verbs. Discuss their relationship to the other verbs or time expressions in the sentences.

B. Exercise: Look at the following pictures and their cues. Using the past perfect continuous, make statements about the lifestyles of the Indians long before the arrival of Columbus.

Example:

COURTESY SMITHSONIAN INSTITUTION

Wichita / construct homes of grass →
Long before the arrival of Columbus, the Wichita Indians had been constructing homes of grass.

COURTESY SMITHSONIAN INSTITUTION

1.   Choctaws / play sophisticated ball games

_____

_____

COURTESY GILCREASE INSTITUTE

2.   Ojibwa / gather wild rice

_____

_____

COURTESY SMITHSONIAN INSTITUTION

3. Mandan / live in complex villages around central plazas

_____

_____

COURTESY SMITHSONIAN INSTITUTION

4. Comanche / make clothing from skins and preserve meat by drying it

_____

_____

5.   Caddo / weave baskets and use animals in their work

_____

_____

Clauses of Time: Past Time (1) with the Past Perfect and Past Perfect Continuous Tenses

In complex sentences, *when, before, until, by the time (that)*, and *after* can relate two activities or situations in the past that occurred at different times. Use the past perfect (continuous) tense with the earlier event and the simple past with the later one.

	Examples	Notes
when	**When** Columbus arrived, Indians had been living in the Americas for thousands of years.	In sentences with *when, before, until,* and *by the time (that),* the verb in the dependent clause is in the simple past tense. The verb in the main clause is in the past perfect continuous tense.
before	**Before** many years passed, thousands of these Indians had died.	The dependent clause may begin or end the sentence.
until	Many tribes had been friendly **until** the Europeans began to take their land.	
by the time (that)	**By the time (that)** the American Revolution began, most Indians had moved west. **By then,** most Indians had moved west.	Note that *before, by, until,* and *after* are also prepositions of time and may begin phrases.
after	**After** the Europeans had settled the Atlantic Coast, they began to move west.	With *after,* the verb in the dependent clause is often in the past perfect (continuous) and the verb in the main clause is in the simple past.

C. Exercise: Change the following sentences to include the past perfect continuous by adding *By the time the Europeans arrived . . . already . . . for centuries.*

Example: Some North American Indians used sophisticated farming methods. →
By the time the Europeans arrived, some North American Indians had already been using sophisticated farming methods for centuries.

1. Indians grew tobacco, potatoes, and corn.
2. Hopi Indians raised cotton and used it to make cloth.
3. Indians throughout the Americas made pots, jars, and baskets.
4. Indians in the Southwest and Mexico created beautiful gold and silver objects.
5. Pueblo Indians in the Southwest constructed large, apartment-style buildings.

D. Exercise: Combine the following pairs of sentences. Use the connecting word in parentheses and punctuate your sentences correctly.

Example: The Europeans arrived. Indians in the Southwest had been irrigating their farmland for centuries. (when) →
When the Europeans arrived, the Indians in the Southwest had been irrigating their farmland for centuries.

1. Columbus landed in the New World. Many Indians had never heard a European language. (until)
2. Tribes with different languages had been using a common sign language to communicate. The Europeans arrived. (before)
3. The Europeans had settled on the Atlantic Coast. They began trading with the Indians. (after)
4. The Indians had been using sea shells as money for a long time. The Europeans discovered the New World. (when)
5. They began to intermarry with the Indians. The Europeans had been in America for only a short time. (after)

E. Exercise: Combine the following pairs of sentences, adding *when, before, until, by the time (that),* or *after.* (In some cases, more than one time word may be correct.) Pay attention to punctuation.

Example: The Aztecs had already built many sophisticated cities. The Europeans arrived in Mexico. →
By the time the Europeans arrived in Mexico, the Aztecs had already built many sophisticated cities.

1. The Europeans had settled in the Americas. They learned new farming and building methods from the Indians.
2. The Incas had been constructing excellent roads for a long time. The Europeans arrived in South America.
3. Columbus and his men landed on the Atlantic Coast of America. They had never tasted corn.

4. Europeans destroyed the great buffalo herds. Many Indian tribes had depended on the buffalo for their existence.
5. The Indians met the white settlers. They had never suffered from smallpox or other European diseases.

F. Exercise: Complete the following paragraphs about the discovery of the Americas with simple past, past perfect, or past perfect continuous forms of the verbs in parentheses.

Historians believe that Europeans _____ (live) in the Americas

1

long before the time of Columbus. By the ninth century, Scandinavian adventurers

_____ (make / already) long ocean voyages. Some of them

2

_____ (reach) North America and apparently _____

3　　　　　　　　　　　　　　　　　　　　　　　　　　　　　　　　4

(visit) Canada more than six centuries before Columbus _____

5

(travel) to the New World. Furthermore, it seems that they _____

6

(live) in Canada for a short time before the twelfth century. These adventurers

_____ (construct) grass houses, _____ (build) a steam

7　　　　　　　　　　　　　　　　　　　　　　　　　8

bath, and _____ (make) nails from local iron.

9

As far as we know, no one _____ (cross) the Atlantic Ocean from

10

Southern Europe before 1492, when Christopher Columbus _____

11

(sail) to the coasts of Cuba and Hispaniola. According to his journal, he

_____ (see) "mountains that _____ (seem) to reach the

12　　　　　　　　　　　　　　　　　　　　　13

sky" and palm trees that _____ (be) "wondrous to see for their beau-

14

tiful variety." After Columbus _____ (return) to the Old World, he

15

_____ (tell) incredible stories about what he _____

16　　　　　　　　　　　　　　　　　　　　　　　　　　　　　　　　17

(see) during his voyages.

G. Activity: Describing Changes. Use your imagination to try to picture life in the Americas before the Europeans came. Imagine that you were alive at that time. Tell a little about your life then.

Example:　**Before the Europeans arrived, we had been living peacefully in our villages. We had made our own systems for community life. We had even made a system of money. After the Europeans had begun to settle here, everything changed. . . .**

PART THREE

CLAUSES OF TIME: PAST TIME (2); PRESENT AND PAST TIME

What do you know about the immigrants who came to the Americas? Share your information and ideas while answering the following questions about the picture.

1. What ethnic groups do you recognize in the picture?
2. When did the various groups arrive in North America?

America: "A Nation of Nations"

In the late 1800s, when Walt Whitman said that America was not just a nation, but a "nation of nations," he was living at a time of major immigration to the United States. Immigration had begun long before then, and it has continued steadily ever since. America is a nation of immigrants: today, one in every five Americans is either foreign born or a child of foreign-born parents.

Since the English founded the colony of Jamestown, Virginia, in 1607, more than 50 million people have begun new lives in the United States. When the first immigrants arrived during the 1600s, they settled along the Atlantic coast. Later immigrants moved west to the Allegheny Mountains. In the nineteenth century, immigrants eventually reached the West Coast.

© OWEN FRANKEN/STOCK, BOSTON

America's immigrants are of all races, religions, cultures, customs, and traditions. Although each group has had difficulties, most immigrants have chosen to stay. The United States is one of the few countries in the world where so many different groups live side by side.

Discussing the Passage

1. Where did the earliest immigrants to the United States settle? Later immigrants?
2. In your opinion, do immigrants have an easier time adjusting today in comparison to one hundred years ago? Why or why not?

Clauses of Time: Past Time (2) with the Simple Past and Past Continuous Tenses

When and *while* can relate two activities or situations that happened (or were happening) at the same time in the past. *When* can also relate events that occurred in a sequence.

	Examples	Notes
when	**When** Columbus **discovered** America, he **believed** he was in the Orient.	Clauses with *when* are normally in the simple past tense. *When* means "at the time that" or "after."
while	**While** Columbus **was exploring** the Americas, Portuguese sailors **were exploring** the coast of Africa. Columbus **was exploring** the Americas **while** Portuguese sailors **were exploring** the coast of Africa.	Clauses with *while* are normally in the past continuous tense. If both verbs in a sentence are in the past continuous, it means that the two actions were in progress at the same time. In such sentences, *while* can go at the beginning or in the middle.
when or while	Columbus **was looking** for India **when** he **discovered** the Americas. Columbus **discovered** the Americas **while** he **was looking** for India.	The simple past and the past continuous may appear in the same sentence. In these cases, *while* begins clauses with the past continuous and *when* begins clauses with the simple past. One event began before the other one and was in progress when the second event interrupted it.

A. Exercise: Combine the following sentences with *when*. Make any other necessary changes and use correct punctuation.

Example: Columbus arrived in the Americas.
Columbus believed he was in the Orient. →
When Columbus arrived in the Americas, he believed he was in the Orient.

1. Europeans first arrived in the Americas.
    They knew nothing about the land or its inhabitants.
2. Over fourteen million Indians were in Central and South America.
    European explorers reached the New World.
3. There were only about a million Indians in today's United States.
    Europeans began to colonize North America.
4. People in Europe heard about the new continent.
    They left their homes to begin a new life in the New World.
5. Some colonists bought land from the Indians.
    Some colonists arrived.
6. Other colonists arrived.
    Other colonists took the land from the Indians.

B. Exercise: Use the following chronology of immigration to America to form sentences with *while*. Form as many sentences as possible for each time period. Pay attention to your use of verb tenses and punctuation.

Example: 1619–1630
British Puritans settled in Massachusetts.
Dutch settlers built New Amsterdam (New York)
Portuguese boats brought the first black slaves to Virginia. →
While British Puritans were settling in Massachusetts, Dutch settlers were building New Amsterdam.
Portuguese boats were bringing the first black slaves to Virginia while British Puritans were settling in Massachusetts.
While Dutch settlers. . . .

1. 1630–1640
    The Puritans founded the Massachusetts Bay Colony.
    Swedes built log cabins in Delaware.
    British Catholics constructed settlements in Maryland.
2. 1640–1690
    The first Jews arrived from Portugal.
    German families came to Philadelphia.
    British Quakers founded Pennsylvania.
    French Protestants traveled to South Carolina.
3. 1690–1760
    The French explored the Great Lakes area and the Mississippi Valley.
    The Spanish built settlements in the West.
    English settlers moved to Georgia.

Africans being brought to North America to be slaves

C. Exercise: Combine the following sentences with *when* or *while*. Use correct punctuation. You may want to add, omit, or change some words when you join the sentences.

Example: Columbus reached North America.
At least a million Indians were living there. →
When Columbus reached North America, at least a million Indians were living there. *or*

At least a million Indians were living in North America when Columbus reached it.

1. Europe was changing from an agricultural to an industrial society.
    Europeans began to settle the New World.
2. The population of Europe was increasing.
    Farmland was becoming scarcer and more expensive.
3. Life became too difficult.
    Many Europeans decided to come to the New World.
4. Many people became ill or died.
    Many people were sailing to the Americas.
5. The first settlers arrived on the East Coast.
    Indians were living all along the East Coast.
6. Conflicts and fighting began.
    Settlers took Indian lands.
7. The immigrants were building a new world in the Americas.
    The Indians were fighting to save their way of life.

D.   Activity: Paragraph Writing. Read the sentences you wrote in Exercise C. They tell a story. Rewrite your sentences in the form of a paragraph.

Clauses of Time: Present and Past Time with the Present Perfect and Simple Past Tenses

Since can join present and past time clauses. The main clause must be in the present perfect or present perfect continuous tense. The clause with *since* is normally in the simple past tense. *Since* (and *for*) may also begin prepositional phrases.

	Examples	**Notes**
clause	I **have lived** here **since I moved** in 1983.	*Since* appears with a specific beginning time in both clauses and phrases.
phrase	I **have lived** here **since** 1983.	
	I **have lived** here **for** several years.	*For* appears in phrases indicating a period of time.

E.   Exercise: Combine the following cues with *since* or *for*. Use the correct tense (present perfect or past) of the verbs.

Example: Germany / send / 7 million immigrants to America
the first German families arrive / in 1683. →
Germany has sent 7 million immigrants to America since the first German families arrived in 1683.

1.   over 13 million British / come / to the United States
the Napoleonic Wars / end / in 1815
2.   1978
thousands of immigrants / arrive / in the United States from Iran
3.   the last several years
most immigrants / come / from Southeast Asia or Mexico and Central America
4.   the first immigrants / arrive / from Europe
millions of people from every continent / immigrate / to the United States
5.   these immigrants / make / many contributions to American culture
they / begin / arriving

F. **Activity: Giving Information.** Have immigrants come to your area or country? Where have they come from? How many have come? Why and when did they come? As a class or in small groups, share your information with your classmates.

G. **Exercise:** Use the simple past, past continuous, or present perfect forms of the verbs in parentheses to complete the following sentences about the exploration and settlement of the Americas.

Example: Columbus ___*discovered*___ (discover) the Americas while he ___*was looking*___ (look) for India.

1. When Columbus _____ (see) the native people of America for the first time, he _____ (call) them *Indians*.

2. While the first immigrants _____ (settle) on the East Coast of the United States, Champlain _____ (explore) French Canada.

3. When settlers first _____ (arrive) in the New World, many of them _____ (die) of illness or hunger.

4. Since the first English colonists _____ (land) in 1607, the population of the United States _____ (grow) to over 230 million people.

5. People from every country in the world _____ (come) to the United States since the first settlers _____ (begin) their new lives here.

6. Since the beginning, different groups of immigrants _____ (have) different goals.

7. As a result, they _____ (settle) in different areas of the United States.

8. For over two hundred years, the cultures and traditions of the settlers _____ (influence) the development of each region in America.

H. **Activity: Describing Historical Events.** All countries experience changes. Think of a change that particularly affected your culture. Then, individually or in small groups, prepare a brief (three-to-five minute) report on this important historical event. If you prepare your report as a group, each member should contribute information and opinions.

PART FOUR

REVIEW

What do you know about colonial life in the Americas? Share your information and ideas while answering the following questions about the picture.

1. When and where do you think this scene took place?
2. What tools or equipment do you see in the picture?
3. What were some of the time-consuming daily tasks?

The Making of a Country

The United States began its life as a nation modestly. Its early immigrants lived in a wild land. Life was hard, and living conditions were poor. Most of the early settlers started farms even though the land along the East Coast was not good for farming. There were resources such as coal, iron, gold, and copper deep in the soil, but they remain undiscovered for much of the country's early history.

In the beginning, the United States was the poorest of Britain's colonies. The only thing that made money for Britain was tobacco. As a result, Britain paid little attention to the colonies, and the American settlers developed their new homes without much interference.

COURTESY BETTMANN ARCHIVE

Slowly, the early settlers worked the land and made it fruitful. In fact, after a relatively short period of time, both rich and poor were living better than they had in Europe. When people worked hard, they could improve their standard of living. Eventually, many men and women shared in the "American Dream": They achieved economic security and lived as they chose to.

Discussing the Passage

1. Why did the British leave the early colonists alone?
2. Why were the early settlers able to improve their standard of living?
3. What is "the American dream"?

A. Exercise: Review of Tenses. Complete the following passage about the American Revolution with the simple past, past continuous, present perfect, or past perfect forms of the verbs in parentheses. Indicate any sentences where more than one form is appropriate.

Approximately 2.2 million people *had already settled* (settle / already) in the thirteen British colonies when the first movements toward revolution _____ (begin) in 1770. These colonists _____ (build / already) homes and communities, and they _____ (establish) a new way of life.

The first protests _____ (start) in Boston, Massachusetts. In the beginning, these _____ (be) only demonstrations. Then, on March 5, 1770, the first fight _____ (take) place when British soldiers _____ (shoot) at an angry crowd and _____ (kill) five people. This _____ (become) known as the Boston Massacre.

While the British _____ (try) to keep Bostonians calm, settlers in other areas _____ (start) protest movements. Soon people _____ (protest) throughout the colonies. While farmers _____ (fight) the first battles, the politicians _____ (plan) a new government. By 1775, colonists _____ (organize) a Congress, _____ (create) a small army, and _____ (print) money. Finally, on July 4, 1776, the Americans officially _____ (declare) their independence. Since then, Americans _____ (celebrate) July 4 as Independence Day.

B. **Exercise:** **Review of *Because* and *Although*.** Combine the following sentences with *because* and *although*. Add or omit words to improve your new sentences and be sure to use commas when necessary.

Example: People came in family groups to New England.
                  They planned to stay. →
                  People came in family groups to New England because they planned to stay.

1. New England settlers built schools and churches.
    New England settlers wanted to start communities.
2. New England was very different from England.
    Many English immigrated to New England.
3. Northern Europeans moved to the mid-Atlantic states.
    The land and the climate were similar to those in their homelands.
4. Parts of Pennsylvania were very much like Germany.
    German colonists felt at home in Pennsylvania.
5. There was no real gold in Virginia.
    Tobacco, "green gold," grew well in Virginia.
6. Large landowners in the South wanted a lot of cheap labor.
    The people in the South brought men from European prisons and slaves from Africa to work.

C. **Exercise:** Rewrite your sentences from Exercise B to use transitions of reason or result—*therefore, as a result, as a consequence, for this (that) reason*—or of concession—*however, nevertheless.* Remember to punctuate your new sentences correctly.

D. Exercise: The following information is listed in chronological order. Combine the sentences with connecting words: *after, before, until, when, by the time (that), although, because, however, nevertheless, on the other hand.* In many cases, more than one connecting word is possible. Add or omit words to form better sentences and change verb tenses if necessary. Remember to use appropriate punctuation.

> *Example:* Thousands of years ago, Asians traveled to the Americas. For centuries, people believed that Europeans had been the first to reach the New World.
>
> **Thousands of years ago, Asians traveled to the Americas; nevertheless, for centuries people believed that Europeans had been the first to reach the New World.** *or*
>
> **Although Asians had traveled to the Americas thousands of years ago, for centuries people believed that Europeans had been the first to reach the New World.**

1. Adventurers from Northern Europe reached North America before 1100. Many people still think Columbus was the first European to reach the Americas.
2. The early settlers lived in the New World for a short time. The early settlers became very different from their relatives in the Old World.
3. Settlers had been living in the wilderness for some years. Settlers learned independence and self-reliance.
4. Many French people lived by fishing and hunting. Most English people started farms.
5. The American colonists valued their freedom. The American colonists rebelled against British taxes.
6. The American Revolution began in 1776. It seemed that the colonists would not win.
7. The Revolution ended. The new country did not begin to grow immediately.
8. Few settlers moved west of the Allegheny Mountains. Then railroads and canals were built.
9. Railroads and canals were built. Railroads and canals carried hundreds of thousands of immigrants to the West.
10. The area between the Alleghenies and the Rockies had tremendous natural resources. Settlers soon began to develop industries there.

E. Activity: Researching Historical Events or People. Choose an event in American or Canadian history or a famous American or Canadian that you would like to know more about. Do some research on this event or person. You may want to ask a fellow classmate, a friend, a co-worker, or a teacher for help or additional information. At another class meeting, give a brief report telling what you learned and how you found the information.

8

TASTES AND PREFERENCES

Adjectives and Adverbs; Clauses and Phrases of Comparison

PART ONE

REVIEW OF PARTICIPLES; CLAUSES WITH (*NOT*) *AS ... AS* AND *SO ... THAT*

What do you like to do in your free time? Share your opinions while answering the following questions about the pictures.

1. What are the various people doing?
2. Which of these leisure-time activities do you prefer?

Leisure Time and How People Spend It

In the past, people rarely had as much leisure time as we have now. Traditionally, work took so much time that very little was left for any sort of recreation. Fortunately for us, however, life has changed. With more free time today, most of us are able to pursue other interests. We have a great many choices: music, dance, drama, movies, sports, travels, painting, and so on.

What do most people do? The choices usually depend on personal tastes and preferences.

"I'm a factory worker. My work is really boring, so I fill my free time with as much excitement as possible. I'm interested in sports . . . and danger! I like to skydive."

"I'm a biologist, and I like my work so much that I take it home with me. On the weekends, I spend time in my garden as often as possible. I'm developing several new varieties of roses. It's fascinating. . . ."

"I'm independently wealthy . . . I don't need to work. I have so many possibilities that it's difficult to make choices. I'm fascinated with a wide variety of things: the environment, politics, the arts . . . you name it."

Discussing the Passage

1. What is *leisure time?*
2. What does *independently wealthy* mean?
3. What are *the arts?*

Participles Used as Adjectives

In Chapter 5, you began to study participles (*boring, bored*), focusing on the variety of prepositions that may follow them. This section focuses on the difference between the present and past participles when they are used as adjectives.

	Examples	Notes
Verb	The movie **bored** us. The language **confused** us. The plot **didn't interest** us.	See Chapter 5, Part Four, for a list of verbs commonly used in this way.
Present Participle	The movie was **boring**. The language was **confusing** (to us.) The plot was not **interesting**.	The present participle expresses how the subject affects someone or something.
Past Participle	We felt **bored**. We were **confused** (by the language). We weren't **interested** in the plot.	The past participle expresses how the subject feels about someone or something.

A. Exercise: What were these people's reactions to the movie they had just seen?

Example: The older woman was _interested_ in the movie.

1. The little girl was _____ by the movie.

2. The little boy was _____ by the monsters.

3. The older gentleman was _____ .

4. The young man was _____ by the plot.

5. The young woman was _____ by the special effects.

B. Exercise: Complete the following sentences by using the present or past participle of the verb in parentheses.

Example: I am _intrigued_ (intrigue) by the history of Japan.

1. Some Japanese stories are very _____ (amuse).

2. Travelers are rarely _____ (bore) when they visit Japan.

3. However, they sometimes show _____ (bore) pictures to their friends when they get home.

4. Traveling is _____ (tire) but _____ (excite).

5. Because I am _____ (fascinate) by Japan, I try to see as many Japanese movies as possible.

6. When I told her that I had seen a movie about her country, Takiko looked _____ (surprise).

7. The movie told an _____ (interest) story about life in Japan.

8. Parts of the movie were _____ (confuse), though.

C. **Activity: Giving Opinions.** What was the last movie you saw? What was your reaction to it? Briefly summarize the story and then talk about your reactions. Was it exciting? Boring? Were the characters and the plot interesting? Was the language confusing to you?

Comparisons with (*Not*) *As . . . As*

As can be used with adjectives, nouns, and adverbs to compare two things. *As . . . as* means that two things are equal in some way. *Just* is often used to emphasize that the two things are *exactly* equal. *Not as . . . as* means that the first item is less or smaller in some way than the second. **Not quite as** is often used to show that two things are almost equal.

	Examples	Notes
As + **Adjective** + *As*	Is the music **as loud as** it was last night? Is the music **as loud as** last night? Is the music **as loud?**	A subject and verb or appropriate auxiliary verb may follow *as . . . as*. The second subject and verb are often omitted. The second *as* is also omitted if nothing follows it.
As + **Adjective** + **Noun** + *As*	There are **just as many people** tonight **as** there were last night. Is there **as much noise** tonight **as** there was last night?	*As many* or *as few* may come before count nouns, and *as much* or *as little* may come before noncount nouns.
As + **Adverb** + *As*	Tonight, the band isn't playing **as loudly as** it played last night. The band is**n't** playing **as loudly as** (it did) last night. Tonight, the band is**n't** playing **quite as loudly.**	Note that in conversation you may hear adjectives instead of adverbs in these expressions (*The band isn't playing as loud . . .*).

D. Exercise: Julio Heartbreaker used to be a very popular singer, but "things have changed." Tell about Julio by completing the sentences. Choose from the following adjectives and use *as . . . as* in your sentences. Create as many sentences as you can.

creative	exciting	handsome	popular	slim
elegant	expensive	hard to get	romantic	young

Example: Julio isn't . . .

Julio isn't as slim as he used to be.

1. His concerts aren't . . .
2. He isn't . . .
3. His music isn't . . .
4. His love songs aren't . . .
5. The tickets aren't . . .

E. Exercise: Everyone is nervous about Julio's concert tonight because there are many last-minute problems. Complete the speakers' sentences with *as . . . as* and an appropriate adverb.

Example: Julio is talking on the phone with his agent. His agent says, "I can't come right now, but I'll come *as soon as I can* ."

1. Julio is very nervous, and he wants his agent to stay with him until the performance. His agent says, "I can't stay all afternoon, but I'll stay _____ ."

2. The stage is not ready for the concert. Julio wants the stage people to work faster. They tell him, "We can't work any faster. We're working _____ ."

3. The microphones aren't working. Julio can't hear the other singers. He tells them to sing louder. They say, "We can't sing any louder. We're singing _____ ."

4. It's almost concert time. Julio doesn't feel ready. He wants more help from his agent. His agent answers, "I can't help you anymore. I've helped you _____ ."

5. The concert has finally started, and the box office has closed. The ticket seller says to Julio's agent, "We can't sell any more tickets. We've sold _____ ."

F. Exercise: What do you know about different types of music—their similarities and differences? Pick two items from the column on the left. Then pick an adjective from the columns on the right. Give your ideas, using *(not) as* + adjective + *as*. Form at least eight sentences, giving both affirmative and negative statements.

Examples: **Classical music is not as loud as rock music.**

  For me, jazz is just as relaxing as classical music.

Types of Music	Adjectives	
classical	loud	enjoyable
rock	relaxing	quiet
jazz	complicated	sophisticated
folk	popular	violent
fusion (rock and jazz)	easy to listen to	peaceful
punk rock	boring	entertaining

G. Exercise: Do you have as much free time now as you did before you came to this school? Has studying changed your lifestyle? Form complete sentences about the following, using *(not) as* + adverb + *as*.

1. List three things that you don't do now *as often as* you used to.
2. List several foods that you don't eat *as frequently as* you would like to.
3. List several people that you don't get to see *as often (frequently, much) as* you would like to.

Example: **Now that I am a student, I don't go to movies as often as I used to.**

H. Activity: Using Similes. English has many idiomatic expressions using *as . . . as*. Does your language have similar ones? In small groups, discuss the meanings of the following expressions and compare them to expressions in your own language.

as blind as a bat	as quiet as a mouse
as free as a bird	as red as a beet
as hard as a rock	as strong as an ox
as light as a feather	as stubborn as a mule
as old as the hills	as white as a ghost (a sheet)

Adjectives and Adverbs with *So . . . That*

You can use adjectives and adverbs with *so . . . that.* In these sentences, the main clause expresses a cause or reason. The clause with *that* tells the effect or result of the situation in the main clause.

	Examples	Notes
So **+ Adjective** **+ That**	The music was **so loud that** I couldn't hear the conversation.	This sentence means "The music was very loud. Therefore, I couldn't hear the conversation." Note that *so* (not *very*) is used to join the two sentences.
So **+ Adjective** **+ Noncount** **Noun** **+ That**	We paid **so much money** for the tickets **that** we decided to stay.	*So much* or *so little* comes before noncount nouns.
So **+ Adjective** **+ Count Noun** **+ That**	There were **so few people** at the show **that** the theater was almost empty.	*So many* or *so few* comes before count nouns.
So **+ Adverb** **+ That**	The band played **so loudly that** I couldn't hear the conversation.	Note that in conversation you may hear adjectives instead of adverbs in these expressions.

I. **Exercise:** Rewrite the following sentences as two sentences with *very* and *therefore*.

Example: The music was so loud that I couldn't hear anything. →
   The music was very loud. Therefore, I couldn't hear anything.

1. There was so much noise in the restaurant that we decided to leave.
2. The singer gives so few concerts that it is almost impossible to get a ticket to one of his shows.
3. The waitress spoke so quietly that we couldn't hear what she was saying.
4. The menu had so many items on it that I couldn't decide what to order.
5. I was so full from dinner that I didn't order dessert.

J. Exercise: In pairs, take turns making suggestions and responding to them. Using the cues, follow the model.

Example: loud / hear anything there →
    S1: **Would you like to go to Pepper's Disco tonight?**
    S2: **Actually, I'd rather go to The Bistro. The Bistro is never as loud as Pepper's. Pepper's is always so loud that you can't hear anything there.**

1. crowded / get a table there
2. smoky / breathe
3. expensive / afford to buy anything
4. noisy / talk
5. hot / dance

K. Exercise: Make other comparisons of Pepper's and The Bistro, using the cues below. Following the examples as a model, use singular verbs + *much* or *little* with noncount nouns and plural verbs + *many* or *few* with count nouns.

Examples: (−) parking places / park →
   There are so few parking places at Pepper's that we won't be able to park there.

   (−) parking / park →
   There is so little parking at Pepper's that we won't be able to park there.

1.   (+) noise / talk
2.   (+) people / dance
3.   (−) tables / find one

4.   (+) smoke / breathe
5.   (−) space / dance

L. Exercise: Imagine that you went to the opening of a Broadway show last weekend. Tell about the events of the evening and your reactions to them by completing the following sentences. Use *so . . . that* or *(not) as . . . as*. Use *much* or *many* when necessary.

1.   The tickets were . . . expensive . . .
2.   The theater was . . . crowded . . .
3.   The show was . . . exciting . . .
4.   The hero was . . . handsome . . .
5.   The music was . . . good . . .
6.   After the show, there was . . . traffic . . .
7.   There were . . . Rolls Royces in front of the theater . . .
8.   There were . . . wealthy people . . .

M. Activity: Comparing Activities. What do you like to do with your free time? In pairs or in small groups, ask each other some of the following questions. Use these expressions as you discuss your own preferences: *as often (frequently) as I can, as seldom as possible, as much/little (many/few) as possible.*

1.   Do you like to dance? What types of dancing do you enjoy? How often do you go dancing? Which club has the best bands?
2.   Do you enjoy going to movies? How often do you go?
3.   Do you like to visit museums? Do you prefer science museums, natural history museums, or art museums? How often do you go?

PART TWO

COMPARATIVE ADJECTIVES

What types of food do you like best? Share your opinions while answering the following questions about the picture.

1. Describe the picture, telling the different types of food available along this street.
2. Which do you think are inexpensive? Why do you think so?

© PETER SOUTHWICK/STOCK, BOSTON

Eating in New York

New York is a city of extremes. The goods are better. The bads are worse. There's more of everything in New York, and above all there's more food. The restaurants are more numerous, and there are more unusual foods available in New York than anywhere else. Would you like to try Norwegian salmon, Maine lobster, or Peruvian anchovies? You'll find them in New York.

There is a wider range of choices in New York. The restaurants are more varied and more plentiful. You can choose among nightclubs, the automat, bistros, street vendors, and ethnic restaurants. The ingredients may be fresher and more authentic in New York, but the prices are probably higher. And the waiters are perhaps less friendly than almost anywhere else in the world!

Nevertheless, neither the prices nor the service will stop a true food lover. If you love food, New York is the place for you.

Discussing the Passage

1. What is the writer's opinion about food and restaurants in New York?
2. In your opinion, what makes one restaurant better than another?

Comparative Adjectives

To compare two things, add *-er* to all one-syllable adjectives and to some two-syllable adjectives. Use *more* or *less* with other two-syllable and all longer adjectives. See pages 50–51 for spelling guidelines for *-er* endings. A list of irregular forms is at the end of this chapter.

	Examples	**Notes**
One-syllable Adjectives	This restaurant is cheap, but the one across the street is **cheaper.**	Add *-er* to one-syllable adjectives to form the comparative.
Two-syllable Adjectives	This café is dirty, but the other is **dirtier.**	Add *-er* to most adjectives that end in *-y* to form the comparative.
	The waiters in this café are help-ful, but the waiters in the place next door are much **more helpful.**	Other two-syllable adjectives take *more* or *less* in the comparative.
Multisyllable Adjectives	This restaurant is interesting, but the other one is much **more interesting.**	All longer adjectives take *more* or *less* in the comparative. *Much* may appear as an inten-sifier with either form.

A. **Exercise: Rapid Oral Practice.** After your teacher reads each adjective, give its comparative form.

Examples: T: nice
  S: **nicer**

  T: beautiful
  S: **more beautiful**

1.	lazy	6.	funny	11.	old
2.	colorful	7.	interesting	12.	boring
3.	pretty	8.	noisy	13.	happy
4.	crowded	9.	good	14.	sad
5.	tall	10.	bad	15.	enjoyable

Comparison of Nouns

The comparative form of adjectives may be used with nouns. *(Much) more,* *(many) more, less,* and *fewer* may also be used to compare nouns.

	Examples	Notes
All Nouns	This restaurant has **lower prices,** but that restaurant has **more interesting food.**	The appropriate comparative form of the adjective comes before the noun.
Noncount Nouns (More/Less)	This restaurant has **less atmosphere,** but it gives you **much more food.**	Use *less/more* with noncount nouns. *Much* may appear as an intensifier with noncount nouns.
Count Nouns (More/Fewer)	That restaurant is crowded today. There are **many more customers** today. Yesterday there were **fewer people** in the restaurant.	In standard English, *fewer/more* is used with count nouns. *Many* may appear as an intensifier with count nouns. Note that you may use *more* with either count or noncount nouns.

B. Exercise: Complete the following interview with Mr. Alfred Charles, restaurant critic, with the comparative forms of the adjectives in parentheses.

INTERVIEWER: Mr. Charles, what general comments can you make about American restaurants?

MR. CHARLES: Obviously, American restaurants come in a variety of styles and sizes. Compared to most other kinds of restaurants, American fast food restaurants are *more boring* (boring). The food is always the same: hamburgers, fries, shakes, and colas. On the other hand, American night-clubs that serve dinner are

_____ (good) and
          1
_____ (interesting) because
          2
they can combine great food with great entertainment.

INTERVIEWER: Other countries are known for their fabulous restaurants. Compared to them, what is special about the United States?

MR. CHARLES: Above all, the United States offers a _____ (wide) variety
3
of restaurants. The choices are _____ (great) here. I think
4
you can find every type of food in the world in a city like New York,
for example.

INTERVIEWER: What are your favorite kinds of foods, and where do you find them?

MR. CHARLES: My favorite dishes are Middle Eastern. Compared to American food,
Middle Eastern food is _____ (flavorful), _____
5   6
(spicy), and _____ (colorful). I find these restaurants
7
_____ (appealing) because the people are _____
8   9
(cosmopolitan), the decor is _____ (exotic), and the
10
atmosphere is _____ (intimate).
11

C. **Activity: Making Comparisons.** What are your own personal preferences about restaurants? In pairs, take turns asking and answering the questions from Exercise B. Role-play your interview for the class if you wish.

Comparisons with *Than*

Than may be used to compare two ideas in one sentence. *Than* may be followed by a subject and verb or a noun or pronoun.

	Examples	**Notes**
Than + **Subject and Verb**	Joe's Café is **more expensive than** Sam's Grill is. Joe charges **higher prices than** Sam does.	A subject and verb may follow *than;* however, the verb is often omitted or the auxiliary is used instead.
Than + **Noun**	Joe's food is **better than** Sam's food. Joe's food is **better than** Sam's.	Possessives are often used without the noun(s) they modify.
Than + **Pronoun**	Sam is not very friendly. Joe is **friendlier than** he (is). Joe is **friendlier than** him.	In formal English, a subject pronoun normally follows *than*. In conversational English, object pronouns are often used instead.

D. Exercise: Use the picture to help you complete the following comparisons.

Examples: Sam's Grill is busier . . . →
Sam's Grill is busier than Café Allegro (is).

The customers at Café Allegro look happier . . . →
The customers at Café Allegro look happier than the customers at Sam's (do).

1. Café Allegro has nicer decorations . . .
2. Café Allegro is cleaner . . .
3. Café Allegro looks more expensive . . .
4. Sam's Grill is more crowded . . .
5. Café Allegro has a more romantic atmosphere . . .
6. Café Allegro looks more appealing . . .
7. The service at Café Allegro is better . . .
8. The customers at Sam's are spending less money . . .

E. Exercise: Make more comparisons of Sam's Grill and Café Allegro. Choose adjectives from the list to form sentences with the cues that follow.

messy	appealing	flavorful	spicy
expensive	intimate	exotic	bad
happy	busy	smelly	interesting
greasy	tasty	good	appetizing
formal	noisy	cheap	attractive

Example: the waiter →
The waiter at Sam's Grill is busier than the waiter at Café Allegro.

1. the tables
2. the food
3. the dishes
4. the atmosphere
5. the prices
6. the customers

F. Exercise: In general, how do the eating habits of North Americans compare to those of people from your cultural background? Make sentences with *more, less,* and *fewer* using the following nouns and others of your own.

Example: **Generally, people from Argentina eat *more meat than* Americans do. They also drink *less milk than* Americans do.**

vegetables	snacks	meals
rice	desserts	soda
wine	bread	tea
fruit	coffee	

G. Activity: Comparing Food and Eating Habits. Separate into small groups of students from different areas or cultures, if possible, and discuss styles of cooking. Are your traditional foods similar or different? Make a chart like the following to help you in your discussion. Finally, prepare a short report for the entire class on how the cooking in one country or culture compares to that in another culture.

Country or Culture	Meal and Time (breakfast, lunch, dinner, special occasion)	Typical Menu	Ingredients (fresh, seasonal, frozen, etc.)	Style of Dining (place, utensils, company, etc.)

PART THREE

COMPARATIVE ADVERBS

What is body language? Share your opinions while answering the following questions about the picture.

1. Describe the man on the right. What can you say about the way he is talking?
2. Describe the couple on the sofa. What is their relationship?
3. Now describe others in the picture. What gives you information about these people? What does this tell you about body language in communication?

Culture, Personality, and Communication

Communication involves much more than just speaking a common language. Non-verbal messages are also important. Because we speak with our eyes, gestures, and movements, our body language plays a major role in communication.

Our culture determines at least some of our body language. Thus, communication between people from different countries may be more difficult than necessary if neither is aware of the body language of the other. A South American prefers more eye contact and speaks more rapidly than a North American, for example. He or she also gestures more frequently. In the Middle East, people stand nearer to each other than North Americans are accustomed to, and they often touch each other during a conversation. These differences can make people who are not from the Middle East uneasy, and they may even cause distrust or disapproval.

Cultural differences often make communication complicated. In addition, personal styles and preferences affect our behavior with others. Even within the same culture, people stand, talk, and act very differently. Although our culture determines some things, our own personality determines many others.

Discussing the Passage

1. What are some cultural differences that influence communication?
2. How might these differences affect a conversation?
3. Have you noticed differences in body language among the students in your class?

Comparative Adverbs

Comparative forms of adverbs appear in comparisons of two actions. Add *-er* to one-syllable adverbs and *more* or *less* to almost all multisyllable adverbs to form the comparative. See pages 50–51 for spelling guidelines for *-er* endings. A list of irregular forms is at the end of this chapter.

	Examples	**Notes**
One-syllable Adverbs	She lives **closer** to the museum than I do. I live **nearer** to campus.	One-syllable adverbs (*fast, hard, late, soon*, etc.) and *early* take *-er* in the comparative.
Multisyllable Adverbs	I go to the museum **more frequently** than she does.	All other adverbs take *more* or *less* in the comparative.

A.   Exercise: Reread the opening passage of this section. Underline all the comparative forms. Decide if they are comparative nouns, adjectives, or adverbs.

B. Exercise: Complete the following passage about cultural differences with the comparative forms of the adjectives and adverbs in parentheses.

Do some of your classmates from other countries appear *friendlier*

(more friendly) (friendly) than others? Do some stand or sit

_____ (close) to you than others? Do some look you in the eye
    1

_____ (frequently)? These may reflect cultural differences.
    2

Do some people speak _____ (rapidly) than others?
                                        3

Do some talk _____ (freely) about politics? Is it
                        4

_____ (easy) for others to learn English? Not all of these
    5

differences are cultural. Some are personal, and others may be political.

Take, for example, North Americans and Northern Europeans. Many North

Americans have European ancestry, but they have developed their own social hab-

its. People often think that Americans are _____ (informal)
                                                            6

while Europeans are _____ (conservative), yet people of all
                                7

types live on both sides of the Atlantic. It is true that many Americans talk, dress,

and act _____ (casually) than Europeans. However, some
                8

Americans dress _____ (conservatively) and dine
                            9

_____ (formally). No one can really say where cultural differ-
    10

ences end and personal preferences begin. Perhaps the two can never be separated.

C. Exercise: These charts give some general cultural differences in body language. Use this information with the cues that follow to form sentences with comparative adverbs. Write three sentences for each one.

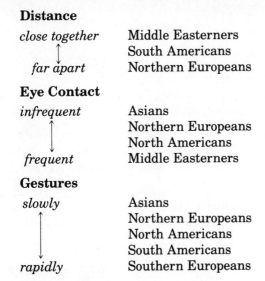

Distance

close together   Middle Easterners
        South Americans
far apart   Northern Europeans

Eye Contact

infrequent   Asians
        Northern Europeans
        North Americans
frequent   Middle Easterners

Gestures

slowly   Asians
        Northern Europeans
        North Americans
        South Americans
rapidly   Southern Europeans

Example: stand →
        Middle Easterners stand closer together than South Americans do.

1. stand
2. look into other people's eyes
3. move their hands (arms, etc.)

D. Exercise: Using the cues that follow, make five general statements about behavior in your culture. Then compare your own personal style or preferences to your generalization about your culture.

Example: **In general, Venezuelans eat rapidly. I eat much more slowly than most people from my country.**

1. eat (slowly / rapidly)
2. talk (slowly / rapidly)
3. stand / sit (close to / far from) other people
4. make gestures (frequently / infrequently)
5. use facial expressions (more / less often)

E. Exercise: Each individual is different from others in the same culture. In fact, even people in the same family differ greatly. Compare yourself to two people in your family: one who is quite similar to you and one who is very different from you. Use the following qualities to help you write at least ten sentences in total, five for each person.

Height: tall, short
Weight: heavy, light, fat, thin
Skin and hair coloring: light, dark, etc.
Personality: friendly, shy, talkative, quiet, serious, funny, easygoing, tense, etc.
Interests: likes sports, keeps active, enjoys studying, reads, is artistic, dates, etc.

Example: **My older brother is very different from me. We don't even look alike. He is much darker and heavier than I am. He takes life more seriously than I do. He reads much more and he studies harder than I do.**

F. Activity: Making Cross-Cultural Comparisons. Using the following list of adverbs, make several comparisons of customs in different cultures. You may want to work in pairs or in small groups.

often	smoothly	formally	quickly
slowly	closely	far	easily
widely	vigorously	frequently	intensely
well	hurriedly	rapidly	

Here are some ideas of things you can compare.

waving good-bye	separation of sexes at family or social
style of walking	gatherings
number of women in public places	places for social communication
arriving late	conducting business or business
dining customs	meetings
dating	informally

PART FOUR

SUPERLATIVE FORMS

What do you do for excitement? Share your experiences while answering the following questions about the picture.

1.   Can you say which trip would be the most dangerous?
2.   Would you take any trips like these? Why or why not?

Excitement!

Everyone has different ideas about the most enjoyable way to spend free time. Some people prefer to stay at home and relax, while others enjoy leisure activities, spending their time at local clubs, museums, theaters, or sports arenas.

These activities may be personally rewarding for "normal" people, but they will not suit the most adventurous. The truly adventurous look for excitement. They take up sports and before long become "the best." They can ski the fastest, climb the highest mountains, run the farthest, dive the deepest.

When these people run out of possibilities close to home, they travel. Of course, their trips are never ordinary! They will go to the most remote areas of the world to find the greatest danger with the least amount of personal comfort! In fact, in recent years these thrill-seekers have made some of the most unusual trips on record. For instance, a young woman crossed the Australian desert alone, accompanied only by a few camels. Three British men kayaked the length of the Nile River, braving crocodiles, hippos, and rushing water. And a group of adventurers from the United States piloted a balloon across the Atlantic Ocean.

Discussing the Passage

1. What are some other examples of "leisure activities"?
2. What are "thrill-seekers"? Do you know people like that?
3. What are some of the most interesting or most difficult trips you have heard of?

Superlatives

Superlative forms of adjectives and adverbs occur in comparisons of three or more things. See pages 50–51 for spelling guidelines for -*est* endings. A list of irregular forms is at the end of this chapter.

	Examples	**Notes**
One-syllable Adjectives and Adverbs	He is **the fastest** runner of all of us. He runs **the fastest** of all of us. She is **the hardest** worker that I have ever met. She works **the hardest** of anyone here.	One-syllable adjectives and adverbs take -*est* in the superlative. *The* normally comes before a superlative. These expressions often follow superlatives: *of all* (*of us, them,* etc.), *that I know, that I have met* (*tried, visited,* etc.)
Two-syllable Adjectives Ending in -*y*	She is **the friendliest** person that I know. Her brother is **the least friendly,** though.	It is also possible to say *the most friendly,* but this form is less common. The opposite is *the least friendly.*
Other Adjectives and Adverbs	He is **the most reckless** skier that I know. He skis **the most dangerously** of anyone.	Longer adjectives and adverbs use *the most* or *the least* to form the superlative.
Nouns	He has **the fewest accidents** of any skier. He has **the least free time** of anyone.	Use *the most* or *the fewest* with count nouns. Use *the most* or *the least* with noncount nouns.

A. Exercise: Rapid Oral Practice. As your teacher reads the following adjectives, give their superlative forms.

Example: T: happy
            S: **the happiest**

1. quick
2. careful
3. pleasant
4. easy
5. dangerous
6. noisy
7. reckless
8. far
9. slow
10. fast

Now make any necessary changes to form the adverb and then give the adverb's superlative.

Examples: T: happy
S: **happily; the most happily**

T: early
S: **early; the earliest, the most early**

B. **Exercise:** What unusual things could you see on an adventure? Animals? Plants? Buildings? Gems? Paintings? Consider some of the following. Tell about them by forming complete sentences with the cues. Use the example as a model.

Example: In Africa, you'll see the giraffe. (giraffe / tall animal) →
The giraffe is the tallest animal in the world.

1. In Africa, you'll see the African elephant. (African elephant / large land animal)
2. In Chicago, you'll see the Sears Tower. (Sears Tower / tall building)
3. In the Arctic and Antarctic, you'll see the blue whale. (blue whale / heavy animal)
4. In India, the Middle East, and Africa, you'll see the cheetah. (cheetah / fast land animal)
5. In London, you'll see the "Star of Africa" diamond. ("Star of Africa" / large diamond)
6. In the Americas, you'll see the three-toed sloth. (sloth / slow land animal)
7. In Japan, you'll see the Seikan Tunnel. (Seikan Tunnel / long tunnel)
8 In California, you'll see the bristlecone pine tree. (bristlecone pine tree / old living thing*)

C. **Exercise:** In pairs, form questions and answers about world geography. Use the example as a model.

Example: hot place / El Aziziyah, Libya →
S1: What is the hottest place in the world?
S2: **The hottest place in the world is El Aziziyah, Libya.**

1. low point of land / the shore of the Dead Sea
2. wet place / Tutunendo, Colombia
3. large freshwater lake / Lake Superior
4. high mountain / Mt. Everest
5. dry place / the Atacama Desert in Chile
6. cold place / Antarctica
7. long river / the Nile
8. deep canyon / the Colca River Canyon in Peru

---

*Some bristlecone pines may be as much as 5,000 years old.

D. Activity: Describing Adventures. Where would you go to find adventure? Choose one of the places from Exercise C or think of another place. Tell why you would go to the hottest, coldest, highest, etc. place on earth.

E. Exercise: What can you do for excitement? Some people find their excitement in being the best (or worst) at some thing. The following is a sample of some unusual world records from *The Guinness Book of World Records*. Using superlative adverbs, make questions and responses from the following cues.

Example: dive / far
           Mexican* / 118 feet →
           S1: **Who dove the farthest?**
           S2: **A Mexican. He dove 118 feet.***

1. throw a boomerang / far
    Australian / 375 feet
2. whistle / loud
    Australian / at 117 decibels
3. jump / high
    American / 7 feet 7¼ inches (23¼ inches above his head)
4. dive / deep
    Frenchman / 282 feet (without scuba equipment)
5. drive / badly
    seventy-five year old American
    (In twenty minutes, he got ten traffic tickets, drove on the wrong side of the street four times, and had four hit-and-run offenses.)
6. sail a boat / fast
    Englishman / at 41.5 miles per hour
7. travel / much
    American / to 213 countries or territories
8. reign / long
    the king of Swaziland / for 82 years

---

*Professional divers in Acapulco, Mexico, regularly make this dive.

F. Exercise: Some people will try anything for excitement, even if it hurts! Form superlative adjectives or adverbs from the list (or add your own) to describe Harry's exploits. Try not to use the same form of any word more than once.

slow   reckless   hard
careless   unlucky   poor
dangerous   bad   few

Example: Harry tries *the hardest* _____ of any athlete I've ever met.

1. Harry also is in _____ shape of anyone that I know.

2. Harry is _____ runner that I know. He runs _____ of all the runners in town.

3. He is _____ skier that I know. He skis _____ of all the skiers I have seen.

4. Harry is _____ golfer imaginable. He swings his club _____ of anyone I've ever seen.

5. Poor Harry! He's _____ fisherman I know. In fact, he catches _____ fish of anyone I've ever met!

G. Activity: Describing People. Who is the laziest person you know? The most energetic? Who drives the most recklessly? The most carefully? Who has the worst luck? The best luck? Tell your classmates a little about your family or friends, describing their best and worst sides! Use the following adjectives to help you.

smart   careful   athletic
energetic   funny   hardworking
boring   lucky   nice
intelligent   cheerful   nervous
tense   grouchy   dangerous
thoughtful

H. Exercise: Complete the following passage about driving with the superlative forms of the words in parentheses.

    In many countries around the world, driving is one of *the most dangerous* (dangerous) activities of all. In Central America, you may have

_____ (much) trouble with other drivers who want
               1

to race while they are passing you. _____ (easy) and
                                              2

_____ (good) way to deal with those drivers is to ignore them!
               3

    In South Asia, the people who drive _____ (dangerously)
                                                            4

are the ones who force you off the road because they refuse to get off the narrow

center strip. Other problems on these narrow roads are truck drivers with

_____ (large) loads imaginable. They speed down mountain
               5

roads in _____ (reckless) way, seemingly without
                       6

_____ (little) care for their own safety. They must be quite
               7

skilled because a traveler seldom sees accidents there.

    Around the Mediterranean, pedestrians have _____ (many)
                                                              8

problems with cars, perhaps. A pedestrian has to be _____
                                                                   9

(careful) when the traffic is _____ (heavy) because drivers often
                                          10

use the sidewalk to pass!

I. Exercise: Review of Comparisons. Complete the following paragraphs with the positive (simple), comparative, or superlative form of the words in parentheses. Be sure to add *the* when necessary.

1. The ____*fastest*____ (fast) way to get anywhere is certainly by plane. The Supersonic Transport (SST), for example, is so ____*fast*____ (fast) that a person can travel from New York to Paris and back in one day! However, many people don't like flying. To them, traveling by plane is _____ (comfortable) way to go anywhere. A long plane ride is _____ (bad) than staying home!

2. Flying used to be _____ (expensive) way to travel, but now most cruise ships are even _____ (expensive) than planes. Ships are not as _____ (fast) as planes, but they are much _____ (comfortable), and the food is _____ (good) because it doesn't have to be prepared ahead of time. Ships are also not as _____ (crowded) as planes, and there are _____ (many) things to do during a cruise than during a plane flight.

3. Most people agree that _____ (good) way to travel is by car because it is _____ (restricting). You can go whenever you want. It isn't as _____ (cheap) as a train, as _____ (fast) as a plane, or as _____ (luxurious) as a ship, but most people prefer car travel because it offers them _____ (much) freedom.

J. Activity: Reporting Records. What "unusual records" has your class set? First, separate into small groups and think of a topic such as sports, food, music, study habits, or clothing. Then write five questions to gather information from your classmates.

Example: (food) →

How many hamburgers have you eaten in one day (week)? How long have you ever gone without eating? What is the most expensive meal you've ever had?

Rank the information that you gather according to *the most, the least, the fastest, the longest,* etc. Finally, give a report on the "unusual records" set by your classmates.

FOR YOUR REFERENCE

Comparative and Superlative Forms of Adjectives and Adverbs

Note: See pages 50–51 for spelling rules for the *-er* and *-est* endings.

Rules	Positives	Comparatives	Superlatives
Add *-er* and *-est* to: one-syllable adjectives adjectives and adverbs that have the same form	nice young early fast hard late	nicer younger earlier faster harder later	the nicest the youngest the earliest the fastest the hardest the latest
Add *-er* and *-est* or use *more, less, the most, the least* with two-syllable adjectives	funny* shallow slender	funnier more funny shallower more shallow slenderer more slender	the funniest the most funny the shallowest the most shallow the slenderest the most slender
Use *more, less, the most, the least* with longer adjectives and most *-ly* adverbs	difficult interesting quickly slowly	more difficult more interesting more quickly more slowly	the most difficult the most interesting the most quickly the most slowly

*With words ending in *-y,* the *-er* and *-est* forms are more common, although both forms are used.

Irregular Adjectives and Adverbs

Adjectives	Adverbs		
bad	badly	worse	the worst
good	—	better	the best
well	well	better	the best
far	far	farther	the farthest
—	—	further	the furthest
little	—	less	the least
many	—	more	the most
much	much	more	the most

9

THE SKY ABOVE US

The Passive Voice

THE PASSIVE VOICE: SIMPLE PRESENT AND SIMPLE PAST TENSES; USES OF *BY* + AGENT; *IT* WITH THE PASSIVE VOICE

What do you know about our solar system? Share your information and ideas while answering the following questions about the picture.

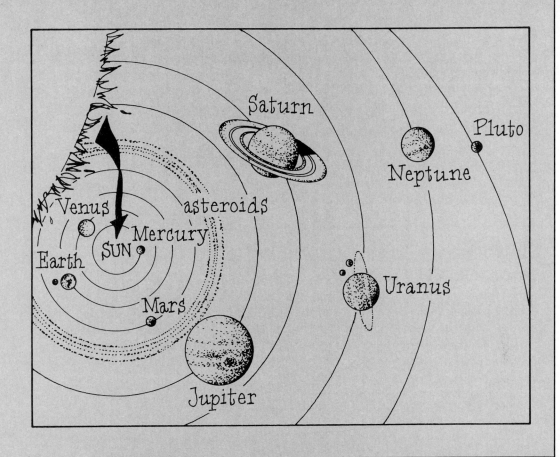

1. What is the center of our solar system?
2. How many planets are there in our solar system?
3. Do the planets and moons move? To your knowledge, how long have we known this information about our solar system?

Our Knowledge of the Universe

For centuries, it was believed that the earth was the center of the universe and that every object in the sky revolved around it. These beliefs were not changed easily. In the 1500s, Copernicus suggested that the sun was the center of the universe, but few people listened to him. Later in 1609, Galileo defended Copernicus' theory. Through his use of a telescope, Galileo realized that the earth was only one of several planets that revolved around the sun. Because he stated this publicly, Galileo was sent to prison in 1633.

Since Galileo's time, astronomers have made tremendous advances in our knowledge about the universe. Today, we know that the earth is one of nine planets that orbit the sun. Our galaxy, the Milky Way, is made up of over two hundred billion stars like our sun. The universe is filled with millions of similar galaxies and countless other extraterrestrial objects.

Discussing the Passage

1. Through most of history, what was believed about the earth and the universe? What do we know differently today?
2. Who gave proof that the sun was the center of our solar system? What happened to him? Why?

Introduction to the Passive Voice

The passive voice occurs in both spoken and written English, and it is used very frequently in technical writing. Most verbs that take an object can be used in the passive voice. In sentences in the active voice, the primary focus is on the subject (the *agent* or doer of the action). To give primary focus to the object of the sentence, the sentence can be changed to the passive voice. Compare:

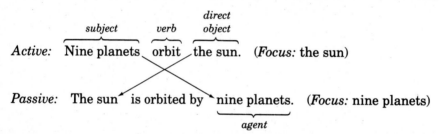

Active: Nine planets orbit the sun.   (*Focus:* the sun)

Passive: The sun is orbited by nine planets.   (*Focus:* nine planets)

In this section, you will study the passive form of simple present and past tense verbs. In Parts Two, Three, and Four you will cover other tenses and modal auxiliaries. In all cases, the verb forms have the same time frame in the passive voice as they do in the active voice.

The Passive Voice: Simple Present and Past Tenses

To form the passive voice, use *be* + the past participle of the main verb. For the simple present tense, use *am, is,* or *are* + past participle. For the simple past tense, use *was* or *were* + past participle. The passive voice subject determines whether the verb *be* is singular or plural. The **agent** can be included in the passive sentence in a phrase with *by.*

	Active	Passive
Simple Present Tense	Nine planets **orbit** the sun. Moons **orbit** some of the planets.	The sun **is orbited** by nine planets. Some of the planets **are orbited** by moons.
Simple Past Tense	The Dutch **invented** a simple telescope. The Italians later **developed** several telescopes.	A simple telescope **was invented** by the Dutch. Several telescopes **were** later **developed** by the Italians.

Note: The following verbs are frequently used in the passive voice. *By* + agent is not normally used; instead, other prepositions follow these verbs.

The movie **was based on** the book.

The moon **is not composed of** / **is not made (up) of** green cheese.

She **is known for** / **is noted for** her scientific discoveries.

Machines **are used to** measure distances in space. / **are used for** measuring distances in space.

A. **Exercise:** Form passive sentences from the following cues. Use the simple present tense.

Example: the sun / orbit / by nine planets →
  The sun is orbited by nine planets.

1. some planets / orbit / by moons
2. the universe / fill / with many galaxies
3. astronauts / send / into space to learn more about the universe
4. high-powered telescopes / use / to study other galaxies
5. new discoveries about the universe / make / every year

B. Exercise: Underline the direct object in each of the following sentences. Then use the direct object as the subject and change the sentences from the active voice to the passive voice. Pay attention to verb tenses.

Example: Scientists around the world study <u>the moon</u>. →
   The moon is studied by scientists around the world.

1. The moon reflects sunlight.
2. The reflection of sunlight produces moonlight.
3. Large craters cover the moon's surface.
4. Volcanos made some of the craters.
5. Meteors probably caused other craters.
6. Most small telescopes reveal the details of the moon's surface.

C. Exercise: Complete the following passage about the moon with either present or past passive forms of the verbs in parentheses.

The distance to the moon *was calculated*

(calculate) long ago when measurements

_____ (make) by ancient astronomers.
       1

Observations _____ (take) from two
                        2

different places on the ground. The moon and these two

locations on the earth formed a triangle. This imaginary

triangle _____ (use) by ancient
                  3

astronomers to calculate the real distance to the moon.

   Although this method was fairly accurate, it

_____ (not use) anymore. Today,
           4

laser beams _____ (use) instead.
                     5

In the 1970s, mirrors _____ (place)
                              6

on the surface of the moon. Now, laser beams from the

earth _____ (reflect) by the mirrors, and the
            7

moon's position _____ (measure) to the nearest few centimeters.
                        8

Its average distance from earth is 384,000 kilometers (equal to traveling around the

earth ten times).

By + Agent

By + noun (or pronoun) can be used in a passive voice sentence to tell who or what performed the action of a verb. However, many passive sentences do *not* include *by* + agent.

Use *by* + agent with new or important information.

	Examples	Notes
Active	Galileo first **used** the telescope in astronomy.	The subject *Galileo* is important to the sentence. It cannot be omitted from the passive sentence.
Passive	The telescope **was** first **used** in astronomy **by Galileo.**	

Do *not* use *by* + agent with information that is obvious or unimportant.

	Examples	Notes
Active	People **make** telescopes with a series of lenses.	The subject *people* is obvious. It is not important to the sentence. It can be omitted from the passive sentence.
Passive	Telescopes **are made** by people with a series of lenses.	

D. Exercise: In the following sentences about the solar system, decide whether you can leave out *by* + *agent* without changing the meaning of the sentence.

Example: The sun is orbited by nine planets. →
   The phrase with *by* must be used in this sentence.

1. Until recently, little was known by scientists about the closest planet to the sun, Mercury.
2. Mercury is rarely seen by people because it is often obscured by the sun.
3. The planet Venus is covered by a heavy atmosphere.
4. Radar is used by scientists to get information about the surface of Venus.
5. Seventy-one percent of the earth's surface is covered by water.
6. For a long time, it was believed by people that Mars was inhabited by little green men.
7. No life was found on Mars by the Mariner space missions.

E. Exercise: Change the following sentences from the active to the passive voice. Decide whether the agent is necessary. If it is, include it in a phrase with *by*.

Example: Nine planets orbit the sun. →
The sun is orbited by nine planets. (*By nine planets* is necessary to the meaning of the sentence.)

1. Sixteen moons orbit Jupiter.
2. Galileo discovered the four largest moons.
3. Christian Huygens first saw Saturn's rings in 1655.
4. William Herschel identified Uranus on March 13, 1781.
5. Astronomers found many irregularities in the orbit of Uranus.
6. Astronomers calculated the size of Neptune before anyone saw it.
7. Clyde Tombaugh discovered Pluto in February 1930.
8. Astronomers use powerful telescopes to observe Pluto.

COURTESY NASA

The planet Saturn and its rings

It with the Passive Voice

It is sometimes used with the passive voice to avoid naming the agent or source of the information. This construction is often used with verbs such as *believe, feel, hope, report, say,* and *think.* A clause with *that* follows the verb.

ACTIVE	PASSIVE
People believed that the earth was the center of the universe.	**It was believed** that the earth was the center of the universe.
Some people thought that everything revolved around the earth.	**It was thought** that everything revolved around the earth.

F. **Exercise:** The following statements were once believed to be true. Now they have been disproven. Change the quotations to the past. Begin each statement with, "It was believed (said, thought, etc.). . . ."

Examples: "The earth is flat." →
            It was believed that the earth was flat.

1. "The moon is made of green cheese."
2. "Little green men live on Mars."
3. "The stars are holes in the sky."
4. "The earth is the center of the universe."
5. "A comet in space causes bad luck on earth."

G. **Activity: Explaining Beliefs and Superstitions.** Most cultures have traditional beliefs or customs regarding the moon, the planets, the stars, the weather, and so forth. Some are superstitions, but others may be true. What beliefs or superstitions are common in your culture? Try to list at least five beliefs.

Examples: **In my culture, it's believed that the full moon makes people crazy.**

            For a long time, it was believed that eclipses were signs from God.

H. Exercise: Complete the following passage on the exploration of the moon with active or passive past tense forms of the verbs in parentheses.

During the 1960s, the first spaceships _were sent_ (send) to the moon. These American spaceships _____ (call) Rangers. Each spaceship _____ (carry) six television cameras. Each ship _____ (design) to send back pictures to earth just before it _____ (crash) on the moon. The first six missions _____ (end) in failure. Finally, a Ranger _____ (reach) its goal in 1963. People on earth _____ (watch) the first "live" T.V. pictures from the moon. Between July of 1964 and March of 1965, 17,000 pictures of the lunar surface _____ (send) back to earth.

From 1966 to 1968, ten spaceships _____ (launch) to land on the moon or to orbit it. Then on July 20, 1969, humans _____ (touch) the moon for the first time. On that historic day, Neil Armstrong and Edwin Aldrin _____ (walk) on the lunar surface. Between December of 1968 and December of 1972, twenty-four people _____ (send) to the moon. Twelve actually _____ (walk) on the moon's surface.

I. Activity: Describing Equipment and Processes. Every type of work has equipment that is helpful or necessary in order to do the job. For example, a thermometer and a blood-pressure gauge are important equipment to a doctor or nurse. A balance sheet is important to an accountant. A tennis racket is absolutely necessary for a tennis player. In pairs or in small groups, think of equipment that is important in a hobby or field that you are interested in. Use the following questions to help you describe the equipment.

1. When and where was it developed?
2. What is it made of?
3. How is it made?
4. How is it used?

Give a brief (two-to-four minute) presentation, individually or as a group. Then save your notes to use in the activity at the end of Part Two.

PART TWO

THE PASSIVE VOICE: THE PRESENT PERFECT TENSE

What do you know about our galaxy? Share your information and ideas while answering the following questions about the picture.

1. What is the name of our galaxy?
2. Is our galaxy unique? How do we know this?

New Discoveries

Much has been learned about our universe since the time of Copernicus and Galileo, but most of the discoveries have been made during this century. During the last several decades, powerful telescopes, satellites, and spaceships have been developed. Through these advances in technology, many of the mysteries of the universe have been solved.

Until forty years ago, it was believed that our galaxy, the Milky Way, was unique. It was believed that our galaxy *was* the universe. In recent years, through improved technology, these ideas and many others have been disproven. It has been estimated that trillions of galaxies like our own fill the universe. The universe itself is calculated to be between fifteen and eighteen billion years old.

COURTESY NASA

Satellite trail in the Milky Way

Discussing the Passage

1.   Who has made these recent discoveries?
2.   What new space technology has been developed?
3.   What is now known about the age and size of the universe?

The Passive Voice: The Present Perfect Tense

To form the passive voice of the present perfect tense, use *has* or *have* + *been* + past participle. The passive voice subject determines whether the verb is singular or plural.

	Active	**Passive**
Present Perfect Tense	The Soviet Union **has launched** many spaceships. Scientists **have improved** technology.	Spaceships **have been launched** by the Soviet Union. Technology **has been improved.**

A.   **Exercise:** Underline all verbs in the present perfect tense, passive voice, in the passage "New Discoveries" at the beginning of this section. In each case, try to tell who or what the agent of the action was.

B.   **Exercise:** Change the following sentences from the active voice to the passive oice. Omit the agent to avoid repetition.

Example: Astronomers have learned much about the universe. →
              Much has been learned about the universe.

1.   Astronomers have discovered new stars.
2.   Astronomers have designed powerful new telescopes.
3.   Astronomers have launched spaceships.
4.   Astronomers have sent astronauts into space.
5.   Astronomers have photographed the solar system.
6.   Astronomers have mapped many parts of the sky.
7.   Astronomers have measured the distance from the sun to each of the planets.
8.   Astronomers have calculated distances throughout the universe.

C.   **Activity: Giving Information.** What else has been learned about the universe in recent years? Do you know of any other major breakthroughs in space study? Briefly share your information with your classmates.

D. Exercise: Rapid Oral Practice. Colonel Mariko Kanno of Aerospace Control Central is reading a checklist to the astronaut in a spaceship that is about to be launched. In pairs, take turns asking and answering questions based on the following cues. For your answers, use "abbreviated" speech. That is, use the past participle as an affirmative answer.

Example: speed / calculate →
              S1: **Has the speed been calculated?**
              S2: **Calculated!**

1. computers / program
2. rockets / test
3. windows / close
4. oil / check
5. radar / set
6. food / load
7. doors / lock
8. engines / start

This is Control Central to Moonbeam. This is our final checklist.

E. Exercise: Colonel Kanno is giving a talk about Operation Moonbean. Complete it with either the active or passive form of the present perfect tense of the verbs in parentheses.

"Good morning. I am here today to announce our newest space program, Operation Moonbeam. We *have completed* (complete) plans for a space colony on the moon. At this point, all the necessary technology _____₁ (develop). A spaceship _____ (build) to carry the astronauts and their equipment.

"In addition, a dome _____ (construct) to cover a small part of the moon's surface. Machines _____ (design) to 'produce' weather. With the help of these machines, we _____ (produce) wind and rain.

"We _____ (begin / also) to select astronauts for this mission. To date, twenty members of the team _____ (choose) by our staff. So far, one physicist, five biologists, four chemists, and ten astronomers _____ (select). We _____ (include) both single people and married couples. But there will be no children on this first mission.

"Are there any questions?"

F. Exercise: In small groups, choose one person to "be" Colonel Kanno. Ask "her" questions about the upcoming Operation Moonbeam. Form questions from the cues following, using the passive voice in the present perfect tense. Then add some questions of your own. "Colonel Kanno" will have to use his or her imagination for some of the information for the answers.

Example: How many spaceships / build? →
         S1: **How many spaceships have been built?**
         S2: **Ten spaceships have been built.**

1. pilots of the spaceships / train?
2. what kinds of safety measures / take?
3. special clothing / design?
4. special food / develop?
5. the weather dome / test?
6. colony managers / choose carefully?
7. what kind of entertainment / plan for the colonists?
8. the space station / check for safety?

G. Exercise: The following passage gives you information on star formation. First, read the passage for meaning, checking any vocabulary that may be difficult for you. Then complete it with simple past, simple present, or present perfect tense, active or passive, of the verbs in parentheses. In some cases, more than one tense is appropriate. Try to give all possibilities.

Gas and dust ___*exist*___ (exist) throughout space, and new stars ___*are formed*___ (form) from this gas and dust. First, gas and dust _____ (form) a sphere or ball, and the "ball'
1
_____ (begin) to rotate. When the pressure and temperature
2
_____ (rise) inside the "ball," it _____
3   4
(begin) to produce radiant energy—light. At this point, the "ball"

_____ (become) a star.
5

Young and middle-aged stars _____ (fuel) by the burning of
6
hydrogen. Radiant energy _____ (produce) when hydrogen
7
_____ (burn). During this nuclear reaction, mass
8
_____ (change) into energy.
9

After the hydrogen _____ (use up), the star
10
_____ (begin) a different nuclear reaction. Heavier elements
11
_____ (burn) until all sources of fuel _____
12   13
(exhaust). At that point, smaller stars _____ (burn out) and
14
_____ (collapse). Medium-sized stars, on the other hand,
15
_____ (explode) in a fiery death. Giant stars
16
_____ (collapse). They _____ (become)
17   18
"black holes."

When the universe _____ (form), only hydrogen and helium
19
_____ (exist). Everything else in our universe
20
_____ (compose) of heavier elements that
21
_____ (create) by star explosions. These star explosions, which
22
_____ (burn) brighter than a billion stars,
23
_____ (call) supernovas. Our planet and all of its continents,
24
seas, and living things _____ (form) from the gas and dust that
25
_____ (leave) in space by the explosion of nearby dying stars.
26

H. Activity: Describing Equipment and Processes. Use the information and notes that you prepared for Activity I in Part One to plan a follow-up presentation. Again, you may do this individually or in small groups. Give more detailed information, including the following:

1. Give a brief summary of your first presentation.

    a. When and where was the equipment developed?
    b. Who developed it?

2. Now give information on the changes that have taken place?

    a. How has this equipment been improved?
    b. Why have these improvements been made?
    c. How have they changed the way the equipment is used?

Finally, use all of this information to write a short composition on your topic.

PART THREE

THE PASSIVE VOICE: THE PRESENT CONTINUOUS TENSE

Do you enjoy science-fiction movies or books? Share your opinions and ideas while answering the following questions about the picture.

1. What kind of story is the man going to write?
2. Have you read stories like these?

Space-age Technology

Only a few years ago, science-fiction writers were writing amazing stories about spaceships, ray guns, robots, and satellites. Even more amazing: today these things are no longer part of science fiction. They exist, and they are being used!

Today, spaceships are being launched regularly. The space shuttle is being perfected. Satellites are being sent into orbit to beam radio, television, and telephone signals worldwide. Space stations are being designed. And lasers, powerful rays of directed light, are being used in all areas of high technology.

Yesterday's science fiction has become today's reality. Perhaps today's science fiction will be tomorrow's reality. It is not impossible!

Discussing the Passage

1. What type of space exploration is taking place today?
2. Did some science-fiction writers predict this activity?

The Passive Voice: The Present Continuous Tense

To form the passive voice of the present continuous tense, use *am, is,* or *are* + *being* + past participle. The passive voice subject determines whether the verb *be* is singular or plural.

	Active	**Passive**
Present Continuous Tense	The Soviet Union **is sending** ships into outer space. Researchers **are launching** a new rocket today.	Ships **are being sent** into outer space. A new rocket **is being launched** today.

A. Exercise: First underline all the examples of *by* + agent in the following sentences. Then change them from the passive to active voice. If a sentence does not have an agent, use *scientists* as the active subject.

Example: New discoveries are being made almost daily. (no agent) →
Scientists are making new discoveries almost daily.

1. Joint research projects are being developed by several countries.
2. Jets are being designed to fly above the atmosphere.
3. Communication satellites are being used by many countries.
4. Space shuttles are being tested.
5. Computer technology is being improved.
6. Space colonies are being planned by many countries.
7. Spaceships are being launched.
8. Robots are being programmed to run spaceships.

B. Exercise: Rapid Oral Practice. Form passive statements from the following cues.

Example: food / load → **The food is being loaded.**

1. control panel / check
2. computers / program
3. radar / set
4. radio / test
5. doors / close
6. climate control / adjust
7. engines / start
8. ship / launch

C. Exercise: Complete the following conversation with either the active or passive voice, in the present continuous tense.

OM: Operation Moonbeam to Control Central. We *are beginning* (begin) our descent to the moon! Can you hear us?

CC: Operation Moonbeam, this is Control Central. We hear you loud and clear! In fact, your voices _____ (hear) by people around the world.
1
People everywhere _____ (watch) you make history!
2

OM: I'm sure everyone wants to know what we _____ (do) right
3
now. At the moment, the ship _____ (prepare) for landing.
4
The spacesuits and oxygen equipment _____ (test) one last
5
time, and the shuttle _____ (check)—just in case. We
6
_____ (plan) to spend an hour on the ground before we
7
actually get off the ship.

CC: Could you describe the scene for us, please? I am sure that everyone
_____ (look) forward to a full description.
8

OM: Better yet, you will have pictures in a moment. Right now pictures
_____ (transmit) directly to you. These pictures
9
_____ (take) by special cameras on the spaceship. The
10
cameras _____ (take) over fifty pictures a minute.
11

CC: Operation Moonbeam, we will let you return to your landing preparations, and we will give the T.V. audience a chance to see these fascinating pictures. Over and out. . . .

D. Exercise: The following passage gives you information on Sputnik, the first satellites into space. First, read the passage for meaning, checking any vocabulary that may be difficult for you. Then complete it with active or passive forms of the verbs in parentheses. Choose from the simple present, simple past, present perfect, or present continuous tenses.

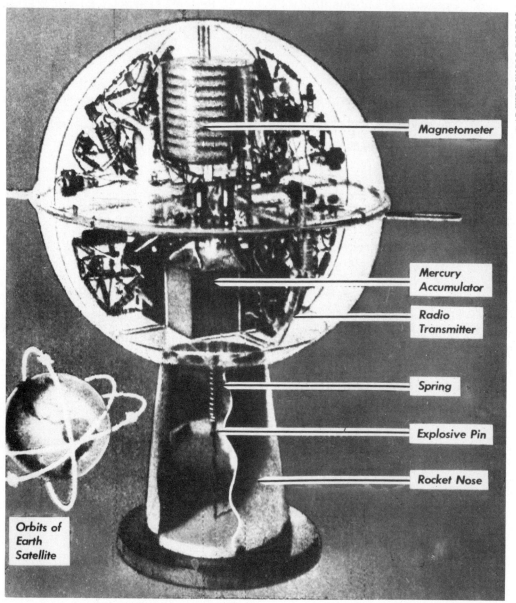

Sputnik: cutaway diagram of the Soviet satellite

On October 4, 1957, a 187-pound sphere (83.6 kilograms) _____
(send) into orbit. It _____*carried*_____ (carry) a radio transmitter and
enough batteries for two weeks. It _____ (launch) into orbit by
the Soviet Union. This satellite _____ (know) as "Sputnik."
                                               2

Sputnik _____ (not be) very sophisticated, but it
                3
_____ (show) the technology of the Soviets. Sputnik
            4
_____ (not carry) any scientific equipment, and it
            5
_____ (not take) any measurements in space. Nevertheless, a
            6
satellite _____ (be) in orbit for the first time, and Sputnik
                            7
_____ (begin) a scientific and technological competition that
            8
_____ (continue) to this day.
            9

People around the world _____ (surprise) by the launching
                                          10
of Sputnik. Five months later, the Americans _____ (finalize)
                                                              11
plans for a space program.

Since 1957, all of those plans and more _____ (finalize).
                                                      12
Hard, soft, and manned landings _____ (make) on the moon.
                                              13
Robots _____ (send) to Mars and other planets. Measurements
                14
_____ (take) and experiments _____
            15   16
(make) in space. Satellites _____ (launch) for worldwide com-
                                          17
munication. Today, these satellites _____ (use) to send radio,
                                                18
television, and telephone signals around the world. Weather forecasting and
map-making _____ (improve) through use of satellites and
                    19
high-flying rockets. New discoveries _____ (make) about distant
                                                      20
stars and galaxies. Lasers _____ (develop) for use in many
                                          21
fields.

It _____ (be) difficult to imagine that all of this
            22
_____ (begin) little more than thirty years ago and that it
            23
_____ (start) with one small satellite: Sputnik.
            24

E. Exercise: Think about one of your hobbies or interests. Write answers for the following questions about new developments in that area. After writing, share your information with your classmates.

Examples: What equipment is being used now? →
My hobby is photography. Both manual and automatic cameras are being used. Many kinds of lenses are available . . .

I'm interested in computer science. Three types of computers are being used now: main-frame computers, minicomputers, and micro-computers.

1. What equipment is being used now in your hobby?
2. What types of things are currently being designed?
3. Are any of these being developed now?
4. What types of things are being tested?
5. What is currently being improved?
6. What is being planned for the future?

F. Activity: Giving "Eyewitness" Reports. In small groups, give an "eyewitness" account of a breakthrough in science or technology. Some of the group members may role-play the event while others are giving the "eyewitness" news story on it. Be sure to include an "anchor person" at your news station, as well as "special correspondents" who are at the scene. You may choose from the following ideas or create your own situations.

1. A flying saucer has just landed outside of your classroom and several extraterrestrials are getting off. Inspect the saucer, describe it, and interview some of the crew members. Find out where they are from, how long they have been traveling, how their spaceship is operated, etc.
2. A famous astronomer has just discovered that the moon is, in fact, made of green cheese. Interview the astronomer and his or her assistants to learn how this discovery was made, what is being done to verify it, and what impact this discovery will have on the future.
3. The first space colony has just been established on the moon. You are being sent to interview the residents of Operation Moonbeam. Ask about their new world and how they like it.

PART FOUR

THE PASSIVE VOICE: MODAL AUXILIARIES (*CAN, COULD, MAY, MIGHT, MUST, SHOULD,* AND *WILL*)

What would life be like on a space colony? Answer the following questions about the picture.

1. Describe the drawing.
2. What purposes could space colonies possibly serve?

Space Colonies

The technology already exists to send people into space and to bring them back to earth safely. Now scientists have started thinking about the next step: building colonies in space. But where will space colonists go? Can a place be found or created that will support human life?

Perhaps space stations could be launched. Or artificial environments might be created on the moon or on another planet. This could be done by building domes and importing air and water. An urban earth environment could be imitated, complete with parks, libraries, even swimming pools!

As countries continue to develop their space programs, a space colony may even be launched during our lifetime. Perhaps technology will be improved so much that ordinary people will have a chance to live in space. Ordinary activities like language classes may someday be conducted in space!

Discussing the Passage

1. Are space stations and artificial environments possible now?
2. Would you like to be one of the first people to live in a space colony?

The Passive Voice: Modal Auxiliaries (*Can, Could, May, Might, Must, Should,* and *Will*)

To form the passive voice of modal auxiliaries, use modal + *be* + past participle. Note that modal auxiliaries have the same functions in the passive voice as they do in the active. See Chapter 3 if you need to review functions of modals.

	Active	Passive
Modal Auxiliaries	We **could launch** space stations. We **should start** space colonies. Scientists **will perfect** the necessary technology soon.	Space stations **could be launched.** Space colonies **should be started.** The necessary technology **will be perfected** soon.

A. Exercise: At a conference, scientists are talking about the technology that is needed for people to live in space. Use the cues to form sentences in the passive voice.

Examples: attractive space stations / develop   (may) →
Attractive space stations may be developed.

In order for people to live in space stations . . .

1. space stations / make safe   (must)
2. an atmosphere / create   (must)
3. station managers / train   (must)
4. comfortable housing / design   (should)
5. parks and other recreation areas / build   (might)

In order for humans to settle on Mars . . .

6. the environment on Mars / change   (could)
7. first, energy / produce   (must)
8. then the Martian icecaps / melt   (can)
9. in this way, a regular supply of water / develop   (could)
10. in addition, oxygen / produce   (must)

B. Exercise: Following are other ideas expressed by scientists at the conference. In each sentence, first underline the direct object. Then change the sentence from the active voice to the passive voice. Omit the agent.

Example: "Someday, something may destroy <u>life on earth</u>." →
"Someday, life on earth may be destroyed."

1. "Then humans must find other places to live."
2. "We will need very advanced technology."
3. "Scientists can plan test colonies now."
4. "We should start training programs for space colonists now."
5. "We can use computers to study life in space."
6. "Governments should spend more money on space research."

C. Exercise: The year is 2020. You are planning to spend your summer vacation on a space colony. The cues are a checklist of things that must or should be done before you leave for your trip. Write each item as a complete sentence using the passive voice.

Example: warm clothes / pack →
My warm clothes must be packed.

1. travel schedule / confirm one week before departure
2. passport / renew
3. camera / repair
4. bills / pay before I leave
5. friends / tell where to write to me

D. Exercise: You've been at the space colony for two weeks now. Life is simple and rather boring. Read the list of complaints below. Then use the cues and any appropriate modal to make suggestions for improving life at the colony.

Example: Mail from home comes only once a week. (mail / deliver twice a week) →
Mail should be delivered twice a week.

1. The food here is tasteless. (hamburgers / import from Earth)
2. There aren't any gardens. (flowers / plant)
3. There isn't any good music. (rock and roll / broadcast from Earth)
4. These dorm walls are colorless. (posters of Earth / hang)
5. It's too hot to go outdoors. (the indoor environment / improve)

E. Exercise: What are your opinions about the "race into space"? Answer the following questions in your own words, using the passive voice.

1. Should space colonies be developed?
2. Should money be spent on this kind of research?
3. In your opinion, what kinds of research should be done?
4. Should people be sent into space for long periods of time?
5. Should tests for ability to survive in space be performed on humans?

F. Exercise: The following passage gives you information on the future of our solar system. First, read the passage for meaning, checking any vocabulary that might be difficult for you. Then complete it by using active or passive modal auxiliaries with the verbs in parentheses.

Life on earth *may continue* _____ (may continue) for a very long time, or it *might be destroyed* (might destroy) by our sun. Sometime, in thousands of millions of years, the sun _____ (will burn) all of its hydrogen. Then, the sun _____ (will expand) into a red giant star. Mercury _____ (will swallow) up by the sun. Venus _____ (may consume) by the expanding sun, and the earth _____ (might destroy).

If this happens, it _____ (will mean) the end of all life in the solar system. Any life on planets near the sun _____ (will destroy). And life on some other planets _____ (will freeze) by the extreme cold. Eventually the sun _____ (will shrink) to a white dwarf star. After the sun shrinks to a white dwarf star, it _____ (will look) like a beautiful, bright diamond in the sky.

G. **Activity: Researching a Topic.** Is there more that you would like to know about the solar system? Other galaxies? Choose a topic and research it. Then report back to the class what you found out. Here are some possible topics:

- black holes
- a mythological story about a constellation
- light
- stars: their birth and death

10

MEDICINE, MYTHS, AND MAGIC

Adjective Clauses

ADJECTIVE CLAUSES WITH *THAT:* REPLACEMENT OF SUBJECTS

What do you know about the way your body works? Share your information while answering the following questions about the picture.

1. What are the major systems of the body?
2. Where does the blood go when it leaves the heart? How does it get to your fingers? Your toes?
3. What are nerves? Do they extend throughout your body?

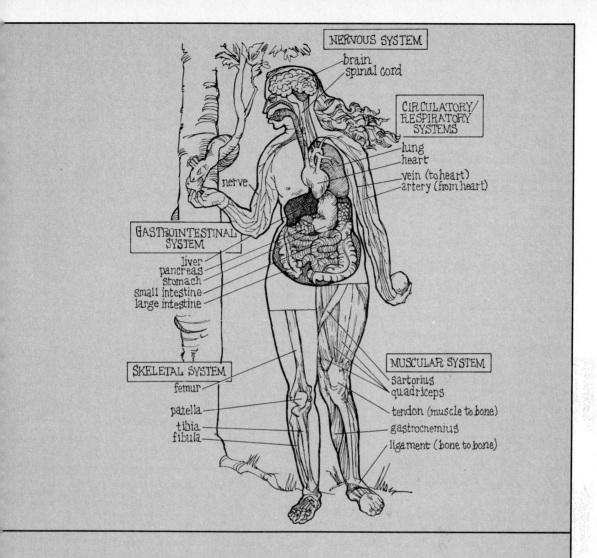

The Major Systems of the Body

During the last one hundred years, medical researchers have discovered a great deal about the way the human body works. We now know about the various systems of the body that keep us alive. The systems that are most important include the circulatory, respiratory, nervous, musculoskeletal, and gastrointestinal systems. Each of these systems controls major body functions. The system that controls the flow of blood through the body is the circulatory system. It includes the heart, the arteries, the capillaries, and the veins. The nervous system connects the brain to the rest of the body through the spinal cord and the nerves. The system that supports the body and allows it to move is the musculoskeletal system. The system that controls breathing is the respiratory system. It includes the nose, mouth, throat, trachea, bronchi, and lungs. Finally, the gastrointestinal system, the part of the body that controls digestion and elimination, consists of the esophagus, the stomach, and the small and large intestines. Two of its most important organs are the liver and the pancreas.

Discussing the Passage

1. Which system connects the brain to the rest of the body?
2. What system includes the liver and the pancreas?
3. What does each of the following systems do: circulatory, respiratory, nervous, musculoskeletal, gastrointestinal?

Adjective Clauses

An adjective clause is a clause that modifies or describes a noun or a pronoun. An adjective clause usually comes immediately after the word(s) that it describes. It begins with a *relative pronoun*. The relative pronouns that are covered in this chapter are *that, which, who, whom, whose, when,* and *where.*

Adjective Clauses with *That:* Replacement of Subjects

To form an adjective clause, *that* may replace the subject of a simple sentence. It may be used to refer to ideas, things, and people. Note that *who(m)* normally refers to people.

Two Simple Sentences

The body is like a complex **machine. This machine** automatically repairs itself.

One Complex Sentence with *That*

The body is like a complex machine **that automatically repairs itself.**

A. **Exercise:** Underline the adjective clauses (*that* clauses) in the opening passage "The Major Systems of the Body." Circle the words that the clauses modify.

B. Exercise: Combine the following sentences to form one sentence with a clause with *that*. Omit words and change *a* or *an* to *the* when necessary. Remember to place the clause after the noun that it modifies.

Example: Blood is a liquid. This liquid circulates through the body. →
Blood is the liquid that circulates through the body.

1.   Blood is a liquid. This liquid distributes our food and oxygen.
2.   The quadriceps is a muscle. This muscle extends the leg.
3.   A thermometer is an instrument. This instrument measures temperature.
4.   Digestion is a process. This process prepares the food we eat for absorption into the body.
5.   The femur is a bone. This bone reaches from the hip to the knee.

C. Exercise: Combine the following sentences to form one sentence with a clause with *that*. Omit words when necessary.

Example: Aristotle wrote *three important books. These books* discuss problems we still face today. →
Aristotle wrote three important books that discuss problems we still face today.

1.   According to ancient Egyptian beliefs, people got sick from certain *spirits. These spirits* were angry and evil.
2.   The Egyptian doctor would put a magic spell on the angry *spirit. This spirit* had caused the person's illness.
3.   The magic spell always included *words. The words* had to be repeated in a certain way.
4.   Egyptian doctors also used *medicine. This medicine* came from the organs of wild animals.
5.   In addition, these doctors used a large number of *drugs. These drugs* included minerals, vegetables, and even beer.
6.   According to the famous Greek philosopher, Aristotle, the brain was an *organ. This organ* cooled the heart.

D. Exercise: Adjective clauses with *that* are often used to define words. Use the following cues to define various parts of the body. Be sure to use appropriate singular or plural verbs in the adjective clauses and to add articles or pronouns when necessary.

Example: heart / organ / pump blood / through / body →
The heart is the organ that pumps blood through your body.

1.   spine / set of bones / support / body
2.   arteries / major blood vessels / carry / blood away from / heart
3.   spinal cord / set of nerves / lead to / brain
4.   nerves / fibers / communicate messages to and from / brain
5.   knees / joints / allow you to bend / legs
6.   tendons / tissues / connect / muscles to / bones

E. Exercise: In pairs, use this diagram of the body and the diagram at the beginning of the chapter to help you give definitions of the following terms. Try to complete the sentences in your own words before checking the words in a dictionary.

1. Your brain is the organ that . .
2. Your eyelids are the pieces of skin that . . .
3. Your stomach is the organ that . . .
4. Your ankle is the joint that . . .
5. Your lungs are the organs that . . .
6. Your veins are the blood vessels that . . .

F. Activity: Giving Definitions. Try to form definitions of the following body parts, as well as four or five others that you may choose.

1. elbow   4. ear
2. eyebrow   5. wrist
3. nose

G. Activity: Giving Definitions. In pairs or in small groups, discuss definitions of the following words. Then try to write the definitions in your own words. Ask your teacher or check your dictionary to change or correct any information.

Examples: **Blood** **is a liquid that circulates through the body. It is the liquid that distributes our food and oxygen.**

           System **is a word that refers to a group of body parts with a common function.**

1. disease
2. pill
3. bandage
4. cast
5. ache
6. circulation
7. thermometer
8. digestion
9. organ
10. infection

PART TWO

ADJECTIVE CLAUSES WITH *WHO* AND *WHICH:* REPLACEMENT OF SUBJECTS; ADJECTIVE CLAUSES WITH *WHOSE:* REPLACEMENT OF POSSESSIVES; RESTRICTIVE VERSUS NONRESTRICTIVE CLAUSES

How has medical care changed during the last century? Share your information while answering the following questions about the picture on the next page.

1. What is shown in the picture?
2. Are any of the treatments useful?

Early Medicine

Medicine and pharmacology are two sciences that have changed a great deal in recent times. Long ago, medicine was a guessing game. Medical care was given by doctors, pharmacists, and even barbers! All of them experimented freely on their patients, who often died as a result.

Early pharmacists depended on plant remedies which had been developed over the centuries. One popular remedy during the Middle Ages was poppy juice, which contains opium (a narcotic). Other remedies were animal fat and even crocodile blood, which was considered a "cure" for poor eyesight.

Other common practices were dangerous and sometimes fatal. For instance, bleeding patients to let out "bad blood" often resulted in death for the patient. A common practice that was equally dangerous involved drilling a hole in the patient's skull. Perhaps this was done to treat head wounds or to relieve pressure inside the head.

People whose diseases were "incurable" often looked for help from the spirit world, astrology, and magic. Astrology, which was valued as a method of diagnosis, was even taught in many medical schools.

Medicine has become a reliable science only in recent times. Even now, however, it still involves a certain amount of experimentation.

Discussing the Passage

1. Why was early medicine a guessing game?
2. What different types of people gave medical care?
3. What were some common early medicines and treatments? Do you know of any other early remedies or treatments?

Adjective Clauses with *Who* and *Which:* Replacement of Subjects

To form adjective clauses from simple sentences, *who* may replace subjects that refer to people. *Which* may replace subjects that refer to things or ideas.

Two Simple Sentences

The **physician** was Dr. Andrews. **He** treated the patient.

One Complex Sentence with *Who*

The physician **who treated the patient** was Dr. Andrews.

Two Simple Sentences

Aspirin is a common treatment for headaches. **Aspirin** is a pain reliever.

One Complex Sentence with *Which*

Aspirin, **which is a pain reliever,** is a common treatment for headaches.

Adjective Clauses with *Whose:* Replacement of Possessives

Whose may also be used to form adjective clauses. It does not act as the subject of a clause. Instead, it replaces a possessive noun or adjective that modifies the subject of the clause.

Two Simple Sentences

The woman thanked **the doctor. His** treatment had cured her.

One Complex Sentence with *Whose*

The woman thanked the doctor **whose treatment had cured her.**

A. Exercise: Use the cues to form sentences with adjective clauses with *who*. Add *a* or *an* when necessary and use appropriate singular or plural verbs in your adjective clauses.

Examples: orthopedist / treat bone, joint, or muscle problems →
   An orthopedist is a doctor who treats bone, joint, or muscle problems.

   orthopedists / treat bone, joint, or muscle problems →
   Orthopedists are doctors who treat bone, joint, or muscle problems.

1. radiologist / read / X-rays
2. surgeons / perform / operations
3. pediatrician / take / care of children
4. ophthalmologist / treat / diseases or injuries of the eye
5. internists / specialize in / diagnosis and treatment of diseases in adults
6. gynecologist / specialize in / functions and diseases of women
7. neurologist / take / care of patients with nerve or brain disease
8. psychiatrists / treat / mental problems

B. Exercise: Use the following cues to form sentences with adjective clauses with *which* or *(that)*. Be sure to add articles when necessary.

Example: rubber hammer / tool / be used for testing reflexes →
   A rubber hammer is a tool that is used for testing reflexes.

1. stethoscope / instrument / be used for listening to a person's heart
2. scalpel / instrument / be used for cutting during surgery
3. opium / narcotic / produce a feeling of great happiness
4. anesthetic / drug / put people to sleep before surgery
5. aspirin / drug / relieve pain

C. Exercise: Combine the following sentences about early medical practices with *who* or *which*. Make the second sentence of the two into an adjective clause when you combine them. Change words when necessary.

Example: Some prehistoric *people* performed brain operations. These *people* lived in Europe in about 10,000 B.C. →
Some prehistoric people who lived in Europe in about 10,000 B.C. performed brain operations.

1. These brain surgeons used simple *knives*. The *knives* were made of stone.
2. Many *skulls* have been found in Europe. The *skulls* had small holes cut into them.
3. The *surgeons* probably removed pieces of bone. *They* operated on the head.
4. In early times, however, some *people* went to magicians rather than doctors. These *people* had physical problems.
5. *People* would ask for help from a magician. *They* thought spirits or magic caused illness.
6. During the Middle Ages, some doctors used different *cures*. These *cures* did not treat the body at all.
7. For example, a *swordsman* was not treated with medicine. The *swordsman* had been hurt in a fight. (The sword was treated instead!)
8. Another *remedy* was to wear a card with the word "abracadabra" on it. This *remedy* became very popular in the Middle Ages.

D. Exercise: Combine the following sentences with *whose*. Make the second sentence into the adjective clause.

Example: The villagers gave a gift to *the pharmacist*. *His* secret medicine had cured their mysterious disease. →
The villagers gave a gift to the pharmacist whose secret medicine had cured their mysterious disease.

1. A *person* sometimes gets well unexpectedly. *His or her* will to live is very strong.
2. Another *person* might die unexpectedly. *His or her* belief in witchcraft is strong.
3. Some *doctors* can be successful. *Their* treatments are not always scientific.
4. Some *people* refuse to see a doctor. *Their* condition is serious.
5. *People* may be afraid of doctors. *Their* faith in modern medicine is not very strong.

Restrictive Versus Nonrestrictive Adjective Clauses

In some cases, commas come before and after adjective clauses. Commas are used with adjective clauses that give additional information about the word(s) they modify. These clauses often modify proper nouns (Dr. Nie, Athens, the Tower of London) or names of unique people, places, or things (the sun, vitamin C, the equator). *Who, which, whom,* and *whose* (but not *that*) may be used in these clauses. They are called nonrestrictive clauses.

In contrast, commas are not used with adjective clauses that specifically identify the word(s) they modify. *That* may be used in this type of clause only; *who, which, whom,* and *whose* may also be used. These clauses are called restrictive clauses.

	Examples	Notes
Nonrestrictive Clauses	Dr. Fox, **who has been a friend of ours for years,** is both a pediatrician and an internist. Dr. Carlson, **who works with Dr. Fox,** specializes in radiology.	Nonrestrictive clauses give additional or extra information about the noun(s) they modify. They do not explain *which* people, places, or things the speaker or writer is referring to—this information is probably known. Commas are used before and after these clauses.
Restrictive Clauses	Doctors **who treat children** are called pediatricians. Doctors **who read X-rays** are called radiologists.	Restrictive clauses explain *which* people, places, or things the speaker or writer is referring to. No commas are used.

E. Exercise: In the passage "Early Medicine" at the beginning of Part Two, reread the sentences with adjective clauses. Try to explain why commas are or are not used with each clause.

F. Exercise: In the following pairs of sentences, underline the adjective clause. Then indicate whether the clause gives essential or additional information. Next, add commas where necessary.

Example: Typhoid and cholera <u>,which have been common problems for thousands</u> <u>of years ,</u>have now disappeared from some areas.
(Additional information—commas are used.)

1. The bubonic plague which is a contagious disease is carried by rats.

2. This plague which was also called the "black death" killed half the population of Europe in the fourteenth century.

3. Physicians who treated plague victims never found a cure for the disease.

4. During the plague, many people who touched the sick or the dead died after a short time.

5. People who lived in major seaports were more likely to become plague victims.

6. Thousands of people died in Marseilles which was a major seaport.

G. Exercise: Combine the following sentences with *who, which,* or *whose.* Change the second sentence into an adjective clause. Be sure to use commas where necessary.

Example: Mumps and chicken pox are not treated with antibiotics. They are diseases caused by viruses. →
Mumps and chicken pox, which are diseases caused by viruses, are not treated with antibiotics.

1. Certain illnesses cannot be treated with antibiotics. These illnesses are caused by viruses.
2. The ordinary cold is a viral infection. The cold is our most common sickness.
3. A careful diet can be a good treatment for people. Their internal organs do not function properly.
4. People can be treated effectively with drugs. These people suffer from tuberculosis.
5. People must take hormone pills every day. Their thyroid glands have been removed.
6. Many people take vitamin C every day. These people are trying to avoid colds.
7. Antibiotics are chemicals. These chemicals are produced from microorganisms.
8. Antibiotics can kill or control some bacteria. Some bacteria causes diseases.
9. Sir Alexander Fleming received the Nobel Prize in 1945. He discovered penicillin.
10. Penicillin is perhaps the most valued medicine today. Penicillin stops the growth of many bacteria.

H. Activity: Giving Definitions. In small groups, test your skills at a vocabulary game. The object of this game is for one person to describe people, places, objects, ideas, and so forth. The other people in the group must guess who or what they are. In this version of the game, the clues must include adjective clauses with *that, who, which,* or *whose.*

Examples: s1: **I'm thinking of an instrument which is used to listen to a person's heart.**
　　　　　 s2: **A stethoscope.**
　　　　　 s1: **I'm thinking of a physician whose specialty is treating children.**
　　　　　 s2: **A pediatrician.**

PART THREE

ADJECTIVE CLAUSES WITH *THAT, WHICH,* AND *WHO(M)*: REPLACEMENT OF OBJECTS

What are "medical myths"? How do such myths originate? Share your opinions while answering the following questions about the picture below.

1.　What is shown in each part of the drawing?
2.　Does your culture have similar myths?

Medical Myths

In the past, people believed a number of medical myths that we laugh at today. During the Middle Ages, for example, many people believed the bubonic plague was caused by arrows that Christ had shot. In eighteenth-century England, even people whom others

considered sophisticated had faith in strange remedies. They believed they could cure an earache by sleeping with a roasted onion in the aching ear. The same people thought a growth on the eyelid could be cured by rubbing it with the tail of a male cat.

Since then, we have learned many things: bubonic plague is caused by bacteria, roasted onions cannot cure earaches, and cats do not cure growths. Nevertheless, there are a number of medical myths that people still believe today. There are many misconceptions about the common cold, for example. People believe they will catch a cold if they sit in a draft or become chilled. Yet, we know a cold is due to a virus which is passed on through personal contact with people who have the germ. There is no myth about this!

Discussing the Passage

1.   What are some ancient medical myths?
2.   What are some modern medical myths?
3.   Do you know of any others?

Adjective Clauses with *That, Which,* and *Who(m)*: Replacement of Objects

That, who(m), and *which* may replace objects. *Who(m)* refers to people and *which* to things or ideas. *That* refers to people, things, or ideas; it may only be used in restrictive clauses.

Two Simple Sentences

Many people believe in **predictions.** Astrologers make **them.**

One Complex Sentence with *That* or *Which*

Many people believe in predictions **that (which) astrologers make.**

Many people believe in predictions **astrologers make.**

That or *which* may replace an object of a verb to form an adjective clause. The connecting word is sometimes omitted in these clauses.

Two Simple Sentences

The woman believed **the astrologer.** She had consulted **the astrologer.**

One Complex Sentence with *Who(m)*

The woman believed the astrologer **who(m) she had consulted.**

The woman believed the astrologer **she had consulted.**

Who(m) replaces the object of a verb to form an adjective clause. *Whom* is correct in formal usage, but *who* is often used in conversation. Either may be omitted in conversational English.

A. Exercise: Underline the adjective clauses in the passage "Medical Myths" at the beginning of Part Three. Indicate whether the clause is restrictive or nonrestrictive. Also note whether the subject or the object of the original clause has been replaced.

B. Exercise: Combine the following either by inserting the adjective clause into the sentence or by putting it at the end of the sentence. Use commas where necessary.

Example: The color red was never used in sick rooms. (which people considered unlucky) →
The color red, which people considered unlucky, was never used in sick rooms.

1. Many societies have a spiritual healer or magician. (whom everyone asks for medical advice)
2. Medical practices differ from culture to culture. (that superstitious people believe in)
3. Copper bracelets are also worn as jewelry. (which many people wear to cure arthritis)
4. Amulets are necklaces. (which some people wear to prevent disease)
5. One belief is that chicken soup will cure any illness. (that many Europeans and Americans have)

C. Exercise: Combine the following sentences by using *that, who(m),* or *which* to form adjective clauses. Use commas where necessary.

Example: There are many medical myths. Even educated people believe them. →
There are many medical myths which (that) even educated people believe.

1. A common saying is "An apple a day keeps the doctor away." Mothers repeat this saying to their children.
2. Most of us think of doctors as special people. We can trust doctors with our most personal problems.
3. In many places, there are no doctors. Sick people can consult doctors.
4. In my town, there was one old woman. Everyone asked her about their health problems.
5. This woman always made herbal tea. She gave the tea to the sick.

D. Exercise: Use the following cues to form questions with adjective clauses beginning with *who(m)*, *which*, or *that*. Work in pairs and take turns asking and answering the questions.

Example: medicine / you take most often →
         S1: **What is the medicine that you take most often?**
         S2: **Aspirin.**

1. doctor / you usually visit when you're sick
2. foods / you eat when you have the flu
3. fruit / you eat most often
4. meat / you like the best
5. mineral / you should take when you feel tired
6. person / people in your family consult when they need medical advice
7. food / you eat to live a long life
8. food / people eat to have healthy hair and nails

E. Activity: Comparing Traditional Beliefs. Are there foods that people from your culture believe have special effects? For example, are there foods that make people live longer, have more children, see better, and so forth? Discuss these questions in small groups. Find out if there are foods that are recommended for a certain purpose in more than one culture. Does science support the idea that these foods are effective for these particular purposes?

F. Exercise: Following the example as a model, use the cues to write definitions. Add connecting words, articles, prepositions, and any other necessary expressions.

Example: flu / illness / many people get / in the winter →
         The flu is an illness that many people get in the winter.

1. sugar / food / people eat for quick energy
2. onion / food / some people eat to live longer
3. black / color / Western societies associate with death
4. mushrooms / plants / many people believe have mysterious powers
5. storks / birds / many children believe deliver babies
6. thirteen / number / many people believe is unlucky

G. Activity: Describing Myths and Superstitions. This activity concerns several "medical myths" and folk remedies that people have believed in. Look at the list of medical problems. Do you know any medical myths about their causes or cures? Where did you hear about them? In small groups, share your stories and information.

colds	skin rashes
flu	allergies
rheumatism	headaches
hiccups	depression

PART FOUR

ADJECTIVE CLAUSES WITH *WHEN* AND *WHERE*

What do you know about medical care in North America? Share your information while answering the following questions about the pictures below.

1. What is shown in each picture?
2. Why is hospital care so expensive today?

Changes in Medical Care

Medical care has changed greatly since the days when the family doctor treated all family members for every type of medical problem. Today's physician is usually a specialist who treats only problems within his or her specialty.

Today's specialists often work together in a large group in order to share costs. The group will buy expensive equipment for its own offices rather than use hospital facilities. The physician's office usually has a laboratory where a variety of medical tests can be done. So, unlike the family doctor, who often visited patients at home, today's doctors normally see patients in their offices, where they can use specialized equipment.

Likewise, many changes are taking place in hospitals, where the cost of medical equipment and care is skyrocketing. Because of the high costs, patients now spend a limited number of days in the hospital, depending on their illness. Even new mothers, who used to have a five-to-ten-day hospital stay after the birth of their babies, are now being sent home in twenty-four hours.

Medical technology certainly has led to great advances in the diagnosis and cure of many illnesses. However, some people want to bring back the good old days when the family physician was also a family friend.

Discussing the Passage

1. What was medical care like in the past? How is it different now?
2. What is one reason why medical care is changing?
3. Are these changes also taking place in your country or area? Why or why not?

Adjective Clauses with *When* and *Where*

When and *where* can introduce adjective clauses if they come after nouns. *When* usually modifies a noun that has the meaning of time or a time period. *Where* usually modifies a noun that has the meaning of a physical place or an abstract area or field.

Two Simple Sentences

The 1950s were a **time.** At that **time,** doctors still made house calls.

One Complex Sentence with *When*

The 1950s were a time **when doctors still made house calls.**

Two Simple Sentences

We can expect continued progress in **the medical field.**

New discoveries are made every day in **the medical field.**

One Complex Sentence with *Where*

We can expect continued progress in the medical field, **where new discoveries are made every day.**

A. Exercise: Combine the following sentences with *when* or *where*. Add commas where necessary.

Example: Treatments for cancer will be more effective in the future. In the future, scientists will know more about the body's immune system. →
Treatment for cancer will be more effective in the future, when scientists will know more about the body's immune system.

1. It's interesting to visit a hospital laboratory. In the laboratory, there is a lot of sophisticated equipment.
2. Teaching hospitals often have the most modern facilities. In these hospitals, new doctors are educated and trained.
3. We are now in an age. Medicine is very specialized.
4. The doctor's office is now a complicated place. In the doctor's office, many tests and even surgery can be performed.
5. Medicine will become a very competitive field in the future. In the future, there will be too many doctors in the United States.

B. **Exercise:** Complete the following sentences by adding adjective clauses with *when* or *where*.

Example: An intensive care unit is a place . . . →
  . . . where critically ill or injured patients are cared for.

1. A hospital is a place . . .
2. The emergency room is the place . . .
3. A laboratory is a place . . .
4. The twentieth century is a time . . .
5. The Middle Ages was a time . . .
6. Your visit to the doctor is the time . . .

C. **Exercise: Review of Adjective Clauses.** Complete the following passage about traditional medicine with the correct relative pronoun.

In most areas of the world, people ___*who*___ are sick are taken to a doctor or a hospital for treatment. But there are still many places _____ patients
1
 are taken instead to a local medicine man, or healer, _____ is a combina-
2
 tion of doctor, priest, and psychologist.

In Western thinking, disease is something _____ people regard as nat-
3
 ural. In tribal cultures, however, people consider illness an unnatural condition; it is a sign of deep anger, hatred, fear, or conflict. To discover the reason for an illness, a healer might use astrology or ask the patient about his dreams. Once the cause of illness is known, the patient may go to a healing shrine or temple,

_____ he cleans himself. After that, he returns to the healer,
4

_____ performs different ceremonies to chase the evil spirits out of the
5
 patient's body. The patient, _____ family also participates in the healing
6
 ceremony, may be put into a trance, _____ is a state of deep, unconscious
7
 concentration. While the patient is in the trance, the healer performs different ceremonies to chase the evil spirits out of the patient's body. Finally, the healer suggests changes _____ the person must make so that the disease does not
8
 return.

Why does tribal medicine work? There are several explanations. Perhaps it works because the people _____ participate in these ceremonies believe in
9
 its power. Or, it may work because the patient sees that all the people

_____ he cares about are involved in making him well. Another reason
                10
may be that the healing ceremonies produce chemical changes in the body

_____ then help to cure the disease. Finally, many of the plants
                11
_____ are used in these ceremonies are known to have healing powers.
                12
People _____ live in westernized societies may be able to learn a les-
               13
son from tribal medicine. In these times, _____ most people no longer
                                                          14
have a strong sense of faith or community, perhaps we need to examine more closely
some of the social and spiritual aspects of healing.

Eskimo drawing of evil spirit entering a house

D. Activity: Playing the Dictionary Game. You will need a dictionary for this
game. First, divide into groups of four. Take turns selecting a word from the dictionary. Choose a word no one in the group knows the meaning of. The person who
chooses the word writes the correct meaning on a piece of paper. The other people
write false definitions that they think "sound" real. Then the person who chose the
word reads all the definitions aloud (without laughing!). Each person in the group
votes for the definition he or she believes is correct. The object is to get your classmates to choose your definition rather than the correct one. You score one point for
every person who voted for your definition.

11

THE MEDIA

Common Uses of Infinitives, Gerunds, and Related Structures

GERUNDS

How has communication changed in the last one hundred years? Share your opinions and information while answering the following questions about the picture.

1. When did each of these scenes take place?
2. What are the people in each scene doing?

Reporting the News

Today newspapers, magazines, radio, and television share the responsibility of reporting the news to the public. However, communicating through printed and electronic media is a relatively new development. For centuries, the news traveled in a wide variety of ways. In Rome, in the fifth century B.C., for instance, Roman

298

barbers were the major sources of news. They reported on recent happenings as they were cutting people's hair. Later, Romans learned the news by reading hand-written reports that were posted on the walls of public buildings. In England and North America in the eighteenth century, the news was delivered by a town crier. His job was shouting out the latest news as he walked the city streets.

In less populated areas, news was often spread by "word of mouth" or other methods. In West Africa, for example, the news traveled from one village to another via the "talking drum." In North America, the American Plains Indians communicated over long distances by sending smoke signals back and forth over hills and plains.

Methods of reporting important events changed when people began printing daily newspapers. For a long time, newspapers were the chief medium for learning about the day's events. The transistor radio, however, revolutionized communication. Nowadays, listening to the latest news on the radio is an event that takes place in even the most remote corners of the world.

Discussing the Passage

1. Can you think of some other traditional ways of reporting news? Some modern methods?
2. How do you usually communicate with other people (letters, telephone, telegrams, etc.)? Why do you prefer these methods?

Gerunds and Infinitives

Gerunds and infinitives are verb forms that may be used in place of a noun or pronoun. This section presents common uses of gerunds; the following section presents common uses of infinitives. Compare:

	Examples	Notes
Noun **Gerund**	I like **books.** I like **reading.**	A gerund is the simple form of a verb + *ing.* See the end of Chapter 1 for spelling rules for *-ing* endings.
Noun **Infinitive**	I like **magazines.** I like **to read.**	An infinitive is *to* + the simple form of a verb.

Uses of Gerunds

Gerunds may replace nouns or pronouns as subjects, objects, or complements. *Not* is used before the gerund to form the negative.

Subject

Reporting the news is the job of television, radio, magazines, and newspapers.

Object of a Preposition

Most newspapers are interested in **reporting** the news accurately.

Object of a Verb

Reggie enjoys **working** for the evening paper.

Complement

His job is **researching** stories.

Negative Gerund

Many people complain about **not getting** accurate news.

Possessive with Gerund*

Reggie's (His) reporting is normally very accurate.

---

*In conversational English, nouns or object pronouns are sometimes used with gerunds instead of possessives. Compare:
   Formal: I don't like *John's (his)* saying that.
   Conversational: I don't like *John (him)* saying that.

A. Exercise: Reread the passage at the beginning of this section. Circle all the gerunds and determine their grammatical function in the sentence (subject, object, object of a preposition, or complement).

Gerunds After Prepositions

These are some common phrases with prepositions that are often followed by gerunds. See Chapter 1 and Chapter 5 for a review of prepositions and phrasal combinations with prepositions.

be accustomed to*	I'm **accustomed to reading** the paper every day.
be used to*	I'm **not used to reading** quickly in English.
look forward to*	I always **look forward to getting** news from home.
angry about	Lois was **angry about losing** her job as a reporter.
bored with (by)	She is **bored with living** in a small town.
certain of	She wasn't **certain of finding** another job.
concerned about	Lois's parents are **concerned about her leaving.**
excited about	She is **excited about moving** to New York.
happy about	Clark was **happy about receiving** her letter.
interested in	Several papers are **interested in hiring** her.
nervous about	The reporter was **nervous about writing** his first article.
responsible for	The publisher is **responsible for hiring** the newspaper staff.
satisfied with	Vince is not **satisfied with being** a sports reporter.
thrilled about (by)	Lois was **thrilled about getting** a job in New York.
believe in	The publisher **believes in publishing** accurate stories.
care about	The reporters **care about writing** good articles.
consist of	A reporter's job **consists of gathering** information and writing articles.
depend on	The reporter **depends on getting** accurate information.
dream about	Many writers **dream about becoming** famous.
insist on	The editor **insists on checking** all the facts.
succeed in	He finally **succeeded in getting** a job at the local paper.

---

*Do not confuse the preposition *to* in *be accustomed to, be used to,* and *look forward to* with the *to* in infinitives.

I am used to getting up early.
not: I am used to get up early.

take care of	As sports editor, he **takes care of checking** the sports section.
talk about	He's **talked about making** some changes.
think about	He's **thought about hiring** new people.
work (hard) at	He **works hard at including** different types of sports.
worry about	He **worries about having** enough variety in his section.

B. Exercise: Gerunds as Objects of Prepositions. Complete the sentences with the gerund forms of the verbs in parentheses.

Example: I finally succeeded in __*getting*__ (get) a job.

1. I'm looking forward to _____ (begin) my new job as a newspaper reporter.

2. I'm excited about _____ (work) for a major newspaper.

3. I'm nervous about _____ (make) mistakes.

4. A reporter must work at _____ (gather) information, _____ (check) all the facts, and _____ (write) a good article.

5. Reporters for major newspapers are used to _____ (work) long hours.

6. They are also accustomed to _____ (get) large salaries!

7. The editor's job consists of _____ (make) corrections, _____ (choose) which stories to print, and _____ (decide) what to put on each page.

8. Editors are also responsible for _____ (write) editorials.

C. **Exercise: Gerunds as Objects of Prepositions.** Complete the following sentences by adding gerunds. Choose from these verbs. In some cases, several choices are possible.

advertise	edit	manage
attract	gather	report
check	get	sell
deliver		

Example: The managing editor is responsible for **checking** all news stories.

1. His job consists of . . . all stories.
2. The advertising manager earns money for the paper by . . . ads.
3. Businesses attract new customers by . . . in the newspaper.
4. A reporter begins his work by . . . facts.
5. The business department is interested in . . . the budget.
6. The circulation department works at . . . new readers.
7. The paperboy is responsible for . . . the paper each day.
8. A sports writer takes care of . . . football games.
9. Newspaper readers are concerned about . . . accurate news.

D. **Exercise: Gerunds as Objects of Prepositions.** Complete the following passage with the missing prepositions and the gerund forms of the word(s) in parentheses. In some cases, you will not need to repeat a preposition that was already used.

Keeping Up on the News

Many people get bored *with (by)* *hearing* (hear) or *reading*

(read) long, detailed news reports. They believe that the media should enter-

tain. These people care only ＿＿＿＿＿＿ ＿＿＿＿＿＿ (listen) to music or
                              1   2

＿＿＿＿＿＿ (watch) entertainment programs.
     3

There are other people who really do care ＿＿＿＿＿＿ ＿＿＿＿＿＿ (be)
                                            4   5

informed; however, they don't have enough time to follow the news in detail. They

have to be satisfied ＿＿＿＿＿＿ ＿＿＿＿＿＿ (watch) the latest news on short
                        6   7

TV programs or ＿＿＿＿＿＿ (hear) ten-second items on the radio. They might
                    8

not be thrilled ＿＿＿＿＿＿ ＿＿＿＿＿＿ (get) such limited information, but
                    9   10

they have little choice.

Of course, some people insist _____ _____ (get) detailed news
                                    11   12
from various sources. They are not only used _____ _____ (read)
                                                    13   14
a morning newspaper, but they are also accustomed _____ _____
                                                          15   16
(receive) one or more news magazines in the mail. They worry _____
                                                                    17
_____ (get) accurate news and believe _____ _____ (be)
      18   19   20
well-informed. They feel each individual is responsible _____
                                                                21
_____ (know) what is happening in the world.
      22

...Our top story today: still no word on the kidnapping...

Common Verbs Often Followed by Gerunds

If a verb form follows these verbs, it must be the gerund form.

avoid	Some people **avoid writing** because it's difficult.
be worth	Good books **are worth reading.**
can't help	I **can't help worrying** about him.
consider	He **is considering applying** for a newspaper job.
enjoy	He **enjoys writing.**
finish	He's finally **finished writing** his first story.
imagine	Can you **imagine working** on a book?
involve	It would **involve doing** a lot of research.
miss	I would **miss having** free time.
spend time (hours, days, etc.)	I would rather **spend time doing** other things.

Common Verbs Often Followed by Either Gerunds or Infinitives (1)

Like gerunds, infinitives may be used as objects of verbs. Either a gerund object or an infinitive may follow these verbs with little or no difference in meaning.

begin	I've **begun understanding (to understand)** most news stories.
can't stand	I **can't stand reading (to read)** late at night.
continue	I've **continued reading (to read)** several papers.
dislike	He **dislikes reading (to read)** the paper.
hate	I **hate being (to be)** uninformed.
like	All of us **like spending (to spend)** hours with the Sunday paper.
love	My brother **loves reading (to read)** the comics first.
prefer	My sister **prefers reading (to read)** the editorial page.
start	I've **started reading (to read)** several different papers.

E. **Exercise: Gerunds as Objects of Verbs and Prepositions.** Complete the passage by adding gerunds; form them from the following list of verbs. In some cases, you'll need to use the same gerund more than once. Finally, mark any instances where either the gerund or the infinitive can be used.

advertise have mix read
buy look notice

When you pick up a newspaper, you can't help *noticing* the amount of

_____ . In fact, the typical newspaper today is 40 percent news and 60
      1

percent ads. At least half of the news is text, but the rest is usually pictures. If you

can't stand _____ at advertisements, read just the front page and the
              2

editorial pages! Normally, these are the only pages without ads.

Editors arrange the newspaper visually by _____ pictures and head-
                                              3

lines with advertisements. In this way, the newspaper does not look dull. Appar-

ently, few people like _____ newspapers without pictures or art work. In
                        4

general, people prefer _____ a lot of art work with the text because they
                        5

enjoy _____ at the pictures. According to marketing researchers, most
       6

people avoid _____ newspapers with "too much print." In fact, the major-
              7

ity of people who buy newspapers spend only a short time _____ the
                                                            8

articles.

F. Activity: Interviewing a Classmate. Using the following cues, interview one of your classmates about his or her newspaper-reading habits. Feel free to add questions besides the ones you form from the cues.

Examples: avoid / read / newspapers in English →
Do you avoid reading newspapers in English?

1. enjoy / read / newspaper / in the morning
2. how much time / spend / read / paper
3. when you are on vacation / miss / read / local paper
4. like / read / the comics
5. prefer / buy / morning paper / or / afternoon paper
6. begin / read / English newspaper / regularly
7. ever / consider / become / journalist

G. Activity: Solving Problems. Imagine that you work for a local newspaper. The paper is in serious financial trouble and may go bankrupt. Some of the problems include: few human-interest stories, boring comics, little advertising, poor circulation, no home delivery, and little material of interest to young people. In small groups, try to find possible ways to save the newspaper and your jobs. Complete the following sentences with gerund phrases and add sentences of your own. Finally, choose one member of your group to report to the class on your recommendations.

In my opinion, people don't like . . .
People are (not) interested in . . .
Our readers are bored with . . .
People enjoy . . .
We should consider . . .
Everyone will have to work hard at . . .
If we don't find a solution, we'll all have to get used to . . .
I don't look forward to . . .

PART TWO

INFINITIVES

Do you know much about moving making? Share your information while answering the following questions about the picture below.

1. What is happening in the picture?
2. What are the responsibilities of the various people shown?

Making Movies

For centuries, people such as Leonardo Da Vinci dreamed about "photographing" objects in motion. Finally, in the twentieth century, inventors succeeded in developing a movie camera.

Leland Stanford was one of the first people to experiment with movement and pictures. Because he wanted to study the motion of a running horse, Stanford asked a friend to take a series of photographs of one. He hoped to find out if the horse ever managed to have all four feet off the ground at the same time. To prove new theories is often difficult, and Stanford's project wasn't easy to do. His photographer needed to use twenty-four cameras set close to each other to take pictures one after the other. After developing the pictures, he was able to report that a running horse did not, in fact, touch the ground at all times.

Later, the inventor Thomas Edison asked Stanford to show him the pictures and to introduce him to the photographer. During this meeting, Edison began to develop his ideas for the first motion-picture camera. It wasn't difficult to interest others in Edison's work. Soon, many kinds of cameras were invented, and within twenty years, filmmaking was a major industry.

Discussing the Passage

1. Who were some important people in the development of the movie camera?
2. What were some important steps in the history of filmmaking?

Uses of Infinitives

Infinitives may replace nouns as objects of verbs and as subjects. They often follow the *anticipatory it* as the subject of a sentence. Infinitives may also be used to show the purpose of an action. In these cases, *in order* is sometimes used before the infinitive. *Not* is used before the infinitive to form the negative. *For* + a noun or object pronoun is often used with an infinitive.

Subject

To make a good movie is not easy.

With *It*

It is difficult **to make** a good movie.

Object of a Verb*

I've always wanted **to learn** more about films.

Infinitive of Purpose

I am taking classes (**in order**) **to learn** more about filmmaking. **To begin,** I've enrolled in three classes.

Negative Infinitive

One of the most important things is **not to shake** the camera.

***For* + Noun or Pronoun**

It's difficult **for me to hold** the camera steady.

A. Exercise: Reread the opening passage. Underline all the infinitives and discuss their grammatical functions.

---

*An infinitive is never used as the object of a preposition. Compare:

      Practice is necessary for learning a new skill.
not: Practice is necessary for to learn a new skill.

B. Exercise: Use infinitives to complete the following passage about the first motion picture. Choose from these simple forms:

attract   go   see
be   keep   study
create   learn   watch

It is interesting _to study_ the history of today's motion-picture industry. In order _____ about its beginnings, we have _____ to New Jer-
₁   ₂
sey in the year 1891. There, at Thomas Edison's workshop, the first movie audience got the opportunity _____ a film of a man bowing to the audience. The
₃
viewers were thrilled _____ able _____ the first movie actor
₄   ₅
smiling, waving, and taking off his hat. Although this first movie was thrilling, it did not contain enough _____ the audience interested for very long.
₆
_____ audiences, moviemakers soon needed _____ film that
₇   ₈
actually told a story.

C. Exercise: Complete the sentences about early movies. Use all of the following.

be   make   take charge
control   produce   view
go   see   watch

Example: In the early days, moviegoers were able _to view_ only short comedies or "newsreels."

1. People liked _____ to the movies because they showed another world.

2. It was thrilling (and frightening) _____ a train thundering toward you on the screen.

3. It was exciting for the audience _____ a "good guy" defeat a "bad guy."

4. In the early days, the actors, actresses, artists, and writers all expected _____ able _____ the content of the films they were making.

5. Later, because of rising costs and competition from radio, bankers began _____ of films.

6. Bankers and businesspeople wanted _____ money-making films.

7. They learned _____ the same types of film again and again because these types were always money-makers.

D. Exercise: Without changing the meaning, rewrite the paragraph by replacing each gerund with an infinitive. Use the *anticipatory it* whenever possible.

Example: Creating new films took a few years. →
It took a few years to create new films.

   After Edison's first movie, creating new films took a few years. The Lumière brothers showed the next motion pictures in 1896. Producing good-quality images was impossible at that time, so the pictures were "jumpy." Also, making films of any length was very difficult, so the Lumière brothers' three "movies" were only 30 to 90 seconds long. Yet watching them was probably a thrilling experience for those early audiences. In the twentieth century, presenting an interesting story became important. Soon, entertaining audiences was the purpose of movies.

Common Verbs Often Followed by Infinitives

If a verb form is used after the verbs below, it must be in the infinitive form.

Verb + Infinitive

These verbs may be followed directly by an infinitive.

agree	My friend **agreed to take** a film class with me.
be (able)	I **was able to find** several good film classes.
decide	I **decided to take** several classes.
fail	My friend **failed to enroll** in time.
forget	He **forgot to enroll** before the first of the month.
have	All students **had to enroll** before the first of the month.
hope	My friend **hopes to take** a class next semester.
know how	I don't **know how to use** a movie camera.
learn (how)	Last night we **learned (how) to load** the film.
manage	Several people **managed to ruin** their films.
offer	The teacher **offered to help.**
plan	I **plan to be** very careful with my camera.
seem	You **seem to be** happy with your new hobby.
wait	I can't **wait to buy** a new camera.

Verb + (Noun or Pronoun) + Infinitive

These verbs may be followed directly by an infinitive, or they may use a (pro)noun object before the infinitive. *Note: For* is not used in this pattern.

ask	I **asked to enroll** in the class.
	I **asked my friend to enroll** in the class.
expect	I **expect to learn** a great deal about early films.
	My teacher **expects me to learn** a great deal.
need	I **need to buy** some film.
	I **need you to buy** some film for me.
promise	We **promised to do** all of the work.
	We **promised our teacher to do** all of the work.
want	I **want to help.**
	I **want you to help.**
would like	I **would like to help.**
	I **would like you to help.**

Verb + Noun or Pronoun + Infinitive

When these verbs are in the active voice, they are not directly followed by an infinitive. A (pro)noun object *must* come before the infinitive. When they are in the passive voice, they may be directly followed by an infinitive. *Note: For* is not used in this pattern.

advise	I **advise you to take** some classes.
convince	A friend **convinced me to enroll** in three classes.
encourage	A friend **encouraged me to buy** a new camera.
force	My budget **forced me to buy** a used camera.
invite	I **invited my friend to attend** a film class with me.
remind	The teacher **reminded us to bring** our cameras.
teach	The teacher **taught us to focus** carefully.
tell	The teacher **told us to adjust** the lights.

E.   Exercise: Decide if the following verbs can be used in patterns A, B, or C.

   A.   He . . . to go to the movies.
   B.   He . . . John to go to the movies.
   C.   Either is possible.

Example: hope →
   Hope is possible only in A.

1.	tell	5.	agree	9.	invite
2.	expect	6.	plan	10.	promise
3.	advise	7.	forget	11.	encourage
4.	ask	8.	want	12.	offer

F.   Exercise: In pairs, ask and answer questions using the following cues. Add a noun or pronoun object when necessary.

Example: advise / not to see *Snake Pit* →
   S1: **Have you advised John not to see *Snake Pit*?**
   S2: **Yes, I advised him not to see *Snake Pit*.**

1. tell / see *Star Wars*
2. remind / not use the free tickets until next week
3. encourage / watch French films
4. invite / come with us Saturday
5. convince / not go out Wednesday
6. promise / not cry during the movie
7. ask / go to see *Dracula*

G. **Exercise:** Complete the following passage by putting the words in parentheses in the correct form and order. Change the appropriate verb to an infinitive.

The first films that *managed to tell* (tell / manage) a story were George Méliès' *A Trip to the Moon* and Edwin S. Porter's *The Life of an American Fireman* and *The Great Train Robbery*. Moviemakers _____

_____ (audiences / expect / enjoy) these early motion pictures, although they
₁

lasted only ten minutes and were actually quite boring. Soon, however, audiences

_____ (producers / ask / make) more interesting
₂

films. People _____ (want / see) short comedies or
₃

newsreels when they _____ (plan / go) to a movie.
₄

Before long, audiences _____ (begin / demand)
₅

even more. They _____ (show / producers / expect)
₆

them a fantasy world in their films. Viewers _____
₇

(create / encourage / moviemakers) illusions on the screen.

Infinitives with *Too* and (*Not*) *Enough*

Adjectives or noun phrases + infinitives are often used in expressions with *too* and (*not*) *enough*. *For* + (pro)noun is often added for clarity.

	Examples	Notes
too	The movie was **too** long (for us) **to sit** through.	*Too* often implies a negative result: *The movie was very long, so we didn't sit through it.*
enough	The film was good **enough** (for me) **to watch** five times.	*Enough* often implies a positive result: *The film was good, so I watched it five times.*
not enough	There weren't **enough people in the audience to show** the movie.	*Not enough* often implies a negative result: *There weren't many people, so they didn't show the movie.*

H. Exercise: Complete the following passage with the infinitive form of the verbs in parentheses and *too* or *enough*.

In the early twentieth century, the motion-picture industry moved to California for one simple reason. The weather in the East was _*too*_ unpredictable _*to make*_ (make) movies outdoors. In the West, however, there was _____ sun year-round _____ (light) the scenes. In those days, technology was not advanced _____ _____ (provide) adequate lighting for indoor scenes. Thus, even indoor scenes were filmed outside in the sun. Unfortunately, the illusion did not work. Outdoor light was _____ strong _____ (seem) like indoor light. Finally, indoor film lighting was invented.

Nevertheless, indoor lighting did not solve all problems. A few important ones remained. For instance, it was _____ hot _____ (use) certain objects under the lights, so substitutions had to be made (for example, mashed potatoes for ice cream). The lights also made some actors _____ uncomfortable _____ (work) effectively.

I. Exercise: Change the following sentences to use *too* or *(not) enough* with infinitives and *for* + (pro)noun where necessary.

Example: The weather in the East was unpredictable, so filmmakers couldn't work outdoors regularly. →
The weather in the East was too unpredictable for filmmakers to work outdoors regularly.

1. In the East, there wasn't very much sunlight in the winter, so producers couldn't film outdoors.
2. In California, there was sun year-round; therefore, producers could make films without worrying about weather.
3. Soon the technology of indoor lighting became more advanced, so filmmakers could begin shooting films inside.
4. The first indoor film lights were so hot that actors couldn't work for long periods of time.
5. Many actors felt so uncomfortable that they couldn't perform well.
6. Some early movies were very good, so people still enjoy them today.
7. Today film technology is very advanced; therefore, we can shoot pictures anywhere, anytime.
8. A few movies are extremely popular, so they bring in millions of dollars in profits.
9. Other movies aren't successful; therefore, they cannot even cover the costs of making them.
10. Some movies would be very expensive, so they are never made.

Infinitives of Purpose

Infinitives can be used to tell why an action is performed. These infinitives may appear at various points within a sentence.

Examples	Meanings
(In order) To create the illusion of blood, filmmakers used chocolate syrup in black and white films.	These infinitive phrases often begin with *in order to*. However, *in order* is not necessary to give this meaning.
Chocolate syrup was used in black and white films **to create** the illusion of blood.	Infinitives of purpose are often used at the beginning of a sentence or after the verb (and direct object).

J. Exercise: Match the events in Column A with their purposes in Column B. Then make the items in Column B into infinitive phrases. Finally, make new sentences by combining the items in Column A with the phrases in Column B.

Examples: **In black and white films, producers used chocolate syrup to produce the illusion of blood.** *or*

To produce the illusion of blood in black and white films, producers used chocolate syrup.

A	**B**
1. In black and white films producers used chocolate syrup.	a. It created an illusion of blood in color films.
2. Red food dye was used.	b. The wires connect the packets to a computer.
3. In old westerns, actors would hit a place on their shirts.	c. It explodes the packet at exactly the right time.
4. Nowadays, packets of blood have small wires in them.	d. It produced the illusion of blood.
5. The computer is programmed.	e. They broke a hidden packet of "blood."

K. Activity: Describing Trends. In pairs or small groups, share information about movies in North America and in your country. What kinds of movies are being produced today? What kinds of movies make a lot of money for the producers? What kinds of movies do people like to watch? As you discuss current trends in filmmaking and in audience preferences, try to use as many of the following expressions as possible.

Today, movies seem . . .	Audiences usually prefer . . .
People in my culture (don't) enjoy . . .	Most people would like . . .
They like . . .	It's (more) exciting . . .
They can't stand . . .	Films today are too . . .
It's boring . . .	It's (not) worth . . .
They're used to . . .	

PART THREE

INFINITIVES VERSUS GERUNDS

What do you know about radios and communication? Share your information while answering the following questions about the picture.

1. What sort of equipment is shown in each picture?
2. What is it used for?

Radio

Like the film business, radio communication seemed to grow overnight. Within a few years, radio developed from an experimental idea into a useful piece of equipment and a huge industry. Today radio technology plays a very important role in many aspects of our lives.

Radio technology is used in a wide variety of ways. The most common is, of course, commercial broadcasting. Radio also has many specialized uses. For example, teletype-writer signals are sent by transmitting radio waves. Another form of radio is radar. Objects of all kinds may be located with radar, which is frequently used for both civilian and military purposes. Armies use short-wave radio to coordinate their activities. Likewise, many political groups have tried to organize their resistance by operating a network of radio communications. Because of the effectiveness of such communication, some governments have stopped allowing private use of radio.

A more common (and less controversial) use of radio is to send and receive emergency information. Professionals such as doctors often carry "walkie talkies" or "beepers." If a hospital needs to contact a doctor, radio waves can be used to signal him or her. In this way, the doctor can be certain of getting emergency calls at any time or place.

Nowadays few people can remember not having radios, and it's difficult to imagine getting along without the benefits of radio technology. Certainly if radio did not exist, we would all miss being entertained and informed by the music, news, and other programs that have come over its waves.

Discussing the Passage

1. What are the major uses of radio? Which do you think are most important?
2. Can you think of other uses of radio?

A. **Exercise:** Reread the opening passage. Circle all the gerunds and underline all the infinitives. Pay special attention to the verbs that are used with both the infinitives and the gerunds.

B. **Exercise: Contrast of Infinitives and Gerunds.** Using the verbs in parentheses, complete the sentences with either infinitives or gerunds. In some cases, either may be possible.

1. In 1920, station KDKA started *transmitting (to transmit)* (transmit) in Pittsburgh, Pennsylvania.

2. By the end of 1922, over 500 radio stations had begun _____ _____ (broadcast) around the United States.

3. The first stations were created by radio equipment companies in order _____ (develop) a market for their products.

4. These companies were concerned about _____ (sell) more radio equipment to stations, and they also wanted _____ (tell) the public about their products.

5. Soon many types of companies were interested in _____ (advertise) their products, so radio stations decided _____ (sell) "air time."

6. Early commercials were very long. In some cases, an announcer would spend ten minutes _____ (encourage) people _____ (buy) cosmetics or _____ (rent) an apartment.

7. Radio became popular very quickly. People throughout the United States dreamed about _____ (have) a radio, and by 1930 12,000,000 Americans had managed _____ (buy) a set.

8. People everywhere enjoyed _____ (listen) to the early radio programs.

9. Americans were thrilled about _____ (be) able _____ (hear) performers like Al Jolson or Amos and Andy in their own homes.

10. People also loved _____ (follow) radio melodramas and looked forward to _____ (hear) their favorite "soap opera" every night.

C. **Exercise: Contrast of Infinitives and Gerunds.** Complete the following passage with infinitive or gerund forms of the verbs in parentheses. In some cases, both may be possible.

Although many radio listeners dislike *hearing (to hear)* (hear) commercials, few noncommercial stations exist in the United States. It is difficult for these stations _____ (survive) because, financially, they have
1
_____ (depend) on _____ (receive) dona-
2   3
tions from their listeners. Sometimes listener-sponsored stations succeed

in _____ (raise) large amounts of money, but often they
4
fail _____ (get) enough funds _____ (cover)
5   6
their budgets. Managers of these stations constantly worry about

_____ (have) enough money _____ (pay)
7   8
their employees and their bills. In fact, financial problems have forced many

listener-sponsored stations _____ (begin)
9
_____ (sell) air time for _____ (advertise).
10   11
As a result, the only major commercial-free station in the United States is

National Public Radio, which receives funds from the U.S. government, in

addition to donations from its listeners.

D. **Exercise: Contrast of Infinitives and Gerunds.** When did you last listen to the radio? Did you listen to the news or weather? Did you hear a commercial? Tell about the radio broadcast by completing the following sentences. Include either an infinitive or a gerund phrase in each sentence.

1. The weatherperson advised people . . .
2. It (the weather) should continue . . .
3. The newscaster said that the government plans . . .
4. The government will avoid . . .
5. The president (governor, mayor, etc.) hopes . . .
6. He or she expects . . .
7. The sportscaster was excited (nervous, angry) about . . .
8. The sportscaster reminded people . . .
9. The commercial tried to convince me . . .
10. It encouraged me . . .

Common Verbs Often Followed by Infinitives or Gerunds (2)

In Part One you saw that some verbs can take either an infinitive or a gerund object with little or no change in meaning. The following verbs may take either an infinitive or a gerund object, but the meaning of the verb changes, depending on which is used.

	Examples	**Notes**
Infinitives with *Remember*	Did you **remember to buy** the tickets?	*Remember* tells the first (or earlier) action, and the infinitive tells the second (or later) action.
Gerunds with *Remember*	I **remember telling** you about that.	The gerund tells the first (or earlier) action, and *remember* tells the second (or later) action.
Infinitives with *Try*	I **tried to buy** several tickets.	When *try* is followed by an infinitive, it means "attempt."
Gerunds with *Try*	I **tried calling** the theater, **going** to the box office, and **asking** all my friends for extra tickets.	When *try* is followed by a gerund, it means "experiment with different possibilities or alternatives."
Infinitives with *Quit* **and** *Stop*	He **stopped to have** coffee. He **stopped** at Mary's house **(in order) to have** coffee.	When an infinitive follows *stop* or *quit* it means that the subject stopped whatever he or she was doing for the reason or purpose given by the infinitive. *In order* can usually be added: *in order to have coffee.*
Gerunds with *Quit* **and** *Stop*	He **stopped (quit) having** coffee because it made him very nervous. He drinks juice, instead.	When a gerund follows these verbs, it tells "who" or "what" was stopped—often a habit or custom that had existed for a long time.

E. Exercise: Complete the following passage with infinitive or gerund forms of the verbs in parentheses.

When I was a child, we had a radio, but we didn't have a T.V. set. The radio was important to our family life. I remember *sitting* (sit) down in the living room after dinner to listen to the evening news. We always remembered _____ (turn) on the radio when there were important events in the world,
₁
and I remember _____ (look) forward to family evenings when we
₂
listened to our favorite comedy or quiz shows. When it was time for them, we stopped _____ (work) or _____ (read) to concentrate on the
₃   ₄
programs. We each tried _____ (sit) in the chair closest to the radio. I also
₅
remember _____ (get) upset whenever the radio wasn't working well. We
₆
tried _____ (fix) it ourselves, but sometimes we couldn't. Then we had to
₇
stop _____ (have) our evenings around the radio until we could get it to a
₈
repair shop. We tried _____ (talk) to one another or _____
₉   ₁₀
(play) games, but we all missed the radio entertainment. Then, a few years later, we bought our first television set. Gradually, we stopped _____ (listen)
₁₁
to radio programs on a regular basis.

F. Exercise: Contrast of Infinitives and Gerunds. Rephrase the following people's opinions by completing the sentences. Use infinitive or gerund phrases in your new sentences.

1. This woman enjoys . . .
2. She's looking forward to . . .
3. She encourages everyone . . .
4. She would like . . .

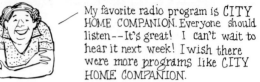 My favorite radio program is CITY HOME COMPANION. Everyone should listen—It's great! I can't wait to hear it next week! I wish there were more programs like CITY HOME COMPANION.

5. This man avoids . . .
6. He prefers . . .
7. He plans . . .

I don't like sports on radio. TV's much better. Tonight there's a great baseball game on the tube.

8. These girls are interested in . . .
9. They spend a lot of time . . .
10. For the girls, it's fun . . .
11. According to their mother, the radio is too loud . . .
12. According to the girls, they're used to . . .

 We always listen to the TOP FORTY so we know the most popular songs. Our mom always complains about the volume. She says the radio is so loud that she can't think. We like loud music—it doesn't bother us.

G. Activity: Persuading. Individually, in pairs, or in small groups, create your own commercial or political advertisement. In either case, you will try to convince your audience to do something. Use as many expressions with infinitives and gerunds as possible in your ad. Finally, perform your ads for the class.

Example: **Homemakers everywhere! Do you want to avoid ironing hundreds of shirts each year? Can you imagine not having to iron another shirt again? Then buy . . .**

H. Activity: Conducting a Talk Show. Many radio stations have talk shows that give advice or information on a wide variety of topics. Conduct a talk show in your class, taking turns being the host of the show, the guest speaker(s), and radio listeners. The guest speakers may want to "be" counselors, political figures, or "experts" on dating, sports, etc. If possible, make arrangements with your local phone company to use a Telezonia Telephone Kit for your "radio" listeners to call in on. (Just ask the telephone company about this.)

Example: **"Hello, Linda Lovelorn? I would like to get your advice on how to meet women and have more dates. . ."**
"Well, if you want to have a date every night, I advise you to learn how to dance. Women everywhere love to dance, but most men are too embarrassed to learn well. A man who knows how to dance well. . ."

PART FOUR

CAUSATIVE AND STRUCTURALLY RELATED VERBS; VERBS OF PERCEPTION

How do televisions work? Share your information while answering the following questions about the picture below.

1. Describe the process of sending a television picture.
2. Describe the process of receiving a television picture.

Television

Television broadcasting began in the United States and England in 1926. Radio stations let the scientists who were experimenting with television use their radio transmitting equipment for these early broadcasts, which lasted only a few minutes and did not include sound. Early broadcasters had difficulty getting investors to support their experiments because few people believed at the time that television had any future.

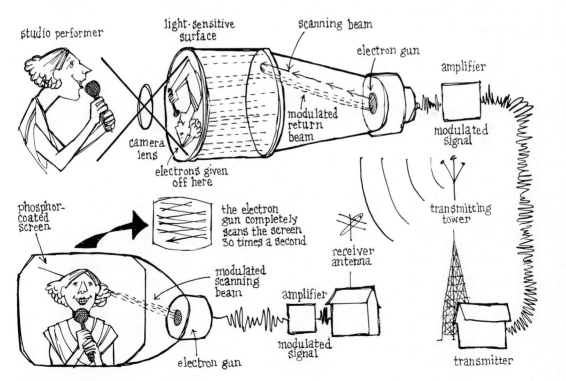

Obviously, T.V. did have a future, and today life without television is almost unimaginable. Television provides us with entertainment and lets us know what is happening around the world. For example, we can watch an orchestra performing in Rome or see athletes swimming in Moscow. Television also educates; it has helped people to learn everything from languages to cooking, and it has gotten all of us to experience new things, ideas, places, and people without even leaving our living rooms.

But television may also affect us negatively. For example, it has been suggested that violent T.V. programs might make some people go out and commit similar violent acts. Many parents also worry that watching a lot of television may make their children become passive. As a result of these concerns, some governments have tried to have T.V. viewing limited. Various countries, for instance, do not let television stations broadcast during daylight hours. Naturally, some people are angry about having their freedom of choice limited in this way.

Discussing the Passage

1. What are some positive and negative effects of T.V.?
2. In your opinion, should governments regulate how much T.V. people can watch?

Causative and Structurally Related Verbs

The verbs *get, have, help, let,* and *make* are often called "causatives." They are followed by a direct object and then an infinitive, a simple form (the infinitive without *to*), or a past participle.

	Active Sentences	Passive Sentences	Notes
Get **Have**	I **got** him **to wash** the car. I **had** him **wash** the car.	I **got** the car **washed.** I **had** the car **washed.**	*Get* and *have* are similar in meaning: "arrange for." Note that *get* is followed by an infinitive in the active form.
Help	I **helped** him **wash** the car. *or* I **helped** him **to wash** the car.		*Help* means "aid" or "assist." Note that *help* can be followed by the simple form or the infinitive of a second verb.
Let **Make**	I **let** him **wash** the car. I **made** him **wash** the car.		*Let* means "allow." *Make* is similar in meaning to "force."

A. Exercise: Appliances and other machines often break down. Using the cues, suggest solutions for the following common problems. Use modal auxiliaries (*ought to, should, could,* etc.) and the causative verb *have* in your suggestions.

Example: The picture on my television set is very poor.
television / repair
picture tube / replace →
You should have your television repaired.
You could have the picture tube replaced.

1. My television set isn't working well.
   T.V. / fix
   antenna / install
2. The sound on my stereo is very poor.
   stereo / repair
   speakers / replace
   wiring / check
3. The lights go out when I use more than one major electric appliance at the same time.
   house / rewire
   new fuse box / put in
4. My car isn't running well.
   engine / tune
   oil / check
   spark plugs / replace

B. Exercise: In pairs, form questions and answers using *get.* Follow the example.

Example: car / wash →
S1: **Do you normally wash your car yourself?**
S2: **No, normally, I get my car washed.**

1. typewriter / clean
2. hair / cut
3. suits / dry-clean
4. piano / tune
5. watch / repair
6. computer / fix

C. Exercise: Which of the following things did your parents let you do when you were fifteen years old? Compare your answers with those of your classmates.

Example: drive the car →
When I was fifteen years old, my parents wouldn't let me drive the car.

1. watch television until midnight during the week
2. go out alone in the evening
3. stay home from school if I felt like it
4. choose my own clothes
5. drink wine with dinner

D. Activity: Discussing Rights. In your opinion, which of the following things do governments have the right to make people do? Compare your opinions with those of your classmates.

Examples: limit the number of children people have →
In my opinion, governments do not have the right to make people limit the number of children they have.

1. serve in the military
2. pay taxes
3. vote
4. wear seat belts in the car
5. quit smoking in public places

E. Exercise: Two local television executives are discussing a change in sports programming. Complete their conversation by using *get, let, make,* or *have.* In some cases, more than one verb may be appropriate.

JACK: People have stopped watching our Saturday afternoon sports show. How can we ____*get*____ more viewers to watch on Saturdays? Perhaps we should offer different sports programs. I think everyone is tired of football and baseball.

ANDERS: I think we should _____ our viewers decide which sports we televise. Why don't we _____ our viewing audience write us letters?
₁
₂

JACK: We've already received a lot of letters requesting more soccer games on T.V. Do you think we can _____ the national T.V. networks to broadcast more soccer matches? How can we _____ them understand that people want more soccer on T.V.? The national networks think that soccer has only a few fans. How can we _____ them change their minds?

ANDERS: That will be difficult. Well, here's an idea. Let's _____ our viewing audience to write letters to the national networks, too!

Verbs of Perception

The verbs *feel, hear, listen to, look at, see, smell,* and *watch* can be followed by a second verb. Depending on the meaning, the second verb can be a present participle or the simple form. A noun or object pronoun is used after the main verb.

	Examples	Notes
Simple Form	I saw **them film** the commercial. I heard **them discuss** the price.	In most cases, there is little difference in meaning between the simple form and present participle. The simple form can imply that the action was completed, however.
Present Participle	I saw **them filming** the commercial. I heard **them discussing** the price.	The present participle may refer to an action in progress. This sentence means "I saw them *while* they were filming the commercial."

F. **Exercise:** Complete the following passage with the present participles or simple forms of the verbs in parentheses. Be prepared to discuss any difference in meaning when both forms are possible.

Most of us have been watching entertainers *perform (performing)* (perform) on T.V. for most of our lives. We have listened to musicians

_____ (sing) or _____ (play) instruments,
1   2

have seen dancers _____ (move) to music, and have heard actors
3

and actresses _____ (say) their lines. We have probably learned
4

a lot from television programming.

Our children are also learning a lot from television, but what exactly are they

learning? Many people are afraid that children are learning violence. Children

today spend hours watching actors _____ (be) hurt or killed.
5

They see and hear people _____ (fight),
6

_____ (hit) each other, _____ (shoot) guns,
7   8

and _____ (use) other weapons.
9

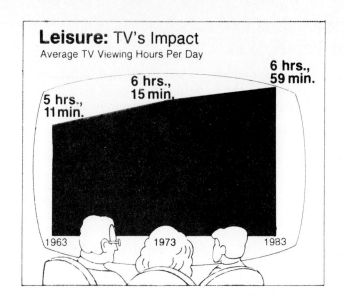

Because of the types of programs on T.V. today, some parents believe that we should not let our children _____ (watch) whatever they want
                                                                    10
on T.V. Instead, we should help them _____ (choose) valuable
                                                              11
shows and make them _____ (think) and
                                                12
_____ (talk) about what they have seen.
           13

G. **Exercise:** Imagine that you could visit the filming of your favorite television show. Describe your visit by completing the following, telling everything you saw, heard, etc.

Example: I saw the stagehands . . . →
              I saw the stagehands setting up the scenery.

1. I saw cameramen and women . . .
2. I heard the director . . .
3. I watched the actors and actresses . . .
4. I listened to the stars . . .
5. I heard the studio audience . . .
6. I watched my favorite actor (actress) . . .
7. I looked at the crowd of fans . . .
8. I felt my heart . . .

H. Exercise: Review of Gerunds and Infinitives. Complete the following passage about television transmission with either gerund or infinitive forms of the verbs in parentheses.

Scientists know how _____ (transmit) T.V. pictures from the moon

1

to earth. But within the earth's atmosphere, we have learned _____

2

(send) a T.V. picture only a short distance. Most stations are able

_____ (transmit) just a little beyond the horizon—as seen from the

3

transmitter.

Very high frequency T.V. waves travel in straight lines. They continue

_____ (travel) right out into space, or they strike the earth and are

4

absorbed. Thus, stations need _____ (build) high antennas in order

5

_____ (transmit) over long distances.

6

For _____ (transmit) over very long distances, T.V. stations use

7

either cables or microwave relay stations, depending on the landscape. Stations

prefer _____ (use) microwave relay when there are mountains

8

or large bodies of water to be crossed. In cities or across level areas, it is easier

_____ (use) cables.

9

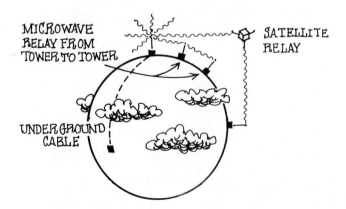

TELEVISION TRANSMISSION

I. **Exercise: Review of Gerunds, Infinitives, and Related Structures.** Fill in the blanks with the correct forms of the verbs in parentheses. In some cases there may be two correct answers.

This is the story of a family that did a very unusual thing: They decided

_____ (stop) _____ (let) television _____
　　　　1　　　　　　　　　　　　　　2　　　　　　　　　　　　　　　　3

(control) their lives. In fact, they agreed _____ (not watch) television
　　　　　　　　　　　　　　　　　　　　　　　　　4

at all for a while. How did they make this decision?

It was dinnertime on a typical day. Jane Wilkins was starting

_____ (prepare) dinner for her family. She could hear the evening
　　　　5

news _____ (blare) in the next room. Suddenly, there was a loud
　　　　　6

BOOM! Then silence. The television set had fallen on the floor and broken.

The Wilkins family had been accustomed to _____ (watch) televi-
　　　　　　　　　　　　　　　　　　　　　　　　　　　　　7

sion four or five hours every day. It was normal for them _____ (eat)
　　　　　　　　　　　　　　　　　　　　　　　　　　　　　　　　8

or _____ (do) homework in front of the T.V. But now the T.V. was bro-
　　　　9

ken. Jane Wilkins had a thought: What would their family life be like if they didn't

have the T.V. _____ (fix)?
　　　　　　　　　10

She remembered that when her children were little, they all used to

_____ (take) walks and play together. She had enjoyed
　　　　11

_____ (read) to her children. It also seemed that she and her hus-
　　　　12

band had spent a lot more time _____ (talk).
　　　　　　　　　　　　　　　　　　　13

Jane thought it would be worth _____ (try) to go a week without
　　　　　　　　　　　　　　　　　　　　　14

_____ (watch) T.V. When she suggested this to her husband and
　　　　15

children, they agreed _____ (do) it. During the week, the family did
　　　　　　　　　　　　　16

things together. Jane was thrilled about _____ (have) time to be with
　　　　　　　　　　　　　　　　　　　　　　　17

her husband and children again. At the end of the week, the family had another

meeting, where they decided _____ (try) another week without T.V.
　　　　　　　　　　　　　　　　　　18

One of the children said, "I thought I would miss _____ (watch) T.V.
　　　　　　　　　　　　　　　　　　　　　　　　　　　19

every day. But I don't. _____ (not watch) television lets me
　　　　　　　　　　　　　　　20

_____ (have) more free time for other things. I really like that."
　　　21

J. Activity: Expressing Opinions. What do you think about the types of programs shown on North American T.V.? On T.V. in your area or country? What would you change? What would you offer more or less of? In pairs, small groups, or as a class, share your opinions by completing the following sentences. Be sure to add original sentences, too.

> I (don't) like . . .
> I (don't) enjoy . . .
> Personally, when I turn on the T.V., I (don't) want to watch actors and
>   actresses . . .
> I prefer (not) . . .
> It's (not) good . . .
> I would have networks . . .
> In my opinion, the government should(n't) let . . .
> It should(n't) make T.V. networks . . .
> It's important . . .

Then, as a group, write a letter to the local station telling them what you like (that they already do) and what other programs you would like to see in the future.

12

PREJUDICE, TOLERANCE, AND JUSTICE

Hope, Wish, and Conditional Sentences

PART ONE

HOPE AND *WISH*

What are human rights? Do you know about any international organizations that work for human rights? Share your knowledge as you answer the following questions about the picture.

1. What does UNESCO mean?
2. What kind of work do you think it does?
3. Who pays for this work?

Peace Organizations

Most of us wish that we could end war, poverty, and hunger; we wish there were no censorship and no political prisoners; and we wish we had more power to change

The United Nations Education, Scientific and Cultural Organization funds educational projects around the world.

conditions in the world. But how many of us actually spend any of our time working to make such changes happen?

There are several outstanding organizations that work to solve these problems. One important one is UNESCO. The purpose of this United Nations organization is to promote peace. Its constitution says: "Since wars begin in the minds of men, it is in the minds of men that the defenses of peace must be constructed." UNESCO hopes that education will help build a peaceful world based on human rights.

Amnesty International is also working to protect human rights. It began in 1961, and it has groups in about 110 countries. Each of these groups adopts at least two political prisoners in other countries. By pressuring governments, writing letters, and demonstrating, they hope they can free these prisoners.

Most "peace demonstrations" need help from many individuals in the countries where they operate. So if you wish that we could solve the world's problems, get involved!

Discussing the Passage

1. How does UNESCO work for peace?
2. What kind of work does Amnesty International do?

Hope and *Wish:* Present and Future

Hope and *wish* express different points of view about the present and future. *Hope* refers to real possibilities. *Wish* is used to express impossibility or improbability—that the speaker or writer wants reality to be other than it is. Compare:

Hopes Versus Wishes	Inferences
I **hope** that they **will (can)** help us.	It is possible that they will (can) help us.
I **wish** that they **would (could)** help us.	They probably will not (cannot) help us.

Hopes: Present and future hopes are expressed by using present or future verbs or modal auxiliaries such as *can* in the dependent clause.

Wishes: Present and future wishes are expressed by using *would, could,* or a special verb form—the subjunctive—in the dependent clause. In most cases, this form is the same as the simple past tense. In formal English, *were* is used for all forms of the verb *be*. However, in informal English, *was* is sometimes used with *I, he, she,* and *it,* although it is not considered correct. Use of *that* is optional in these sentences.

	Examples	Inferences
Wishes About the Present	I wish (that) they **were** here.	They aren't here.
	I wish (that) they **were coming.**	They are not coming.
	I wish (that) they **came** here more often.	They don't come here very often.
	I wish they **could come.**	They cannot come.
Wishes About the Future	I wish they **were going to come.**	They are probably not going to come.
	I wish they **would (could) come** next week.	They probably won't (can't) come next week.

A. Exercise: *Hope* **Versus** *Wish* **in Present Time.** Complete the following by using either the present or past tense of the verbs in parentheses.

Example: I wish there __*weren't*__ (not be) so many problems in the world.

1. The teacher hopes that the students _____ (understand) her explanation.

2. The students wish that they _____ (understand) English grammar better.

3. Everybody wishes there _____ (be) peace in the world.

4. I hope there _____ (be) enough time to discuss this problem.

5. The representatives at the peace conference wish they _____ (not disagree) about so many things.

B. Exercise: *Hope* **Versus** *Wish* **in Present or Future Time.** Complete these sentences with *can, could, will, would,* or *be going to* + the simple forms of the verbs in parentheses.

Example: My friend and I wish we __*could work*__ (work) together, but we can't.

1. I hope we _____ (be able to) work together some day.

2. After meeting at the conference, the two delegates hope they _____ (meet) again soon.

3. I wish I _____ (meet) you this evening, but I have to go to a meeting.

4. I wish they _____ (call) us.

5. I hope they _____ (come) with us to the meeting.

C. **Exercise:** Complete the sentences with the correct forms of the verbs in parentheses. Add modal auxiliaries when necessary. (In which sentences are both **could** and **would** correct?)

Example: There are many conflicts among nations, but we wish there _weren't_ (not be).

1. We wish we _____ (know) a way to end wars forever.

2. We wish we _____ (establish) a permanent peace.

3. We wish governments _____ (agree) to stop the arms race.

4. Many people wish governments _____ (ban) nuclear weapons.

5. We wish there _____ (be) more organizations working for peace.

6. We wish we _____ (be able to) protect human rights for everyone.

7. We wish more individuals _____ (work for) peace.

8. We wish that somehow we _____ (guarantee) the survival of the human race.

D. **Exercise: Error Analysis.** Correct the following sentences.

1. I wish I ~~would be~~ *were* in Mexico now.

2. I wish I can talk to Maia now.

3. I hope I would see you tomorrow.

4. I wish I will be in college next semester.

5. I wish I went to New York next year.

6. I hope I could feel better now.

E. Exercise: The Peace Corps is an organization that sends volunteers to developing countries to help people improve their living conditions. In the following passage, a Peace Corps volunteer in East Africa describes her experiences. Complete the passage with the correct forms of the verbs in parentheses. Add modal auxiliaries when necessary.

"I came here two years ago because I wanted to teach people about modern health care. I will be leaving in about two months; I wish I *could stay* (stay) longer, but it's time for me to go home.

"My work here has been very interesting. I am learning so much. I always wish that there _____ (be) more hours in the day so that I could do
₁
more. Maybe it's silly, but I worry about what will happen to the villagers after I leave. I hope that my students _____ (remember) the things I've
₂
tried to teach them. I hope that in the

future there _____
₃
(be) less disease and that the children

_____ (be)
₄
healthier. And of course, I hope that

they _____
₅
(not forget) me. I've become so close

to the people here, I wish I

_____ (take)
₆
them home with me! But of course

that's impossible, so I hope I

_____ (visit)
₇
them in the future. I wish more

people _____
₈
(join) the Peace Corps. It's so

rewarding, and there's so much

work to be done.

© JAMES FOOTE

An American and several Africans work on making a concrete building block that will be used for a maternity clinic.

F. Exercise: Several students are talking about the problems in their countries. Complete the sentences with statements expressing their *hopes* or *wishes*.

Example: "My city is very big, so people drive their cars everywhere. We have terrible traffic jams. We need better public transportation."

a. This student wishes *people wouldn't drive their cars everywhere.*

b. She hopes *that the government will develop a better public transportation system.*

1. "We don't have enough schools or teachers in my country. Few people can get a good education. This is one of our biggest problems, something we want to change."

a. This student wishes _____

   _____

b. He hopes _____

   _____

2. "We have a serious problem with medical care in my country. There aren't enough doctors, and hospital care is very expensive. I want to study medicine so that I can help my people."

a. This student wishes _____

   _____

b. She hopes _____

   _____

3. "My country is fighting a war right now. I don't know what is happening to my family. I want this war to end soon."

   a. This student wishes _____

   _____

   b. He hopes _____

   _____

4. "We didn't have enough rain last year, so this year we are having a food short-age. Many people are hungry. Maybe next year we will have more rain."

   a. This student wishes _____

   _____

   b. He hopes _____

   _____

G. **Activity: Expressing Hopes and Wishes.** Does your city or country have a problem that particularly concerns you? Have you done any work to help solve the problem? What would you like to do? What do you hope will happen? Discuss this problem with your classmates. Briefly state the problem. Tell what you wish you, personally, could do. Then say what you hope will happen.

   Example: **Inflation is my country's biggest problem. Prices keep going up and people are uncertain about the future. I wish that people would try to stop buying so many foreign products. I hope that we can solve this problem soon.**

PART TWO

IMAGINATIVE CONDITIONAL SENTENCES: PRESENT OR UNSPECIFIED TIME

What are *civil rights?* Where do they come from? Share your knowledge while discussing the answers to the questions about the picture.

1.   What are some basic rights in the United States?
2.   What is freedom of speech?

If there were no freedom of speech in North America, people might go to jail for speaking against the government.

Civil Rights

Civil rights are the freedoms and rights that a person may have as a member of a community, nation, or state. For Americans, these rights are described in a part of our Constitution that is called the *Bill of Rights*. A few of these rights are explained below.

Freedom of speech: The Constitution guarantees freedom of speech. If Americans did not have this freedom, someone who spoke against the government could go to jail.

Freedom of religion: The Constitution also guarantees freedom of religion. If Americans did not have this right, it would be possible to discriminate against people because of their religious beliefs.

Due process: This means that a person accused of a crime must receive fair treatment. For example, the police must have a reason for arresting someone. In addition, an accused person has the right to be represented by a lawyer. Due process is a very important part of the American legal system. If the United States didn't have due process, accused persons wouldn't have any legal protection at all.

Discussing the Passage

1. What important rights are guaranteed by the Constitution?
2. What do you think *freedom of speech* means?
3. What is *due process?*

Conditional Sentences: Present or Unspecified Time

"Imaginative" conditional sentences express conditions that the speaker thinks of as unlikely, untrue, or contrary to fact. They may be wishes and dreams, or they may express advice to others. The following conditional sentences refer to the moment of speaking or to habitual activities, depending on the context. In these sentences, a modal auxiliary (usually *would, could,* or *might*) is used in the main clause. The subjunctive form is used in the *if* clause. In most cases, the subjunctive form is the same as the simple past. For the verb *be,* however, *were* is used for all persons in formal English.

Examples	Inferences
If we **had** more police, there **might be** less crime.	We don't have enough police. Because of this, there is a lot of crime.
If the government **spent** less money, it **could lower** taxes.	The government spends a lot of money; therefore, it cannot lower taxes.
I **would lower** taxes if I **were** president.	I'm not president, so I can't lower taxes.

A. Exercise: What could we do if we raised taxes? Or do you believe taxes should be lowered? Complete the sentences with *would, could,* or *might* + the simple forms of the verbs in parentheses.

Example: If I were president, I _*would raise*_ (raise) taxes.

1. If the government did not have enough money, it _____ (not protect) people's rights.

2. If we raised taxes, we _____ (improve) schools.

3. If we had no taxes, rich people _____ (get) richer.

4. If there were no sales tax, some poor people _____ (not pay) any taxes.

5. If tax laws were simpler, more people _____ (calculate) their own taxes.

B. Exercise: Laws protect citizens in many ways. What would happen if we didn't have this protection? Complete the following statements with the correct forms of the words in parentheses. Be sure to pay attention to the order of the clauses; add *would, could,* or *might* to the main clauses.

Example: If there _*were*_ (be) no police, crime _*would be*_ (be) worse.

1. If we _____ (not have) freedom of speech, people _____ (not criticize) the government.

2. If we _____ (not have) laws, people _____ (behave) in any way they liked.

3. An accused person _____ (have to) defend himself or herself in court if there _____ (be) no lawyers.

4. If we _____ (not have) trial by jury, all cases _____ (be) tried by judges.

5. If all cases _____ (be) tried by judges only, then judges _____ (have) too much power.

C. **Exercise:** First, think about the ideal society and the ideal place to live. Then, in pairs, take turns asking and answering the following questions. Give reasons for your answers. Finally, add a few of your own questions.

Examples: If you could live anywhere, where would you live? →
If I could live anywhere, I'd live on the top of a very high mountain where I could watch everything surrounding me. And only people who really cared about me would climb up to see me . . .

1. Where would you live if you could live anywhere in the world?
2. If you had all the money in the world, what would you build or create there?
3. If you could choose the people who would live there, who would you choose?
4. If you had to create laws, what types of laws would you want?
5. If you could live at any time in history, what time might you choose?

D. **Exercise:** Complete the following sentences with your own ideas. Pay attention to verb forms.

Example: If I had more time, . . . →

If I had more time, *I'd read more books.*

1. If I won $1 million in the lottery, . . .
2. I might get married if . . .
3. The world would be a better place if . . .
4. If I didn't eat for a week, . . .
5. If I were president, . . .
6. We wouldn't need to learn English if . . .
7. If I were an American citizen, . . .
8. If people had wings, . . .
9. You could borrow my car if . . .
10. I might go to China next year if . . .

E. Activity: Planning a New Society. If you had the opportunity, how would you organize a legal system? What laws would you put into effect? Consider the following issues; several positions have been listed for each. Choose one of these or state your own position on the topic. Make at least two statements about your position. Use *if* clauses that explain your choice.

Example: control of handguns →

      a. It would be legal for anyone to have a handgun.
      b. I would ban all handguns.
      c. Only the military and police would have handguns.

In my system, only the military and police would have handguns. If only the military and police had handguns, there would be fewer violent crimes, murders, and assassinations. If criminals could not obtain handguns, our society might be safer.

1. education

      a. All education would be free.
      b. Only primary education would be free.
      c. Everyone would pay for education. There would be no scholarships.

2. religion

      a. All religions would be allowed.
      b. Only one religion would be allowed.
      c. All religions would be prohibited.

3. voting

      a. Every person, including children, would be allowed to vote.
      b. Everyone over age eighteen would be allowed to vote.
      c. There would not be any elections.

4. censorship

      a. I would allow complete freedom of the press.
      b. I would form a government agency to monitor the press.
      c. The government would control (and censor) all newspapers, magazines, television, and movies.

PART THREE

PERFECT MODAL AUXILIARIES

What are the largest minority groups in the United States? What special problems do they have? Share your knowledge while discussing the following questions.

1. What is happening in the photo?
2. How do you think the students feel?

© OWEN FRANKEN/STOCK, BOSTON

The Bakke Case

In the past, members of minority groups without a good educational background were not admitted into good universities. To help minority students, some universities now have "affirmative action" programs. These programs give special consideration to minority applicants. This help may include scholarships or special admission requirements. Many Americans support these programs, but there are also many who oppose them.

The famous Bakke case questioned the use of affirmative action programs in universities. In both 1973 and 1974, a California medical school refused to admit Allan Bakke, who was a white engineer in his mid-thirties. The school said that Bakke's grades and test scores should have been higher. With a better academic record, the school might have accepted him. However, Bakke discovered that his grades and scores were higher than those of some minority students who had been accepted as part of a special affirmative action program. So Bakke sued the university. He said that the university would have accepted him if he hadn't been a white male.

In the end, the Supreme Court decided that Bakke was right. It said that the medical school should have accepted him and that the affirmative action program was unfair. Of course, many people disagreed with the Court. They believed that the Court should have supported the special affirmative action program for minorities.

Discussing the Passage

1. What is *affirmative action?*
2. Why didn't the medical school admit Bakke?
3. Why did Bakke sue the university?

Perfect Modal Auxiliaries

Perfect modal auxiliaries describe past activities or situations that were not real or that did *not* occur. Often, they express our wishes about these past events. Perfect modals follow this pattern: modal + *(not) have* + past participle.

	Examples	**Notes**
would have	He **would have gone** to medical school, but his grades were too low.	*Would have* refers to past intentions that were not fulfilled.
should have	He **should have applied** earlier, but he didn't.	*Should have* refers to actions that were advisable, but that did *not* take place.
could have	He **could have gone** to any school he wanted.	*Could have* refers to past possibilities or choices. In many cases, the speaker or writer is uncertain if the action occurred.
might have	He **might have gone** to Harvard; I'm not sure.	*Might have* refers to past possibilities. In many cases, the speaker or writer is uncertain if the action occurred.

A. **Exercise:** You applied for a job, but you didn't get it even though you were very well qualified. You think the interviewer may have discriminated against you because of your age. What would you have done differently? Make statements using the following cues.

Example: wear a new suit for the job interview →
I would have worn a new suit for the job interview.

1. be enthusiastic about working for that company
2. ask a lot of good questions about the company
3. describe my work experience in detail
4. discuss my good health and high level of energy
5. explain why I was a good candidate for the job
6. try to relax more

B. **Exercise:** You were fired from a job you had had for many years, so you stopped working and left quietly. Now you are beginning to question your decision and you ask your friends what they would or would not have done. In pairs, ask and answer questions using the following cues.

Example: sue the company →
S1: **Would you have sued the company?**
S2: **Yes, I would have.**

1. write a letter to the company president
2. talk to someone in the personnel department
3. ask for another job in the same company
4. tell your co-workers about the problem and ask for their advice
5. discuss the case with a lawyer
6. ask for a meeting with a company representative

C. **Exercise:** In the following situations, a friend of yours tells you what he or she did or didn't do. You think your friend made a mistake; respond with *should (not) have.* In pairs, take turns making the statements below and responding to them.

Example: S1: I didn't get the job I wanted, so I just gave up. Now I'm receiving unemployment insurance. →
S2: **You shouldn't have given up. You should have looked for a job with a different company.**

1. I didn't vote in the last election.
2. I drove home from a party after drinking nine bottles of beer.
3. I saw somebody shoplifting in a department store, but I didn't tell anybody about it.
4. I was fired from my last job. I don't think it was fair, but I didn't complain about it.
5. When my boss criticized me, I got angry and shouted at him.
6. I quit my job because I didn't get a raise.

D. Exercise: Read the following situations. For each one, think of other things the person in the situation *could have* done.

> Example: When Allan Bakke wasn't accepted by the medical school, he sued the school. What other choices did he have? →
> a. **He could have applied to another medical school.**
> b. **He could have continued working as an engineer.**

1. The nurses at Community Hospital were complaining about their working conditions. They felt that their salaries were too low. However, nobody did anything to change the situation. What could they have done?

   a. (go on strike)
   b. (quit)

   c. _____

2. A foreign student wasn't accepted at a famous university because her TOEFL score was only 450. As a result, she went back to her country.

   a. (take the TOEFL again)
   b. (apply to a different university)

   c. _____

3. George M. works for a large corporation. Recently it was discovered that a large sum of money had been stolen from the company, and George was blamed for it. George knew that one of his co-workers actually stole the money, but he had no proof. George was fired. What could he have done?

   a. (tell his boss the truth)
   b. (go to the police)

   c. _____

E. Exercise: Following are several short "mysteries." Decide what *might have* or *could have* happened in each case.

1. Charles H. was hired by the XYZ Corporation. He was supposed to start work on Monday, but he never showed up. The secretary called him at home, but he never answered the phone. By Wednesday, he still had not appeared.

    a. (have accident)
    b. (get another job)

    c. _____

2. Mr. Purl feeds his cat every evening at exactly six o'clock, as soon as he comes home from work. On this particular evening, Mr. Purl's cat has not come home for dinner even though it is already seven o'clock. Mr. Purl is very worried; what happened to his cat?

    a. (find better food at the neighbors' house)

    b. _____

    c. _____

3. Mr. and Mrs. Yan have spent the evening at the opera, and they are now walking back to their car. To their great surprise, their car is not where they left it. What happened to it?

    a. _____

    b. _____

    c. _____

F. Exercise: John Q. applied to law school and was rejected seven years ago. Now he is talking about it with Bill, his next-door neighbor. Complete the conversation with *would, could, should,* or *might + have +* past participle. In some cases, more than one answer may be correct.

JOHN: When I didn't get into law school, I was shocked. All my dreams were ruined. I didn't know what to do, so I went to work in a bank.

BILL: What do you think you _could (might, should) have done_ (do) differently?

JOHN: Looking back, I think there were several possibilities. First, I _____ (work) for a year to get some legal experi-
1
ence and then applied again. I also _____ (take)
2
the entrance exam again; I _____ (get) a higher
3
score the second time. Finally, I _____ (apply) to
4
more schools instead of just the university. I'm sure I _____ (be)
5
accepted somewhere. Anyway, I _____ (not give
6
up) so easily.

BILL: Why didn't you try harder?

JOHN: Well, I was already married at the time, and we didn't have much money. I felt that I couldn't afford to waste another year. But now I'm sure that we _____ (find) a way of supporting ourselves if I'd
7
been accepted.

BILL: Did you ever think of trying again?

JOHN: As a matter of fact, yes. I'm taking the entrance exam again next week.

BILL: Good luck!

G. Activity: Expressing Regrets and Giving Advice. Have you made any mistakes—large or small—since you've been in this country? Think of a specific event or action and tell the members of your group what happened and what you might, could, or should have done differently. The members of your group will comment on what you should, could, or might have done, and what they would have done instead.

Example: S1: **When I came to this city, I took the first apartment I found. I didn't know that it was in the most expensive part of town. I think I should have looked at some more apartments. Unfortunately, I also signed a year's lease.**

S2: **You shouldn't have done that. Now you have to pay a high rent for a whole year. I would have asked somebody for advice before I signed anything. You could have saved yourself a lot of money that way.**

PART FOUR

PAST WISHES; IMAGINATIVE CONDITIONAL SENTENCES: PAST TIME

Do you know about anyone who has won the Nobel Peace Prize? What special thing did this person do? Share your ideas and information while answering the following questions abut the pictures below.

1. Who are the people in the pictures?
2. What did they do?

The Nobel Peace Prize

What kind of person wins the Nobel Peace Prize? Almost always, these are individuals who have worked all their lives to fight injustice, poverty, and discrimination. Here are three famous examples.

Albert Schweitzer (1875–1965) was a German physician, philosopher, musician, clergyman, missionary, and writer. In 1913, he established the first hospital in the rural areas of West Africa. After many years of humanitarian work, he received the Nobel Peace Prize in 1952. Schweitzer used this award money to help Africans who had leprosy. If Schweitzer had not gone to Africa, thousands of Africans that Schweitzer treated might have died.

Martin Luther King, Jr. (1929–1968) received the 1964 Nobel Peace Prize for his efforts to create social, political, and economic equality for American black people. He encouraged people to oppose discrimination by using nonviolent methods. As a result of the efforts of Dr. King and other civil rights workers, Congress passed the Civil Rights Act of 1964 and the Voting Rights Act of 1965. These laws might not have passed if King had not spent years fighting for them. Sadly, King was assassinated in 1968.

Albert Schweitzer

Martin Luther King, Jr.

Mother Teresa

Mother Teresa is the Yugoslavian-born nun who started the Missionaries of Charity, a group of Catholic nuns and brothers who serve the poorest people in the world. She received the Nobel Peace Prize in 1979, after starting homes in India for victims of leprosy, homeless children, and retarded people. Would anyone else have helped these people if Mother Teresa had not? It is doubtful. Unfortunately, there are very few Mother Teresas in the world.

Other winners of the Nobel Peace Prize include Willy Brandt, Henry Kissinger, George Marshall, Lester Pearson, René Cassin, and Woodrow Wilson. How would history have been different if these people had never been born?

Discussing the Passage

1. Why did Schweitzer, King, and Mother Teresa win the Nobel Peace Prize?
2. What do you know about the other people mentioned in the passage?

Wishes About the Past

Wishes about the past express feelings or thoughts that did not happen, that are contrary to reality. To show the unreality of the wish, a subjunctive form, which is the same as the past perfect tense, is normally used in the dependent clause.

Examples	Notes
The workers went on strike. I wish (that) there **hadn't been** a strike. The negotiators didn't agree. We wish (that) they **had (agreed).**	In most cases, *had* + past participle is used with past wishes. The past participle can be omitted if the meaning is clear. *That* can also be omitted.
The negotiators couldn't agree. We wish (that) they **could have (agreed).**	In some cases, perfect modals (*could* [*would*, etc.] *have* + past participle) are used to express past wishes.

A.   Exercise: The following sentences express regrets. Complete each sentence with your own ideas. Be sure to use *had* + past participle.

Example: I spent only three years in college. I wish I . . . →
             I wish I had finished school.

1. I started working full time at sixteen. I wish . . .
2. I got married when I was twenty. I wish . . .
3. I left home for good when I was eighteen. I wish . . .
4. I never did any volunteer work. I wish . . .
5. I was never very good at learning languages. I wish . . .

B. Exercise: In the following passages, several people are speaking about missed opportunities. Complete each with the correct form of the verbs in parentheses. In some cases, you may want to add modal auxiliaries.

1. "Last week I had two big exams on the same day. So what did I do the night before? I went to a movie with my friends. Of course, I didn't do very well on my tests. I wish that I ___*hadn't gone*___ (not go) to the movies. I wish I _____ (study) instead. I wish that I _____ (get) better grades on the tests."

2. "I voted for Jack Hopkins for mayor of this town and, as you know, he won. But I'm pretty unhappy with what he's done since he was elected. Taxes are higher, there's more crime, and the schools are more crowded than ever. To tell you the truth, I wish I _____ (vote/never) for him. I wish I _____ (work) for the other candidate. Better yet, I wish that I _____ (be) a candidate myself!"

3. "I really wish that I _____ (go) to college, but my parents didn't have the money to send me to school. I wish there _____ (be) scholarships in my day. I wish that I _____ (got) a job and paid for my own education.

C. Activity: Expressing Regrets. Think of a time when you made an incorrect decision. For example, did you give a friend some bad advice? Did you make an unwise investment? Did you get married too young? Did you ignore your parents' advice about something important? Use one of the following sentence patterns to tell your classmates what you did and what you would have done differently.

> I . . . , but I wish I had . . . .
> I didn't . . . , but I wish I had.

Conditional Sentences: Past Time

The conditional can be used to describe ideas about past situations or events that did *not* take place. The past perfect tense is used in the *if* clause. A modal auxiliary (usually *would, could,* or *might + have +* past participle) is used in the main clause.

Examples	Inferences
If Schweitzer **had not gone** to Africa, he **wouldn't have received** the Nobel Prize.	Schweitzer did go to Africa and received the Nobel Prize for his work there.
Martin Luther King, Jr. **could have worked** for more reforms if he **had lived** longer.	King was assassinated, so he was not able to work for more reforms.

D. Exercise: Read the information about other Nobel Peace Prize winners. Then complete the sentences using the past perfect and *would, could,* or *might + have.*

Example: Dag Hammarskjöld, a Swede, was Secretary General of the United Nations from 1953 to 1961. He helped to solve conflicts in the Middle East and in Africa. He died in a plane crash and was awarded the Nobel Prize after his death.

If Hammarskjöld ____*had lived*____ (live), he ____*would have received*____ (receive) the prize in person.

1. The International Red Cross has won the Nobel Peace Prize three times for its efforts to reduce human suffering. For example, following earthquakes in Nicaragua in 1972 and in Guatemala in 1976, it sent emergency food and medicine to these countries. Fewer people _____ (be helped) if the Red Cross _____ (not coordinate) these rescue operations.

2. Andrei Sakharov, born in 1921, is a Russian physicist who is best known for his efforts to support human rights and world peace. He criticized the Soviet government for refusing to give its citizens basic human rights; as a result, his government arrested him. If Sakharov _____ (remain) silent, he _____ (not go) to prison.

3. Linus Pauling, the famous American chemist, was one of the first people to speak against the dangers of atomic power. Because of his great influence, 9,000 scientists signed a petition to stop atom bomb tests in the late 1950s. Pauling received the peace prize in 1962. If Pauling

_____

(not be) a famous scientist, people _____ (not start) to pay attention to the dangers of nuclear power.

Linus Pauling demonstrating against nuclear testing in the early 1960s

E. Exercise: Complete the following sentences with your own ideas. Pay attention to your use of verb forms and modal auxiliaries.

Example: If I had gotten up earlier this morning, . . . →
            I might not have been late.

1. If I had been born in the United States, . . .
2. He could have gotten a better grade on the test if . . .
3. I couldn't have come to this country if . . .
4. If my family had had more money, . . .
5. We wouldn't have run out of gas if . . .
6. Yesterday I would have stayed home if . . .
7. If I had learned English when I was a child, . . .

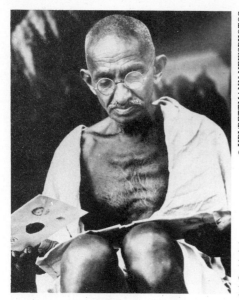

© UPI/BETTMANN NEWSPHOTOS

Mohandas Gandhi in London negotiating for India; he wore traditional Indian clothing even to meet King George at Buckingham Palace.

F. Exercise: Mohandas Gandhi is honored by the people of India as the father of their nation. He helped free India from British control through nonviolent resistance. Gandhi took many risks in his life and often had to suffer the consequences. Read the following information about the life of Gandhi. After each section, write at least one sentence, using the example as a model.

Example: In 1893, Gandhi went to South Africa to do some legal work. There, people would not respect him because he was not white.

The people in South Africa might have respected Gandhi if he had been white. Gandhi might not have had problems with the South Africans if he had been white.

1. Gandhi spoke out against British rule, and he went to prison many times.

_____

_____

_____

2. Gandhi did not stay in Africa. Instead, he returned to India in 1935. Soon, he became leader of the Indian nationalist movement.

_____

_____

_____

3. Gandhi believed that it was honorable to go to jail for a good cause. He spent seven years in prison for political activity against the British.

_____

_____

_____

_____

4. Gandhi wanted people of all races and religions to live together peacefully. He frequently spoke in favor of this. He was assassinated by a man who disagreed with him.

_____

_____

_____

_____

G. **Activity: Describing Turning Points.** Events, experiences, and decisions that change your life in a major way are called "turning points." What turning points have you experienced? Was your decision to study English or to come to this school a turning point? Are you at a turning point now? First, think of a major turning point in your life. How would your life have been different if you hadn't had that experience or if you had made a different decision? How would your life be different now? Are you happy with the outcome? Or do you wish you had done things differently? What are your hopes for the future in this regard? Then share your turning point and the results of it with your classmates—in pairs, in small groups, or in a letter to your class.

Example:

Dear Class:

Now that we are at the end of our session, I want to say good-bye and to tell you how much I've appreciated all of you. Learning to speak another language has changed my life, and you are all part of that change. If I hadn't learned English, I couldn't have come here. And if I had not studied in this program, I would never have met all of you.

Meeting all of you has been a wonderful experience for me, and I only wish I could have gotten to know everyone much better. I wish I had been able to speak more English in order to talk with you more. I wish that the time hadn't gone so fast. Above all, I hope that you will all come to visit me at my home.

Love,

Patricia

(from Argentina)

INDEX OF GRAMMAR AND FUNCTIONS